THE METAMORPHOSES OF
FAT

European Perspectives

EUROPEAN PERSPECTIVES
A Series in Social Thought and Cultural Criticism
Lawrence D. Kritzman, Editor

European Perspectives presents outstanding books by leading European thinkers. With both classic and contemporary works, the series aims to shape the major intellectual controversies of our day and to facilitate the tasks of historical understanding.

For a complete list of books in the series, see pages 263–64.

THE METAMORPHOSES OF
FAT
A History of Obesity

Georges Vigarello

Translated from the French by C. Jon Delogu

COLUMBIA UNIVERSITY PRESS   NEW YORK

COLUMBIA UNIVERSITY PRESS
Publishers Since 1893
New York   Chichester, West Sussex
cup.columbia.edu

Library of Congress Cataloging-in-Publication Data

Vigarello, Georges.
[Métamorphoses du gras. English]
The metamorphoses of fat: a history of obesity / Georges Vigarello;
translated from the French by C. Jon Delogu.
pages cm.—(European perspectives: a series in social thought and cultural criticism)
Includes bibliographical references and index.
ISBN 978-0-231-15976-0 (cloth: alk. paper); ISBN 978-0-231-53530-4 (e-book)
1. Obesity—Social aspects—History. I. Title.

RC628.V5413   2013
362.1963'98—dc23   2012029197

Cover Design: David Drummon

CONTENTS

Introduction   ix

PART 1 THE MEDIEVAL GLUTTON

1.   The Prestige of the Big Person   **3**
Spontaneous Vigor   3
What Insults?   6
From Big to Very Big   7

2.   Liquids, Fat, and Wind   **10**
Matters of Fat   10
The Deviations of Wind and Water   12
Gout and Gout Sufferers   14
The "Simplicity" of Evacuations   15

3.   The Horizon of Fault   **17**
The Clerical Model   18
The Medical Model   19
The Courtly Model   21

4.   The Fifteenth Century and the Contrasts of Slimming   **23**
The Ascendancy of Images   24
A Social Distinction?   25
Lifestyles and Conflicts   26
The "Laborious" Place of Beauty   28

PART 2   THE "MODERN" OAF

5. **The Shores of Laziness**   **33**
    "Modern" Activity and Passivity   33
    From Private Insult to Public Code   36
    Resistances and Fascinations   38
    The Refusal of All Skinniness   41

6. **The Plural of Fat**   **45**
    Dramatizing the Threat   45
    Fear of Apoplexy   47
    Fat Talk, an Abstract Discourse   49
    Specifying Hydropsy   51
    Specifying the Excess of Gout   53

7. **Exploring Images, Defining Terms**   **55**
    Images and Realism of Features   55
    The Choice of Rubens   57
    The Power and Powerlessness of Words   59

8. **Constraining the Flesh**   **64**
    The Beginning of an Evaluation   64
    Only the "High" Size   67
    Diets and "Modern" Restraints   69
    Drying Out   71
    Vinegar and Chalk   73
    Belts, Blades, and Corsets   75

**PART 3   FROM OAFISHNESS TO POWERLESSNESS:
THE ENLIGHTENMENT AND SENSIBILITY**

9. **Inventing Nuance**   **79**
    "Tireless" Measuring and "Fruitless" Measuring   79
    Waist or Weight?   81
    Inventing the Means   82
    The First Specifications of Forms   84
    Masculine "Gravity" and Social "Gravity"   87

10. **Stigmatizing Powerlessness**   **90**
    Introducing a New Word, *Obesity*   91
    The Bad Symptom: Insensitivity   94
    The Criticism of the Affluent   95
    The Big Bad Husband   97

11. Toning Up   99
The Virtue of "Tonics"   99
The Virtue of "Excitants"   101
Electric Dreams   102
The Nerve Regimen   103
Plants or Meats?   105
The Chemistry Revolution   106

PART 4   THE BOURGEOIS BELLY

12. The Weight of Figures   111
The Presence of Numbers   111
Figuring the Waist-Weight Relation   112
The Question of Self-Weighing   113

13. Typology Fever   116
"Gastrophoric" Men, Adipose Women   117
The Bourgeois and the Avowed Belly   120
The Bourgeois and the Lampooned Belly   121
Romantically Thin?   123

14. From Chemistry to Energy   125
The Aqueous and the Adipose: New Distinctions   125
Fat and Fire   127
Fat and "Morbid Imminence"   129

15. From Energy to Diets   131
The Consequences of Energy   131
The Question of Creating an "Art of Living Well"   133
The Archaic and the Modern   134
The "Misfortune" and Me: The New Status of Obesity   135

PART 5   TOWARD THE "MARTYR"

16. The Dominance of Aesthetics   141
The Spread of Weighing   142
The First Conflicts Between Charts   143
The Exposure of Bodies   145
The Ascendancy of Women's Hips   146
From the Masculine Waist to the Muscular "Discovery"   148
From Aesthetics to the Conflict of Images   151

17. **Clinical Obesity and Everyday Obesity**   154

   Forms and Numerically Measured Degrees   155
   Retarding Nutrition and Excess Nutrition   156
   The Degenerative Obsession   158
   The Explosion of Diets   159
   The Socializing and Chemistry of Spa Life   162
   The Ascendancy of Advertisers   164

18. **The Thin Revolution**   166

   The "Defect of Civilization"   167
   The Dashing Slender Male   168
   The Dashing Slender Female   169
   The "Graduated" Anatomy   170
   The Creation and the "Monstrous"   171

19. **Declaring "the Martyr"**   174

   Revolutionizing the First Degrees   175
   The Multiplication of Pathologies   176
   The Multiplication of Therapies   177
   The Evidence of Therapeutic Failures   179
   Between Trial and Martyr   181

**PART 6   CHANGES IN THE CONTEMPORARY DEBATE:
AN IDENTITY PROBLEM AND AN INSIDIOUS EVIL**

   The Affirmation of an "Epidemic"   186
   "Counterattacks"?   187
   The Dynamics of Thinness, the Dynamics of Obesity   188
   The Effects of Thinness   189
   A "Multifactor" Universe   190
   The Self, the Trial, and Identity   193

Conclusion   197

Notes   201
Index   249

INTRODUCTION

In one of her letters from the end of the seventeenth century, Elizabeth Charlotte, the Palatine Princess, gives the reader this image of herself: "my waist is monstrously wide, I am as square as a cube, my skin is red, speckled with yellow."[1] This testimony is precious because physical self-description is rare in old regime France. It supposes a distance, an objectification of the self, a dominating judgment that only a slow process of cultural labor could make possible. The testimony is especially valuable because it confirms that a definitive change in thinking has occurred: big is now only bad. The princess insists on the disgrace, the heaviness, the irremediable descent from "feathery to fat" that "places her among the ugly."[2] Then come anecdotes naming the symptoms of various troubles and ailments: "spleen pain," "colic," "vapors," and a "loss of balance" worsened by bumpy carriages. Being big is a disadvantage, perhaps even a curse.

The big person, however, was not always so strongly denounced—a fact that justifies historical inquiry. Massive bodies can be praised in the Middle Ages, for example, as denoting power and ascendancy. Similarly, in times of hunger, admiring praise is accorded to lands of plenty [*pays de cocagne*] with all-you-can-eat banquets and visions of endlessly stuffing oneself. Force is associated with the large hearty meal. Accumulating pounds is seen as health insurance. And social "privilege" is signified through a display of one's own size. These ideas are probably complicated as well, though, because even in the Middle Ages they are contested by the sermons of clerics and the reservations and beliefs of doctors and even by the delicately phrased demands of courtly codes. Nevertheless, they are impressive, immediately recognizable signs that lend the big person power and conviction.

A definitive break however takes place with the advent of modern Europe. The closely contemporary testimonies of Saint-Simon in France and Samuel Pepys in England denigrate a "lazy, fat priest,"[3] deride a "fat child" called "Punch," "a word of common use for all that is thick and short,"[4] "big, fat creatures,"[5] and "fat and lusty and ruddy" courtiers,[6] while Madame de Sévigné fears above all becoming a "flattened fatty."[7] The big person [le gros] is now only a fat person [le gras]—indolent and collapsed.[8] Prestige and models change. The rough tables of olden times heaped with food are no longer classy, and accumulating pounds of flesh is no longer a sign of forceful reserves but rather of a certain loss of control and grossness.

The history of being big is the story of these reversals. The development of Western societies promotes a tendency toward slimmer bodies, a keener supervision of physical contours, and an increasingly alarmed refusal of heaviness. This of course brings changes in what counts as big and a barely imperceptible but steady privileging of lightness. This in turn strongly exacerbates contempt for big people, who find themselves increasingly discredited. Voluminous individuals fall further and further below standards of refinement, while beauty is ever more associated with the thin and slender.

This same discredit takes on a different content over time and these changes further justify a history of bigness. The vision of the "fault" shifts, thus revealing how much the body's appearance, with its real or supposed flaws, is linked to a history of cultures and sensibilities. Medieval criticisms, formulated by clerics and diffused with some success in the fourteenth and fifteenth centuries in advance of our modern era, insist on the capital or "deadly" sins. These criticisms assail the passions, single out the glutton, and denounce his lack of dignity. They condemn avarice, while modern criticisms insist on a lack of dexterity and efficiency. The big, now fat, person becomes a figure of the inapt, the unfit—flabby and inert. Their fault is a deficit of doing, an insufficiency of power and action. Annibal Carrache's caricature "portraits" from the seventeenth century are the best illustrations: groups of men with oversized stomachs and short limbs stuck in poses of heaviness.[9] The flaw of the fat person in modern times is lack of dynamism and a capacity for doing. The dominant idea becomes *fat = no power*. The fat person can also provoke collective denunciations, as when the full chests of the wealthy are pointed to as a sign either of their rapaciousness or their true inefficiency. With their round tummies and degraded bodies, aristocrats and abbots at the end of the eighteenth century are the classic examples—"profiteers" that revolutionary ideas will squeeze down, then out, thus exposing their uselessness.

Criticisms also become more psychological as societies accentuate individualism and valorize autonomy and self-affirmation. The "losers" in these accounts are more intimate, emotional cases. Hence the "apathy"[10] that weighty anatomies are reproached for in northern countries in the late eighteenth century, or the "egoism"[11] held against the "fat person" in the proto-sociological portraits of Romantic literature; for example, the young bullied kid, "fat and sad," as described by Granville in his *Small Miseries of Human Life* (1843).[12] Size comes definitively to be thought of as correlating with individual attitudes and personality traits and even ways of thinking. At the end of the nineteenth century, Manuel Leven goes so far as to write up a long series of treatises associating neurosis and obesity.[13] The criticism of the fat person thus participates in the immense shift within Western societies that deepens the space given over to psychologies—taking distance from older moral classifications and instead developing an infinite array of personal differentiations and types of behavior.

In other words, this stigmatization reflects above all an accentuation of norms that in Western societies dictated ever stricter rules and precise guidelines for physical appearance and the expression of self. It can also reflect differences that are upheld between male and female genders as well as between social groups. For example, public condemnation is more severe toward the female body, which has been traditionally expected to be supple and fluid. Inversely, judgments have been more tolerant toward the dominant sex whose ascendancy has traditionally allowed for a more imposing voluminous size. The court of the great king in the seventeenth century, for example, does not lack for princes of a certain rotund stature, just as in the nineteenth-century world of the bourgeois there is no shortage of figures whose prestige is marked by a certain hefty, not to say heavy, allure. Here, too, social and cultural polarities, the differences constructed between men and women, inevitably traverse both positive and negative judgments.

Obviously the history of the big and the fat is also the history of the valuations of bodily forms and the work they're put to. For a long time these judgments remain imprecise because of a lack of measurable, statistical criteria. For a long time the intermediary stages or types between "normal" and "very big" are not clearly described. It takes a slow, gradual invention of a set of terms and diminutives between the sixteenth and seventeenth centuries to suggest a scale of chubbiness, posit types, and attempt to formalize them despite the inevitable persistence of imprecision.[14] The increasing variety of terms testifies to the increasing discrimination of the eye, even though its judgment remained rather approximate and even disappointing by today's standards for quite a while. We may note the insistent affirmation in a *Dictionnaire de médecine* from 1827 that fatness "presents a multitude of degrees."[15] A history of the body must give an account of both these evaluations of appearances and the history of their ever more explicit elaboration.

A sign of this growing exactitude is the statistical calculation and report of body weight that becomes customary by the end of the nineteenth century, just as an increasingly industrious vision of bodies and anatomies is also taking hold. It will take time before the bathroom scale and related personal tools arrive in private spaces in the twentieth century, marking a new requirement for self-maintenance that the evidence of periodic self-weighing fulfills. The presence of the scale has become part of everyday life, almost "natural," so spontaneous that it can make us forget how much our judgments of weight developed and refined themselves before the advent of numbers and tests. But it is this refinement and its diversification and individualization that are central to a history of "big" people.

Finally there are the fitness tactics and strategies for fighting fat as priority is gradually given over to slimming within Western societies. These practices also accelerate through the modern era, diversifying over time, revealing that the "fight" against weight is not a new invention but accompanies the gradual refinement of judgment about bodily curves and their modifications. For a long time this battle had as its first principle the constraint exerted on the skin itself: the corset, the girdle, and straps of all sorts. As though the body's forms had to obey the most material manipulations, as though they had to yield to the tightest strictures. At bottom this is nothing but the expression of an archaic belief that targets the body as a passive ensemble, a consummately malleable object, a material submissive to the simplest mechanical corrections.

This fight against fat has a new dimension that has not received much historical attention despite its impact, namely, that a project of getting thin can encounter limits and even impossibilities. Not that it is always deficient. Successes continue to multiply, linked to this or that scientific breakthrough. But the resistances also multiply—curves and weight go unchanged despite the accumulation of treatments. The obstruction can then become an obsession, a site of growing worry as knowledge develops to sophisticated levels, and alarms ring as diet procedures become an obligatory practice. The stigmatization thus shifts from a denigration of fat to a denigration of powerlessness, the inability to change. The reprobation becomes more psychological, more intimate; they are no longer accusations of awkwardness or gluttony, but of nonmastery, a lack of power over oneself as one keeps an "impassive" and ugly body whereas "everything" says it ought to change. The history of obesity is also the history of these "inertias," of a body ever more identified with a person in Western history, and yet that body escapes from certain attempts, apparently simple, to adapt and modify it. An entirely singular image of the obese person thus emerges—one that the growing norms for getting thin along with the ill-understood difficulty to respect them drives toward a singular hardship.[16] The latest new feature is that this hardship can express itself most easily in a society that favors intimate confession and psychologizing.

The history of fat people is first the history of a condemnation and its transformations across differing cultural contexts and socially targeted rejects. It is also the history of the particular difficulties experienced by the obese person: a hardship that has probably been accentuated by the refinement of norms and the growing attention to psychological suffering. Finally it is the history of a body that undergoes modifications that society rejects and that the will is not always able to modify.

THE METAMORPHOSES OF
FAT

PART 1

THE MEDIEVAL GLUTTON

"Bigness" is imposing right away in ancient intuitions.[1] It impresses. It seduces. It is also suggestive as it incarnates abundance, denotes wealth, and symbolizes health. Decisive signs in a universe marked by constant hunger and precariousness. This is demonstrated in the earliest fables: "gluttonous throats," repasts of "great size," "overflowing" feasts, the pleasure of "stuffing one's stomach," "all you can eat and drink" meals.[2] The body is unthinkable without filled up flesh. Health care itself and the first response to sickness cannot be thought except in terms of abundant food. The wounded fox in the *Roman de Renart*, for example, recovers his force by ingurgitating many foods and drinks.[3] The generous silhouette protects, convinces, and dominates forcefully in a confusion of fat and flesh.

This contour, however, can also provoke worry or even disgust, especially if its dimensions grow. Its materials are already composite, suggesting both softness and firmness. These states can also provoke subtler responses including the condemnation of clerics and doctors as well as that of the court elite who are quite sensitive to the odd word here or there about dimensions and reserve. During the Middle Ages a doubt takes hold as to the virtue of bigness, a contest between conflicting images. It is not that the prestige of the big, the massive, or the plump suddenly disappears. A moralistic universe, however, does spend more time contemplating the dangers of "excess." An already old, strongly edifying criticism focuses on the glutton and the overeater who get carried away. It is a criticism of behavior more than one of aesthetics or morbidity.

1. The Prestige of the Big Person

The prestige of the big person derives first of all from a certain context. The world in 1300 is one of hunger, severe restrictions, and food shortages that recur at less than five-year intervals. For several centuries during the Middle Ages, poor degraded soils, inadequate storage, slow and difficult transportation networks, and vulnerability to inclement weather all contribute to raising the accumulation of calories into an ideal. During these times, lands of plenty, the so-called *pays de cocagne*, also become marvelous symbols.[1] These fictional worlds are described as earthly paradises filled with spices, fatty meats, and white bread; dizzying landscapes where beer and wine flow like rivers, stews and roasts seem to pop up out of the soil, and hillsides are perfumed with fabulous nectars. Eating this "world" is a softening dream next to the hard reality of "bad harvests, exorbitant prices, and mortality."[2] The collective imagination dreams of accumulation. Health means a full stomach. Vigor is represented in the compact heft of flesh. These early truths have to be kept in mind to fully understand the future criticisms of "the fat."[3] But one must first take stock of the prestige of volume and big sizes.

Spontaneous Vigor

The words used to describe "beautiful" women in the oldest medieval tales are entirely clear on the matter. Each one is "fat, white, and tender" or "fat, tender, and beautiful,"[4] and the "gentle, beautiful maiden" in the *Romance of the Rose* is "rather big."[5] The words are the same for describing resplendent health. The heroines in the tale *The Heart Eaten*, freed after torments and misfortunes, are alive to the point of drunkenness and, feeding on "blood and flesh," become "big and fat" and thus more attractive than ever in this new appearance.[6] There are also the comparisons between horses and young women in the *Parisian's Household Manual* from the fourteenth century that calls for both to have "beautiful loins and big bottoms."[7] These pronouncements about female "fat" must be read carefully as denoting a lack of leanness more than a big overall size. "Fat" can imply "full" without necessarily meaning "big," which contributes to the ambiguity of the terms and the judgments and perceptions that go along with them.

Similar words crop up in descriptions of men, though perhaps with less nuance and more affirmation. Note what is seductive about the clerics for the bourgeoise woman of Orléans in the thirteenth century:

> The clerics were very big and fat
> Because they probably ate a lot
> They were highly esteemed in the city.[8]

Note the gentleman's lamentation in *The King of Navarre* from the thirteenth century who says he regains his fat by regaining possession of his loves,[9] or the whining about hunger in the Fastoul d'Arras that will produce "bitterness" and prevent "fattening up."[10] Even more striking are the mid-thirteenth-century Southern peasants who find no better term of praise than "ox of Sicily" to describe the beauty of Saint Thomas Aquinas as they abandon their labors to better admire him,[11] "pushed toward him" by his "imposing stature" more than by "his saintliness."[12]

Medieval myths say the same thing. Their giants are of immense size, constantly devouring and unsurpassed in power. Gergunt, for example, the "son of Belen," whose terrifying force is described by Giraud de Cambrie in the twelfth century, dominates Great Britain before Caesar.[13] The patronymics associated with him are themselves symbols that all point to the etymology of "Gargantua": *Gurguntius, Gurgant, Gremagoth*. These names all contain the phoneme [grg] present in all Indo-European languages "to express the idea of ingurgitation."[14] The sound reinforces the idea of vigor, for the source of the gigantic forms is nothing else but constant swallowing. This example mixes together more subtly and confusingly two distinct categories: the volume of muscle tissue and that of fat.

Medieval travelers show this in writings that identify improbable faraway inhabitants whose prodigious force derives from their immense size and unchecked appetites. For example, the men of Zanzibar described by Marco Polo in the thirteenth century are "tall and big" and "more wide than tall,"[15] and each places in his enormous mouth a volume of food that exceeds the total quantity of what several normal men would eat. Whence derives the "immeasurable" force that is attributed to them, their resistance in battle, and the capacity of each one to defeat single-handed "the attack of four other men."[16]

Noble references extend this promotion of bigness further still. The knight in the romances of the twelfth and thirteenth centuries ostentatiously indulges in massive quantities of food. Moniage Renoart "puts away five pâtés and five capons along with two gallons of wine."[17] In an instant Ogier the Dane eats up an enormous side of beef that could have fed "three lowly cart-pullers."[18] Quantity means both ascendancy and power. Medieval romances linger over the interminable meals of noblemen where one dish after another reinforces the idea of power. There is a succession of fifteen courses at the feast of Perceval beginning with "stag served with spicy pepper";[19] an accumulation of "venison, pork, and wild boar" in *Amis et Amiles*;[20] an extensive diversity of meats in the *Gerbers de Metz*; "venison, deer testicles, cranes and other river birds, stuffed bear and many spices."[21] Here force calls forth the accumulation of foods. The manners of the glutton take precedence over those of the gourmet.

The image of the endless meal is the product of dream, but is also symbolic. "In a society ruled by warriors who raise physical force to mythic status, the powerful eat to their full. . . . The one who eats a lot rules over everyone else."[22] Whence the privilege given to quantity as well as to the precise type of food: flesh is preferred over vegetables, for example, and blood over muscle fiber. In the thirteenth century, Helmbrecht, the old peasant of Wermer, expressly acknowledges confining himself to a diet of grains. He says to his son that he leaves meat and fish for the diet of the local lord.[23] Whereas Aldebrandin of Sienna, a thirteenth-century doctor, praises bloody foods because they are "more nourishing," "fattening," and "give force."[24] They make one big and fleshy. Thus there is a great diversity of animals consumed (chickens of all sorts, geese, pigs, sheep, lambs) during the brief stay of Queen Petronila of Catalonia and Aragon in the bishop's palace in Barcelona between 1157 and 1158.[25] The persuasiveness comes from the profusion as well as from the type of foods listed. The cumulative effect and the blood ingested makes for vigor, even if the reality does not always correspond to the idea; for example, the garbage heaps of the powerful of the time do not reveal large quantities of animal bones (only five percent, for example, of deer bones).[26]

The prestige of the bear crowns this honoring of bigness. A royal reference in Arthurian legend, the bear is the emblem of grandeur in ancient tales. He is big and forceful, heavy but also agile. Michel Pastoureau has underscored the importance of twelfth-century texts that magnify these images showing the bear's manifest weight to be accompanied by agility, quickness, and a talent for scampering between obstacles.[27] An omnivorous animal, like man, and capable of standing up as well, the bear is praised for being both adroit and powerful, rapid and massive. Royal weight means weight as model. The legend of "bear-like royalty," in fact, constructs a hybrid figure: a child of noble blood that a chain of obscure circumstances leads to be nursed on bear's milk before ascending to the throne becomes "furry and strong like the animal."[28]

Note this simple and revealing gesture: when the count of Foix falls into apoplexy one day in 1391, servants attempt to return him to his normal self by placing in his mouth "bread, water, spices, and all manner of comforting foods."[29] Only a large quantity is considered capable of restoring force and movement. The lifestyle of the count and his alimentary splendor provides further illustrations with his tables "dressed with abundance,"[30] extensive hours for meals, an overwhelming amount of food and drink, and a wish for "grand enjoyment."[31] Froissart directly links quantity and grandeur. He admires it and affirms it.

What Insults?

The largely "positive" force of a massive physical appearance and powerful eating has a particular effect: the big person is rarely the object of insult in the middle centuries of the medieval period. His image is rarely attacked, as it will be later, with an arsenal of insults and offenses. There is, however, the madness of the mouth, the animality of the glutton, the *gula*, which take on negative values. But even here, the words point more to excess desire than to the physical profile, to a kind of fever more than to the weight itself.

The terms *lecheor*, *lechiere*, and *lechieresse*—all having to do with licking—strikingly recur as signs of gluttony; in other words, behavior is more the focus than being heavy per se. It is as though the big person is incapable of being disgraced. All the words focus on the overall appetite, the attraction, the erotic quality even, more than on body lines. All focus on morals. In the prose version of Lancelot, the expression *lecheor* is used about a man living with a married woman; it is also addressed to Gauvain in the book of Artus to denounce his abuse of amorous liaisons and pleasures.[32] What counts is the transgression of a norm, of a proper attitude toward things and people, more than the physical characteristics, which are not taken seriously into account here.

We may also note the terms *cras* and *crais* and their probable distant relation to the big or the fat.[33] But the disgust for the abject dominates more than the rejection of the heavy. Here again there is a moral allusion rather than a physical denunciation, says Nicole Gonthier in her long inventory of medieval insults.[34] The *cras* quickly becomes the *croy*, in fact, and thus provides a nuance to the immorality, designating as *croy chosa* the intolerable sex pot, the contemptible woman who overrides all rules with her own errant strangeness.

It is important to insist on this ascendancy of the moral. Big people are not yet attracting that sort of attention. The moral ascendancy corresponds to a very specific, almost intuitive way of viewing the body; one where behavioral values remain dominant and mostly take priority over all indications of form or weight. It is not the weight of man but the ways of man that mostly come in for insults—the bawdy, the bastards and the idiots, heretics, prostitutes, and sodomites.

From Big to Very Big

The prestige of the big can yield, however, before the excess of the "very big"—when the enormous becomes the deformed, the ultimate physical disgrace. There is no precise measure of this threshold, no definition, just the allusion hardly ever discussed in twelfth-century Latin chronicles that distinguish *pinguis* ("big") and *praepinguis* ("very big"). There is a penalty, though, when it comes to certain gestures, places, and situations—the impossibility of mounting a horse, difficulty moving, powerlessness to do or accomplish something, and "inaptitude at war" when it comes to Philip the First as noted by Orderic Vital at the end of the eleventh century.[35] The pathology is undeniable. This deformity has always existed, just as it has always been pointed out. The criticisms of the very big concentrate solely on the idea of excess—true bigness is that which hampers mobility to the point of prohibiting it. Only the physical impediment, the difficulty moving become primary traits. A gray area persists, yet the big person can be praised, whereas the very big person may be condemned.

The oldest chronicles evoke the stigma of the extreme when their effects touch the lives of the powerful. William the Conqueror was so enormously fat in 1087 that the French king was led to say that the Englishman must be about to give birth.[36] Louis the Fat was so intensely heavy in 1132 that he contracted an illness that left him "absolutely stiff in his bed."[37] Queen Berthe of France's "extreme fatness" provoked her giving up the crown in 1092.[38] Chronicles also tell of accidents and deaths that allegedly followed from such extreme states including the death of William the Conqueror in 1087 and that of Louis the Fat in 1135. They are allusive, imprecise descriptions, however, that suggest an image-filled world and an obscure logic within which this "too much" finds a meaning.

The explanation given for the death of William the Conqueror is in this way representative, even if the chroniclers hesitate about the precise circumstances—a fall from a horse, a brusque hit against the horn of the saddle during the fury of combat near Nantes in July 1087, or a collapse due to summer heat. The reports are inconclusive.[39] In both cases, however, the accumulated fat would have melted inside the body. The bodily envelope would have let its matter dissolve like butter, creams, or gels. The Conqueror would supposedly have been submerged from the inside, overtaken by a breakdown of substances. The description of the death of Louis the Fat in 1135 is almost identical. The king is no longer able to mount a horse at age forty-six. He has become "the Fat" in the prime of life, thus confirming a clear physical weakening.[40] Louis's friend L'Abbé Suger, the most attentive and laudatory commentator in the manuscript written on the ruler's life, describes the growing "softening" and posits causes and consequences: dysentery, fevers, weaknesses, and disorders all attributed to his excessively "thick and heavy mass."[41] Extremely weighed down, the body of the king supposedly suffocates, losing food, blood, and waters leaking out of distended organs, provoking "stomach movements" and diarrhea.[42]

Two types of bigness therefore exist in these old accounts: the one relates to forms and forces, compact flesh and vivacity; the other extreme one, though without exact numbers, smothers "vital warmth" through its irremediable excess. The first is a sign of opulence, the second of disability. The border between the two is, of course, uncertain, for the distinction makes use of a changeable sentiment of immediate efficacy linked to weight: mass and density elicit dreams of health and vigor. The border is significant, however, since the distinction confirms that in the middle centuries of the medieval period the prestige of bigness really existed. It also confirms the belief in the value of enormous feasts and endless eating.

Still, numerous ambiguities exist where alongside the apparent density of the big person, there are softer, mushier volumes that combine improbable liquids with air and water. The archeology of the big must also contend with these opaque volumes. Thus a double equivocation emerges that will long be a part of the modern vision of bigness: the confused definition of substances and the confused definition of thresholds.

2. Liquids, Fat, and Wind

An initial ambiguity arises around the very existence of the "adipose." Hippocrates is careful to distinguish the big size of the athlete from that of the "fat man." The first weighted down by flesh, the second by fat.[1] The distinction is sometimes difficult to pin down, however. Caelius Aurelianus, one of the rare Latin authors to comment on physical sizes, groups them together under the generic term *flesh* (*superflua carnis incrementa*),[2] thus mixing together fat and that which is not fat exactly, and assimilating this excess to cachexia or wasting syndrome when he insists on the slowness of movement and the debility provoked.

There is no doubt however that medieval texts refer to fat: an oily, pliable and fundamentally aqueous material, sometimes more compact depending on the location, and of a composite, somewhat obscure nature. What are its proportions of water, oil, blood, or phlegm? What is its consistency, its density? It remains difficult to specify its origin and content. All that is certain is the immediate evidence: colors, odors, resistance, and extension that lump together many possible substances as sources of fatness. Even air must be considered since it is thought to move through the body provoking swelling and puffiness, a by-product of body heat as much as smoke from fire.

Matters of Fat

Medical texts hardly concern themselves with this fat. It is not part of the organs themselves, but it is judged useful. Its disappearance is often a sign of illness. It shapes, forms, prevents dryness, aids digestion, and protects from the cold. It also causes a certain delicate moisture. At the beginning of the fourteenth century, Henri de Mondeville offers this rather poetic description: it permits certain parts of the body to be "humidified and bathed in its unctuosity."[3] Fat serves and maintains the body's appearance. This adds to its prestige, even though its excessive presence guarantees enfeeblement. How is its presence in the body to be explained if this material is supposed to be useless? It was impossible to imagine human anatomy without it; impossible to imagine the body properly protected. These views are of course far from the ones we have today. All the more considering that in those ancient times body shape was not a function of muscle, but of obscure layers of fleshy mixtures.

The substance, however, seems impenetrable. Both a necessary and yet degraded material, fat is a waste product. It is what "remains," an accident, "undigested blood," says Bartholomaeus Anglicus in the thirteenth century, who supposes the substance became dense because of super abundance or excessive cold.[4] It is considered as one of those solidified substances that supposes a certain cold environment that hardens it like coagulated milk or frozen dew. It also resembles phlegm, although the difference between these two bodily components is not clearly established. Phlegm results from insufficiently cooked blood, "half-cooked" says Bartholomaeus Anglicus.[5] It is one of the four bodily humors along with blood, bile, and melancholy that together make "the first natural beginning of the body."[6] The milky appearance and thick consistency of phlegm contributes a certain round unctuousness as well. It's a sort of greasy fat, even though this association is never affirmed. A decisive clue that confirms its liquid nature is that phlegmatic people dream of watery landscapes, of streams, rivers, foggy lands, and horizons covered in "snow and rain."[7] Due to their size, they are plunged into a watery universe.

At this time phlegm is still the dominant humor of the female body. It accounts for its whiteness and medium density, while blood is the dominant humor of the male body and accounts for its "darkness" and firmness. Phlegm would seem to be all the more closely linked to fat since its very increase and profusion derives from fatty foods. Do they not all produce a "great phlegm"? asks Aldebrandin of Sienna in 1256. Hildegarde of Bingen offers a similar image when she foresees the most irascible gluttons accumulating a "dangerous and venomous phlegm."[8] Like fat, this humor results in a "weighty, slow" body,[9] a "soft tongue," "heavy, sleepy eyes,"[10] to which is added "spittle" and a "rumbling" tummy.[11]

One sees the inevitable contradiction of two possible attitudes. A large size which by its very imposing mass provokes respect as a sign of attractiveness and health versus a large size whose weighty swollenness saps energy and even disables. There's a borderline most likely that permits the "giant" person of olden times to be appreciated so long as size does not impede mobility, as well as a latent confusion that allows fat to connote density on the one hand and swollenness and fragility on the other. Finally, there is the effect of undifferentiated substances that allows bigness to be described in the most general terms as something "replete with humors,"[12] as Michael Scot puts it in the thirteenth century in his book on physiognomies where he defines the fat person as having an excess of humors that "swell the stomach and slow the body."[13]

In other words, the material poles of bigness range from the most compact to the most porous, from the most condensed to the most spongy.

The Deviations of Wind and Water

The ambiguity is compounded by another size factor that is apparently common, or at least frequently cited, namely, hydropsy (now more commonly called edema), a deformation of the body due to liquid substances alone. The diagnosis was a pathology linked to water. Certain testimonies evoke what modern medicine calls ascites, a condition already described in the second century by Arétée de Cappadoce as including a "sizeable tumor" of the stomach, "swollen feet," and a "moist" appearance of the arms and trunk.[14] This excess of especially abdominal fluid is explained today as originating from infection, cancer, or cardiac and arterial causes that affect especially the kidneys and urinary function. The medieval explanation was simply that a weak liver was pumping water instead of blood. Attention, however, was focused on the symptom and the unmistakable resemblance to fatness.

Other medieval accounts mention a "swelling of the whole body,"[15] "anasarca," a deformation called a "universal tumor,"[16] a general overflowing that sounds a bit like what twenty-first-century medicine might call "a serous invasion of cellular tissue" or what it might also call "obesity," an "adipose invasion"—a symptom that was attributed in ancient times solely to the presence of water.[17] In addition, there was also "leucophlegmasia," an exaggerated swelling of the body's surfaces and articulations.[18] It is of course impossible to specify further any correspondences with today's symptomatology. The old descriptions retain their obscurity.

However, one thing is certain. This hydropsy in various guises is systematically explained as a "disturbance" and, going way back, is ascribed to
the liver secreting this insipid liquid instead of the blood, which according to ancient thinking it ought to produce and circulate through the
body.[19] Instead of the latter there is a water that invades the body to the
point of a general "inflammation."[20] Excess drink, moreover, is sometimes
evoked—liquids that attack the stomach, infiltrate the liver, and impede
the passage of "nutritive material to the other organs."[21]

The image of swollenness is important to keep in mind. Medieval
descriptions and explanations rely on immediate perceptions and
imaginary ones too—the archaic image of receptacles and containers,
swollen bodies, blown up like a bladder or ball, organs that undergo a
process of rounding out. There is, for example, the image suggested
by the thirteenth-century miracle of Saint Douceline whose "sacred"
hands save a young religious Marseillaise girl from an inflammation
of the legs and abdomen so serious that the skin had cracked.[22] Such
accounts contribute to the intuitive vision of liquids causing a deformation of contours.

There is also the vision of other swellings attributed to wind, breath,
and air. This is evidenced by "tympanites" and its "winds,"[23] a special
type of hydropsy recognizable by the characteristic sound produced
when tapping one's fingers against a distended abdomen. In the thirteenth century Arnaud de Villeneuve evokes an imprisonment of excessive "moving winds" inside the body,[24] the difficulty of evacuating "airs,"
and spasms that "inflame all limbs."[25] Wind is one of the materials of
the body just as it constitutes one of the materials of the world. It is
born from heat, disperses, grows, and spreads inevitably throughout the
organs like a smoke that escapes "abundantly from green wood through
the action of a low fire."[26]

The medieval outlook believes in swellings and the possible role of air.
It believes in breaths that distend the skin as much as in quasi-occult
causes. There is the scene described in *The Knight of Landry Tower* (1374),
for example, where a young woman is punished for her sumptuousness
by the invasion of her body. An edifying tale indeed. We're first told
of the "excesses" committed by the "coquette"; then of the necklaces
and jewels, the make-up worn to church, and the disregard of calls for
more humility. The second moment is the shock of the punishment: a
hot wind infiltrates the guilty one and disfigures her shape. The third
moment is the humiliating avowal: "See the vengeance of God. . . . See
what I have become. I am fatter than a bladder."[27] Or consider these

scenes described in the *Visions* of Christine de Pisan a few decades later: turbulent noblemen in the reign of Charles VI are punished by "a wind from the mountains" that causes their bodies to swell enormously so as to better reveal their indignities.[28]

There is probably nothing "real" in these visions Christine relates. All is in the representation—of water and air which both occupy an important place in the medieval imagination. They guide the physical perception of excesses as well as of their possible erasure.

There remains this ambiguity between appearances which are nevertheless different: on the one hand fleshy but firm, on the other flesh that's swollen, soft, and blown up by liquids and winds contained within.

Gout and Gout Sufferers

Finally, there is a type of discreet, quasi-invisible fatness, considered to be linked as well to "excess" food and humors: gout. Its secretions attack the foot, inflame the nerves, infiltrate the joints, and swell up the affected parts immensely.[29] The condition of gout sufferer (*podagre*), in the absence of the reference to uric acid that future biochemists will identify, has long been known as a stigma of opulence. In a twelfth-century translation of the Bible, the king Asa becomes gouty or *podagre* in old age and is anguishing in pain.[30] The *pouacre* in plays of the fourteenth century is a vile bear, *vil et ors*.[31] And Bartholomaeus Anglicus in his descriptions of gout from the thirteenth century targets "those who live deliciously and overly sedentarily."[32]

The causes are liquids of course: "bad humors that descend to the ankles,"[33] "higher humors descending to the feet,"[34] and phlegm provoked by "watery meats on which the sick person is nourished."[35] Erratic substances, mixtures that result from failed digestion, these aqueous things circulate in the body with their obscure origins, their acidities, their localization in lower parts, susceptible of attacking hips, known as the "loin condition" for example—the sciatica of future nosographs, "the wooly condition" of Rutebeuf in the thirteenth century, "a most villainous gout," also called *goute de rain*.[36]

The origins are murky, even if the color of the inflammation sometimes helps differentiate the causes: blood when the color is red, phlegm when it is milky, anger when it is yellow. The sole fact, however, that women cannot be *podagre,* "purged as they are by their flowers,"[37] confirms the possible variety of these mixtures flowing "here and there."[38] A very particular "surplus" exists in the absorption of foods, a traveling accumulation that, without provoking a visible increase in size, does provoke a strong noxiousness. The proposal of curing it with a purge or bloodletting confirms that it has to do with something that is too much, a vision of certain excess.

The gouty person, while not being explicitly a fat person, nevertheless reveals what could be going on within the latter, namely, liquids of varying densities moving about. The "additives" are diverse, more or less visible, heavy, and painful. They all belong to the mixed category of the "fat" person. They are all related to materials whose repression seems totally simplified: expulsion, rejection.

The "Simplicity" of Evacuations

The image of "reducing," of evacuation and emptying, imposes itself as a matter of course. All the more so since the "very big" person is but an extension of the "normal" person. The only recourse then is a drying out, the erasure of this "too much" by expulsive, anti-inflammatory means, powders, "bitters," "astringents" that are intended to reduce humidities and firm up the flesh, such as with the treatment given to Louis the Fat, for example, in 1135. Suger insists on the practice of tightening, praising the courage of the king who was condemned to put up with the "strongest and most disagreeable potions" and the most intense "bitters" administered to dry out the interior.[39] The search for a constriction is thus added to that of an evacuation.

There remains the cure for hydropsy that was sometimes more involved, but with a similar goal in the end: the release of air and water. Jehan Yperman gives the "general instructions": bloodletting, leeches, laxatives, "hot fomentations with parsley and greenweed,"[40] and the usual evacuating gestures. Guy de Chauliac mentions "windy abscesses" whose smoky material "circulates throughout the body,"[41] against which he proposes a double treatment: dieting, thus limiting the production of air coming from "meats full of vapors from heating,"[42] and the application of "evaporating" and "extirpating" substances to eliminate excess air.[43] The procedures can be abrupt, as, for example, with the incisions made in limbs tied beforehand "above and below," pierced "with a razor" to allow for better escaping of the wind,[44] then cauterized finally with oils and gels to better firm up the skin.[45] The "smoke" is thus liberated like that released from some pressurized container.[46]

The imaginary of air, water, bladders, and containers, as well as the looseness and tightness of enveloping skin, all suggest curative practices without ever actually specifying the exact profile of the sick person in question. They are all "simple" measures however: let out what is too much. This shows to what extent thinning down is not considered to be a problem: reducing measures can solve everything. Their success is guaranteed, except of course when the condition is too advanced.

3. The Horizon of Fault

Many types of bigness coexist in the Middle Ages. One is a sickness due to liquid laxness and hydropsy; a second is a sickness due to the worrisome extremity of being "too big"; and a third, "the big person," is the picture of health with a forceful appearance. The latter figure is also the most important, being the outcome of ascendancy and linked to the prestige of accumulation and a tolerance for enormous meals and "endless drinking."[1] It is a figure that translates power and certainty.

Next to nothing is said, however, about the passage from being big to very big. In the eleventh century the "wide and robust corpulence" of William the Conqueror is long considered a sign of vigor,[2] before abruptly changing into a sign of weakness. The same is true for Philippe, William's contemporary, who goes from physical elegance (*elegantis corporis sanitate*) to a total breakdown without any distinguishing of forms or stages.[3]

However, in the middle centuries of the medieval period, a change in attitude occurs around the big person associated with excessive eating and daily rotundity. Criticism of the ordinary big person, no matter how vaguely defined, starts to build. Pressures rise. Different criteria come into conflict. Different groups accentuate what is for them anathema: the clergy preaches control and restraint; doctors do the same, insisting on the dangers of fat; and the medieval courts cultivate refinement.

The Clerical Model

The clergy's discourse and its impact changes during the middle centuries of the medieval period. In the twelfth and thirteenth centuries clerical austerity, for long confined to abbeys and similar isolated spaces, spreads into the heart of cities that have been transformed. The "urban flowering" at the end of the twelfth century renewed the community.[4] The city modified human sociability. Preaching can reach out, and "continence" can become a secular model. Poor friars intensify their message, simplifying it to make it more accessible, pointing out the "abuse" of the stomach as a general indicator of other sins.[5] Thus one gets the dramatic images in the long poem on the "quarrel between the limbs and the stomach" borrowed from the ancient fable of John of Salisbury, the bishop of Chartres who died in 1180. There the stomach is depicted as a "bellows filled with infectious wind," "a sack filled with garbage," "a dirty chasm," "foul receptacle," "an infamous swollen vessel."[6] The conclusion does not change: the stomach is indispensable to the limbs, it nourishes and "upholds" them. The severity, however, is decidedly more pronounced.

The theme sharpens in the thirteenth century. The organizers of confession target especially the new urban public. They reorganize the avowal of faults, playing on simplifications and concretizations.[7] "A pedagogical effort," says Mireille Vincent-Cassey: voraciousness must be contextualized, excess "visualized," suggesting situations and objects. This gives to gluttony and its symbols a clear depiction that they formerly did not have, right up to the bestiary associating the fat pig and the fat person, mud and massiveness.[8] The image, unknown before the thirteenth century, of the abusive eater astride a pig denounces a more vulgar, more passive sinner, carried off by the evil that possesses him. Meanwhile the bear, who will soon be substituted for the pig in this same image, has its prestige contested. The ferocious wild animal that had been a symbol of force is now only a symbol of excess. He carries the glutton and is his reflection.

What also enlivens the evocation of bodily forms in moralizing speeches and sermons is that allusion to the voluminous now implies overeating and avarice. The argument of various *exempla* clearly shows this within a new genre of tale made to concretize the doctrine. Thus, in a tale set around 1220 by Etienne de Bourbon, monks who are ineffective at electing their abbot turn the task over to the king Philippe Auguste. The king accepts, walks among them, inspecting their bodies, and makes his decision. Who is elected? The one whose "ascetic skinniness" triumphs over the redundant "massiveness" of the others.[9] What gets rejected are excessive contours.

There is nothing aesthetic about these criticisms. Ugliness is not central to the debate. What is central is vice: avarice condemned by the body's falling apart, the gravity of sin before all else. However, there may be a nuance of opposition, though limited, for the cleric may compromise somewhat and yield to the privileged, granting a possible normalcy to the "big person." Thomas de Chobbam shows this in his thirteenth-century proposal of "substitute penitence" for those whose status would render abstinence "difficult": "On the powerful and the rich, who are accustomed to the riches of a good table, one cannot impose an overly strong penitence or diet; also for those who, because of bad habits or perhaps also by natural constitution, cannot live without delicate foods, there can be imposed a substitute penitence in the form of donations and prayers."[10] Saint-Louis himself yields without hesitation to the "necessity" of noble tables, despite his sensitivity to the abstinence discourse of the clergy, it being impossible to escape "occasions of feasting."[11]

The slow work of medieval clerics remains constant, however, diffusing the value of abstinence against the culture of feasts, multiplying their texts and sermons. What continues especially is the dominance of the moral risk as evoked by Christine de Pisan who condemns gluttony at the beginning of the fourteenth century by assimilating "fattened flesh" to a stubborn "horse" that its master can no longer control.[12] The medieval transgression is above all getting carried away. Fat is, above all, passion. This "too voluptuously fed body" would remain for Christine de Pisan a "lost" insatiable object,[13] sliding toward an ever growing dissipation. Once again, the question is not one of aesthetics but of a moral failing and its insurmountable consequences.

The Medical Model

Doctors, another group with its particular culture, impose their views in the middle centuries of the medieval period, especially in opposition to the practice of accumulation. Not that the definition of what constituted "big" was any more precise or numerical for them. At the turn of the fourteenth century, Henri de Mondeville, the personal surgeon of Philippe Le Bel, refrains from describing the "big person," evoking the manifest evidence of such a state, the conviction it produces imposed by "sight and touch."[14] However, the doctor acquires more presence as medieval civilization advances. His pronouncements are no longer merely addressed to a single grand personage surrounded by advisers. They become more general, directed toward a public, and are supported by a more formalized university discourse in the course of the thirteenth century during which the idea of a "healthy regime" becomes more widespread.[15]

The originality once again is a question of rhetoric. Medical texts at the end of the thirteenth century do not put forward a general condemnation of the big person. They specify triggers and warning signs. Thus Aldebrandin of Sienna writes that man must eat in such a way that "he does not feel heavy after eating, nor feels his stomach to be swollen or noisy, and can breath deeply."[16] Bernard de Gordon writes that the quantity of food "ought to be such that one's breathing doesn't alter, nor one's pulse . . . and that one feels neither winds, contortions, gravity, or weakness."[17] If size is hardly defined, the palpable negative symptoms are closely surveyed. Sobriety is the central concern, and a sensation of heaviness is what throws it off.

And when a clearer definition of "fat" is attempted by doctors in the middle of the fourteenth century, the image of an extreme condition, of drooping flesh, remains the image most frequently given. The body is called "fat" according to the treatise of Guy de Chauliac in 1363 when "the person has turned into such a mass of fleshy fattiness that he can no longer walk normally, nor touch the ground, nor put on his shoes on account of the girth of his stomach, nor even breath without difficulty."[18] This is a decisive text that shows the difficulty still in the fourteenth century to discuss precise gradations of bigness, including exact amounts of fat and flesh. Guy de Chauliac, the surgeon of the Avignon popes, defines the fat person as the "ultimate," objectifying the thickness in question as enormous and unbearable in light of actions that are visibly impeded more than the forms and contours themselves. He goes for things that are easier to describe obviously, such as the difficulty mounting a horse mentioned in the eleventh century to describe the size of Philippe the First. Guy de Chauliac extends and aligns this procedure with the gestures of walking and touching. In the end he evokes the risk that arteries and veins will be constricted by the mass of flesh and the body will suffer a loss of natural heat due to the absence of blood and spirits.

In this regard, it is clearly the "very big person" and only this person that is being singled out by the doctor of the Avignon popes. This confirms once again the persistent ambiguity and difficulty of the oldest definitions. The result is the erasure of a whole range of degrees of bigness. The mental means that would lead to a designation of stages and gradations is perhaps lacking. There are no images or words to characterize the medium-big person. No excessive volume, no "too big" form is named, except for that which is approaching invalid status. This fact allows a certain "notable" heaviness to be "acceptable" or even "advantageous," though it will be rejected once the art of making finer distinctions is invented.

The Courtly Model

The third cultural pressure comes from the medieval courts and their social scene. Appearance itself undergoes refinement in the middle centuries of the medieval period. The lance carrier and the man on horseback are inevitably confronted with the increasing demands for dexterity and lightness. Models are at odds in the world of combat.[19] There is a growing expectation that power and lightness be united, an association of big and slim, even though social ascendancy is still associated with alimentary accumulation. One shows one's force with a ravenous appetite and one's dexterity with a more slender figure. Tristan, for example, already in the twelfth century has a singular profile: "seeing him so noble and so proud, his broad shoulders and slender hips, all complimented Rohault his father." Or consider Raynaut, the lover of "beautiful Érembourc," in a twelfth-century poem: "big shoulders, flat stomach."[20] Whence comes the implicit limit imposed on volume: excess arises when an activity, a movement, or vigor are impeded.

The art of the knight converges with its images. For example, the force and heft that jousting demands, the assault of lance against lance. Weight is of major importance, as it allows one to throw the opponent off balance and unseat him, causing him to "leave his stirrups." Vigor and heft are united in Galahad in the *Quest of the Holy Grail* where he resists the attack of three knights, "not budging from his saddle even though the force of the lances had brought his galloping horse to a standstill."[21] Besides this, there is the indispensable agility that only narrow hips could make possible. This explains the repetition of the alliance of wide and narrow, big and light that becomes the standard way of evoking a condition of adroit heftiness.

The prestige of the lion comes to compete with that of the bear before eventually replacing it. The royal animal has a powerful chest and mane positioned atop flanks that are as agile as they are slender. In the romance by Chrétien de Troyes, "Lion" is the nickname of Yvain, he whose blows crush opponents' spears to the breaking point.[22]

More generally, the medieval courts initiate a general socialization with dances, table manners, looks, and dress. There is a parallel difference in outlook for the female body, all the while maintaining important differences with the male body: an addition of delicacy and fragility to the limbs and an orientation of the gaze upward more than down. Yvain's damsel is "tall, thin, and straight."[23] The female body is described as more vulnerable, looser, at the same time suggesting a certain fleshiness. A mixture of refinement and tender flesh, of grace and fat. "Only at the end of the thirteenth century in France did beauty begin to be associated with a slim waist and relatively generous bust."[24] The lover of Ignauré in a thirteenth-century poem promotes the image of a "long and chubby" neck, "somewhat wide hips," "a thin waist," and "firm small breasts."[25] In the *Romance of the Rose*, also from the thirteenth century, Fortem has a lace tied around her waist that she raises to support her breasts.[26] Meanwhile, Nicolette allows one to suppose firm breasts with such a fine waist "that your two hands could close around."[27] In other words, thinness becomes an obligatory criterion.

4. The Fifteenth Century and the Contrasts of Slimming

The criticism of "ordinary" bigness increases in the fifteenth century. Access to images with identifiable sizes in illuminated manuscripts and frescoes occurs for the first time by the end of the medieval period, and this brings about a slow but explicit attention to contours, including attempts to specify and stigmatize excess. The theme takes on importance in the fifteenth century. Fat people who are now present in iconography for the first time understandably give rise to a new way of looking at them.

Bigness, for a long time, was hardly ever represented in the medieval universe. If the theme of the big or fat person was present in the language, it was nevertheless neglected in drawings and other representations. The Bayeux tapestries that were made at the end of the eleventh century to celebrate the conquest of England depict innumerable heroic figures, boats, battles, marches, and banquets, but hardly ever distinguish body types. The profile of William, who is known to have been really fat, is similar to that of his thinner companions. The silhouettes are all identical, with coats of mail that mould contours being the most visible.[1] Is this a sign of indifference to thickness or selective attention?

Realism becomes important, however, in the fifteenth century as the early use of perspective gives bodies a denser more three-dimensional quality. A number of scenes place figures here or there in a manner that underscores an attention to contours. The world of images is more discriminating about differences of appearance and size. With these new techniques of display, the body's volumes exist differently, revealing "defects" and suggesting excess.

There are, however, points of resistance. Models of restraint or refinement do not impose themselves all at once. The force intuitively linked to quantities of food as well as the link between ascendancy and physical weight do not yield immediately to vigorous sermons and medical advice. At the dawn of the modern era, the subject provokes conflicts. The greater awareness of physical forms is hardly met with a corresponding unanimity about their meaning or a rejection of the big.

The Ascendancy of Images

Contrast emerges abruptly in the iconography of the fifteenth century. A stomach can show a certain amplitude and the overall form can accentuate contours. In 1460 a figure accompanying the king in *The King of Babylon Giving His Land to His Two Sons* has a silhouette that is curved exaggeratedly in the front.[2] Yet it is a positive element, a rounded effigy ceremoniously accompanying the ruler. King René in Nicolas Froment's *Burning Bush* from 1476 is shown with a massive face and heavy double chin.[3] But this is hardly denunciation or irony—heaviness here remains the sign of ascendancy and authority. Nevertheless, contrasts do appear between silhouettes and drawings that confirm a heightened realistic attention to the disorders of the flesh.

The increased attention to physical traits is accompanied by a more pointed criticism of size. This can be seen in the image of the delighted observer depicted in the wedding of the Virgin in *The Book of Hours of Étienne Chevalier* from the mid fifteenth century.[4] The swollen face, closed eyes, short neck, round shoulders, and prominent stomach confine this person to being a ridiculous outside witness of the marriage between God and the Virgin, an awestruck city dweller clearly excluded from being considered eligible. The importance, of course, is this exclusion along with the exclusivity of the sacrament which together disfavor those who up until then pursued marriage but now no longer can. The depreciating effect of the massive contours is clear: the awkward heaviness, the rustic appearance, and grotesque gape say it all. A similar meaning is attached to the silhouettes of the "sacrificers" that surround Pilate later in the same manuscript: greatly dilated faces, heads hunched into slumping chests—every trait confirms lack of intelligence and wisdom. The criticism of the fat person is even more center stage with the depiction of the glutton in the fifteenth century *Parade of Vices*. The excess of volume is primary. The bear and the bourgeois who rides atop the gluttonous animal appear as symbols in the *Miroir historial* miniature from 1463.[5] The striking association of indolence and fat definitively unite the bear and the glutton.

The miniature takes on more picturely detail in the fifteenth century and the objects depicted become more differentiated. The criticism of size, however, remains largely moral—teasing over behavior and point- ing out faults more than an aesthetic judgment, even if the latter is never totally absent. Here, big = sin.

Stories go along with these criticisms as, for example, when Commynes at the end of the fifteenth century mocks the English king Edward for having been an exaggeratedly big eater, and the king dies in 1483 "choked" by his weight: "He took pleasure more than one ought, fearing no one, became fat and full, and at a young age his excesses overtook him and he died suddenly of apoplexy."[6]

Being big is clearly a dangerous failing.

A Social Distinction?

These contrasting contours also have social connotations. One notes, for example, two types of figures represented in the fifteenth-century minia- ture illustrating the collective banquet in the *Book of the Hunt* of Gaston Phoebus.[7] First, the aides: ordinary people, valets, beaters, grooms, and various other assistants shown making animated gestures and wearing loose, simple clothes. Second, there is the lord and his entourage making more controlled gestures and wearing clothes with fur and velvet. Those of the first group often have round shoulders, heavy faces, and some thick stomachs that contrast markedly with the postures and lines of the lord and his associates who are served at a separate table looking thin with long faces and belts tightened. Popular pounds on the one side versus distinguished slimness on the other? The physical attitudes would seem to confirm this, as one notices in the first group a certain voraciousness with valets and other assistants seated on the ground, tearing apart meat with their bare hands, sharing the same meal, drinking from the spout of a cask with heads leaning back—a sign of the abundance provided by the master but also of the simple spontaneity and abandon of common people. Avarice is behind the gestures just as fat is underneath the con- tours. These features are in stark contrast to the king, who is seated at a high table, possesses a knife and other utensils, approaches the food with reserve, eats small portions, and even seems to push a dish away to avoid any chance of excess. One also notes the raised finger of another figure to his right who might be the his doctor giving advice and especially preaching sobriety.

Illustrations from the fifteenth century depict specific groups within popular culture, notably professions that are synonymous with bigness: cooks, bakers, and butchers. All such figures are clearly shown with large bodies in fifteenth-century miniatures such as in Boccacio's *Decameron*, for example. One can note the cook serving Guiglielmo Rossiglione: thick face, stomach hanging over his belt, and overall heavy looking.[8] Or the baker Cisti, "intelligent and loved by all,"[9] walking in the streets of Florence with his round tummy out front. Here the popular enjoyment of size becomes a motive to literally draw attention to it.

There is nothing more cultural, perhaps, than these oppositions between the popular and the distinguished. They all declare the desire for distance, for a social code that uses these physical markers. These distinctions extend allusions that are already present, though rare, in medieval fabliaux where the villain is "big and stupid"[10] or a "terrible glutton."[11] Above all, they establish a social reference point where the low and the popular are associated with heaviness and the high and distinguished with lightness. The stigmatizing gaze is socially oriented, and a number of reference points get transformed.

Lifestyles and Conflicts

Conflicts remain, however, including among the privileged. The prestige of accumulation of pounds does not always yield to the norms of clerics, doctors, or courtiers. On the contrary—opposition continues in the fourteenth and fifteenth centuries. The exchange of letters between the Florentine merchant Francesco di Marco Datini and his doctor, Lorenzo Sassoli de Prato, around 1380 illustrates both social and cultural resistance. The great cloth merchant whose products traverse the seas practices the popular tradition. He counts on the health that comes with accumulation, takes care of his associates with meats, sends three pairs of guinea hens to comfort a sick servant, and stresses his prescription in a personal note: "Take care to eat them all because you won't find anything better or healthier to fill you, and I will continue to send you more."[12] The wealthy Francesco believes in the virtues of eating enormously: "good soup," "creamy cheese," "fresh eggs," "meats," "good fish," and "large quantities of fully ripe figs." Here health comes from taking care that one is generously and regularly fed. Clearly the old tradition has not been erased.

The doctor, on the other hand, exerts pressure to correct these customs, establish restraint, and associate "gluttony" with "shame" as he tries to sermonize the merchant with a leading question: "Is it proper to praise a mature man by telling him he is a victim of overeating?"[13] The doctor's missives are cast as rules for living, make appeals to "moralists and theologians," and evoke the "greatest sin"—again as much a moral as a medical vision of a body whose humors must be regulated. The exchange of letters highlights the diametrically opposed reference points for the merchant and his doctor.

The tension is the same in 1457 when Ludivico Sforza seeks out a doctor from within the Milan nobility. The prince wants to impose a low-fat diet on his own son, Gianfrancesco, judged too fat by the father, which already proves his acceptance of the principles of restraint. The doctor accepts, proposes a treatment, obtains the consent of the son, but fails to get the job done. It's impossible to successfully carry out the cure for a clear social reason that the doctor relates in simple terms: "Taking into account the variety and amount of foods, and after having presented to him many arguments about how overeating was harmful and unnecessary, his Excellency promised to cut back at his own table, but he told me that he did not want me to impose restrictions at the tables of gentlemen."[14] The doctor made his case and even partially convinced his patient, but still encountered an obstacle: the generous meal remains for many in the fifteenth century an image of force. The "tables of gentlemen" are the social stage, and abundance translates ascendancy and power.

Other signs underscore the permanence in the fifteenth century of a dream of endless ingestion of food: drinks flow like rivers, dishes are oversized and piled on top of one another at banquets of the nobility such as the marriage of Philippe the Good and Isabel of Portugal in Bruges in 1430 where wine "falls" like a fountain "night and day," patés are like buildings that partially block the view of men and animals, and the tables to receive all the food have five layers each two and half feet tall.[15] Only ostentatious abundance is capable of signifying plenitude, ascendancy, and health.[16]

Other examples, however, show the reality of the cure and its acceptance. Around 1430, Conrad Heingarter prescribes a regimen for Jehan de la Goutte, a friend of the Duke of Bourbon, whose great size (clearly noted: *homo pinguis*) becomes the focus of medical attention.[17] Conrad

Heingarter speaks of "big" (*pinguis*) and not "very big" (*praepinguis*)—subtle differences that are noted but not clearly defined. The precautions prescribed confirm the special targeting of a body that is supposed to shed water: do not eat or drink too much, avoid sleeping on your back to prevent humors from stagnating, do not sleep with shoes on in summer so as to allow smoke and vapors to freely leave the body, wash your face and hands with hot water in the winter to aid evacuation through the pores, begin meals with tender and even fat foods to facilitate the absorption of the next foods and avoid blockages. In addition, purges and bloodlettings are prescribed to "lighten" the interior (*medicine laxative frequenter*).

"Clear" and aqueous principles predominate. The suggestion of taking off one's shoes at night in summer evokes a change in lifestyle (from possibly *wearing* one's shoes to bed) as much as a belief about the efficiency of all evaporation no matter how partial or localized. Eliminating smoke and vapors is supposed to purify the skin. In sum, it's a wide assortment of recommended behaviors predicated on the familiar experience of releasing trapped water.

But an ambiguity remains, and will remain for a long time, about what exactly counts as "big" and what is unacceptable because "too big." How much is too much? This ambiguity is more acute in the case of men where the "imposing" stature blends with a massive authority and blocks out all other considerations. There are countless images from the fifteenth century where a full face, round cheeks, and double chin—especially for men—are supposed to evoke nobility, not gluttony. Van Eyck's *Madonna of Chancellor Rolin,* from the middle of the fifteenth century[18], for example, or the dignitaries who accompany Lorenzo the Magnificent in the *Procession of the Magi* by Benozzo Gozzoli from 1459,[19] or the self-portrait by Pietro Perugino at the Collegio del Cambio in Perugia with his intense eyes, voluntary stiffness, and heavy fat neck.[20]

The "Laborious" Place of Beauty

Once again, though, there is no mention of beauty in this will to reduce the big person. The only clearly designated aims are good morals and good health, not good looks. For example, the *Shepherd's Calendar* from the end of the fifteenth century defines the "healthy man" as "neither too fat nor too skinny."[21] The medieval treatises on beauty do not take up the subject of the body's envelope and its possible reduction. Étienne de Fougères's *Book of Manners* from 1175 is concerned with only four practices—applying makeup, care of the eyes, depilation, and skin care—and totally ignores the body's profile.[22] *L'Amiria* by Leone-Battista Alberti from 1470 and *Gli experimenti* by Caterina Sforza from 1490 only consider the face and skin care with no word about the aesthetic aim of bodily forms.[23]

There's no doubt the aim exists, but it is rarely if ever discussed. There are the hot tubs of Isabeau de Bavière, for example, from the fifteenth century, and drinks considered more "purifying" thanks to the presence of boiled gold that are supposed to contribute to "the health of the queen."[24] They are probably meant to enhance beauty as well by reducing her considerable size, which was known to all. But the latter aim is not named; it is a domestic issue that doesn't bear commentary. Persevering work on one's anatomical attractiveness seems not yet able to be acknowledged. All references to Isabeau's hot tubs and golden liqueurs treat them strictly as matters of "health."

One must look to more indirect, simple, and immediate practices to detect any concerted effort at slimming in the fifteenth century, such as, for example, wearing tightly belted clothes to hold in flesh. In 1490 Anne of France tells of a young woman who is "so tightly strapped into her clothes that her heart gives out."[25] There is also the wide belt that strangles the waist of high-status women in the fifteenth century, the two-sided strong belt of noble women in René d'Anjou's *Book of Tournaments* from 1460,[26] and a similar one worn by religious women in the *Théséide* of Vienna from 1480.[27] In other words, there is nothing with which to contain fatness but a sort of sheath applied directly and physically to the flesh—of women's bodies more than men's. Here too the aesthetic code is followed wordlessly.

It is worth repeating once more the relatively indeterminate nuances between "normal" and "too big"—an especially sensitive subject, of course, when it comes to men whose ample robes and coats allow "floating" volumes to appear as normal parts of the anatomy of ample men.[28] There is a scene in the *History of Brittany,* from the end of the fifteen century, depicting the gift of the manuscript to Jean de Malestroit surrounded by his entourage.[29] The full-faced men wearing large robes in contrast to the women strangled by their clothes is perhaps meant to underscore the ascendancy of the former.

PART 2

THE "MODERN" OAF

Criticism of the fat person changes during the Renaissance, becoming more centered on the slowness, laziness, and ignorance about things and people. "Care" for the fat person intensifies as well, becoming more centered on diets and physical constraints, especially belts and corsets that are applied directly over the flesh.

The cultural perspective shifts. Large physical size means above all heaviness. To become rounder is to fall behind, to be unadapted to a world where activity takes on a new value. Not that weakness or slowness had up until then been neglected or ignored; it's simply that medieval attention was most concerned with the moral dimension of overeating and gluttony. It was fixated on capital sins. The modern mind is instead worried about flabbiness and efficiency. La Fontaine's weasel feasting in the granary, who becomes "fat and round" to the point of not being able to get out through the hole by which she entered,[1] captures the no exit predicament and disability to which the big person is condemned. What was formerly a falling off is now worse, becoming stigma and rejection.

There is little change, however, about the representation of the substances, in particular fat. Sixteenth- and seventeenth-century doctors still give rather proximate accounts of its composition, while continuing with the most traditional methods for its evacuation from the body: purgation and bloodletting. The heightened denunciation is not accompanied by more knowledge, although a greater distinction is made between internal fat and water.

A very slow cultural slimming, however enriches the perception of the body's lines and traits during the sixteenth and seventeenth centuries. A few new expressions and diminutives enter into circulation to suggest different states of bigness. The subject is fundamental, even if the regular tendency remains describing the "fat" person in terms of the "very fat" person where the distinction is mostly latent, opaque, glimpsed more than studied.

5. The Shores of Laziness

Renaissance storytellers pause first over the awkwardness of the oaf: for example, the "fat cleric" who provokes a fall and impedes an escape in a story from the *Heptameron*[1] or the "big, heavy Dutchman" whose heavy drinking and general heaviness render all activity impossible in a tale from the *Hundred New Stories*.[2] More clearly still, there is Vauban's refusal in the seventeenth century to give jobs to big eaters and fat people who are judged "incapable of good service and not to be trusted with important affairs."[3] The poles of attention change. What matters now most is incapacity and awkwardness.

Nothing yet specifies the stages of this fat invasion. Nothing yet specifies the thresholds. The stigmatization of heaviness, however, and the faults attributed to the fat person, despite the silence when it comes to details of actual measurements, disrupt everyone's outlook in the end.

"Modern" Activity and Passivity

It is the criticism of the "heavy" and "enormous" person that changes in the sixteenth century. Indolence displeases. The useless is disquieting. Laziness becomes "the plague of human understanding."[4] One representation of this are the beggars fleeing the countryside, the new poor who

are pushed toward cities in the sixteenth century as a result of the widening economic gap between town and country. Another are the vagrants
mentioned by Sixte Quint in 1587 who "overrun all the streets and public
squares of the city looking for bread."[5] Laziness is being targeted here,
along with loitering, inactivity, and weakness. The Renaissance's larger
urban centers become new places of refuge for those condemned to pov-
erty by a general scarcity of resources.

Did the anathema toward laziness and unproductiveness contribute to
the increase in the denunciation of heaviness? There is apparently no connection between the powerlessness of the fat person and the weakness
of the beggar. It is certain, however, that the insistence on activity and
purposeful mobility would not come without consequences. One notes,
for example, the admiring observation of Claude Seyssel who mentions
the multiplication of merchants and professions as a sign of the times—
growing from "one to fifty" between the time of Louis XI and the beginning of the sixteenth century.[6] One can also note the increasingly made
connection between the lazy and the big, the slow and the heavy—an
association sometimes extended to a link between the passivity and the
physical weight of the beggar. Around 1570 Ambroise Paré relates that
women begging will tell lies to fool passersby about their true infirmity.
All are supposedly fat and lazy and all use artifice to hide their disguise
their inertia. "The chubby, fat-bottomed, buxom wench says she's from
Normandy and begs for alms pretending she has a snake in her stomach."[7]
Or the "big chubby lazy person . . . pretending to have an infection of the
breast" who lies spread out at the entrance to a church when really there's
nothing wrong with her.[8] A few decades later, there's the engraving of
Nicolas Guérard of *The Lazy* stigmatizing a central lack that is conveyed
in the response of the beggar to the threats of the policeman: never tire
oneself out or upset one's stomach.[9]

It's a paradox, of course, at a time of intense social segregation and the
nobility's contempt for manual labor, but it is truly the idea of "inactivity," doing nothing, and softness that is stigmatized more than that of
"work."[10] An assortment of references condemning paralysis adds to the
irony of Jacques-Auguste de Thou, for example, when he ridicules women
at court who must ride in carriages because "their overly large breasts prevent them from riding horseback."[11] The nobleman Faret makes the criticism of "voluptuous, flabby individuals who don't know how to occupy
themselves" in his *The Art of Pleasing at Court* from the beginning of the
seventeenth century, noting the necessity of seeming to be constantly
moving and busy.[12]

The court serves as an important model. The extension and diversification of the sovereign's entourage in the modern state reinforces the principles of socialization. "Good manners" become obligatory.[13] In the sixteenth and seventeenth centuries the court multiplies codes of politeness, cultivates particular looks, softens bodies, and increases the stakes of appearance where formerly a warrior code was more dominant. The courtier is no longer the knight. An imposing presence counts more than the former heaviness, as one notes when Thomas Artus makes fun of the worried appearance of old barons in the entourage of Henry III, mocking their slimmed down bodies, pinched shoulders, tightly buckled belts, and the healthy look that supposedly replaces the excess of their former fleshy faces.[14] The exercises pursued confirm this change as well—no longer just military training but attention to promoting ease of movement, posture, and everything belonging to refinement. Their value is symbolic, socially conditioned, and today studied and explored already a hundred times in works devoted to the courtly world.[15]

The meal as spectacle, the feast, and noble festivals do not disappear however. Nor do the massive representations addressed "to the guests and to written and pictorial memorialization" such as the meal offered at Versailles on July 18, 1668, that presented dishes transformed into immense constructions piled high before the wide-eyed stares of those at court.[16] Félibien describes it well, remarking the first tables of the feast of 1668 as a sign of rigorously orchestrated prestige: "Here was a sort of mountain where in all kinds of little caverns there were different sorts of cold dishes; there was the façade of a palace built from marzipan and other sugary cubes; here a table covered with pyramids of candied fruits; another with pitchers filled with all sorts of liqueurs; and one more covered with caramels."[17]

A model of thinness imposes itself in modern social references. The word *light* (*léger*) in particular is repeated frequently in Baldassar Castiglione's *Book of the Courtier* from 1528: "light and adroit," "strong, limber, and light," "force and lightness acquired through practice" are some of the desired qualities that patient apprenticeship will produce according to the treatises.[18] This is summarized by Nicolas Faret in his *Art of Pleasing at Court*: "preferably thinner than too fat, well-formed limbs, strong, supple, limber."[19] The lightness recommended is hardly ever defined in fact, but functions as a denunciation of heaviness and large volumes, as for example, the fat member of the reigning Medici family of Florence who is cited in Castiglione's text with contempt as a counterexample, even if no detail indicating the precise size of the prince is given.[20] There is also the hunting and military boot of the Duke of Saxony: "so extremely large" that it is brought as a trophy to Charles V after a victory against the Protestant princes in 1547, provoking hilarity at the court against the duke, who is judged too "big, fat and full."[21] An imprecise description, certainly, but "fatness" is clearly being rejected.

From Private Insult to Public Code

A more profound new development is that the intensification of contempt touches the language, building new expressions and displacing the horizon of words. A negative culture surrounding size is stated more than ever before, though still indifferent to precise indicators and quantifiable measurements. In the sixteenth century those with wide waists are repeatedly spoken of in strongly negative terms as "lacking spirit," "knowing very little," and "displeasing."[22] It's not even that they are really always fat, but they are considered so by allusions and metaphors: "slow" and "hick" operate as shorthand for physical references. The insult plays on images, suggesting something visible, whereas the Middle Ages ignored it. "Heavy" gets loaded with possible associations, designating those who don't understand much or well, those who show a lack of intelligence or subtlety. The heavyset are the fatheads in the *Hundred New Stories*, the simple ones with no discernment. The spouse of the knight of Haynau, for example, is a naive woman, chosen precisely on account of her "slightly wide waist"[23] so that she'll be more easily directed and shaped by her husband.[24] Or the people of Champagne with generous waists who are unthinking and unaware, like the country merchant from Reims who was long incapable of physical intimacy with his wife because he was too ignorant or stupid.[25]

From the start of the sixteenth century, the word *heavy* (*lourd*) elicits linguistic inventiveness, stigmatizing awkwardness and torpor. Many variations are created, *lourderie*, *lourdise*, *lourdeté*, and *lourdaut*—the latter designating in Bonaventure Des Périers's *New Recreations and Joyous Estimates*, from the middle of the sixteenth century, a badly educated, imprudent person, a man lacking principles and precaution.[26] There is also the person described as *grosse lourdière* or more simply as *grosse loudière* in the inventory done by Étienne Pasquier in 1560 to describe heaviness as well as vulgarity (*grossièreté*).[27] And there is a decisive accumulation of insults toward Shakespeare's Falstaff at the end of the sixteenth century where Prince Henry pours out an endless battery of insults on his fat victim:

How now, wool-sack! what mutter you? (*Henry IV*, part 1, act 2, scene 4, 129)

. . .

Why, you whoreson round man, what's the matter? (134)

. . .

These lies are like their father that begets them;
gross as a mountain, open, palpable. Why, thou
clay-brained guts, thou knotty-pated fool, thou
whoreson, obscene, grease tallow-keech (213–216)

. . .

I'll be no longer guilty of this sin; this sanguine
coward, this bed-presser, this horseback-breaker,
this huge hill of flesh (229–231)

. . .

Thou art violently carried away from grace:
there is a devil haunts thee in the likeness of an
old fat man; a tun of man is thy companion. Why
dost thou converse with that trunk of humours, that
bolting-hutch of beastliness, that swollen parcel
of dropsies, that huge bombard of sack, that stuffed
cloak-bag of guts, that roasted Manningtree ox with
the pudding in his belly, that reverend vice, that
grey iniquity, that father ruffian, that vanity in
years? Wherein is he good, but to taste sack and
drink it? Wherein neat and cleanly, but to carve a
capon and eat it? Wherein cunning, but in craft?
Wherein crafty, but in villany? Wherein villanous,
but in all things? Wherein worthy, but in nothing? (429–442)[28]

The dominant impression is one of overall heaviness, an invasive encroachment well beyond the stomach involving the entire body.

It must be said that popular songs also participate in the denigration of unpleasant fatness. A complaining song from 1633, for example, lists the displeasing features of the "Beautiful Alison" whose every bodily feature, by virtue of its excess size, demoralizes her husband:

> She has chubby arms
> Like a mustard barrel
> Her stomach is a frozen cabbage
> And her thighs like halberds.[29]

By this time a standard style has taken hold that fuses stupidity with heaviness, stigmatizes the useless, and fertilizes the language with a host of terms that can ornament the religious diatribes or the possible passions of literary texts. In 1539 Sagon does not hesitate to call Marot a "lazy, heavy, cowardly ass," "a fat ass," and "an ignorant calf."[30] A few decades later, the Catholics of Montauban readily describe the death of Pastor Daniel Chamier as the breaking of a "stuffed belly" or "rotten belly."[31]

Illustrations also confirm this tendency. In religious polemic, for example, Catholic iconography represents Bibles crushed under Luther's stomach, which is so big that he needs a wheelbarrow to get around;[32] while Protestant iconography represents the pope blown up to grotesquely huge proportions by a devil whose flesh is itself sagging all over.[33] Softness, but also debauchery and filth—the fat person definitely focuses the negative, incarnating in his appearance disabled movement and a disabled state in general. It is still a matter of opposition between "thinness" and "fatness" whose limits are felt more or less intuitively. This opposition sharpens contrasts. It plays with excesses more than it specifies actual traits. It most likely targets the very fat. It denounces that category with plenty of force, but with little definition or nuance.

Resistances and Fascinations

This allows the Rabelaisian giants to be symbols of mocking resistance. The figure of Gargantua, with his "good face" with "eighteen chins," his immense stomach, his belt of "three hundred ells and a half of silken serge," his marvelously phlegmatic complexion, stands out all the more as the ironic counterillustration of modern thinness. It revives the old fascination for lands of plenty, generous feasts, and endless eating. It literally incarnates a direction lineage with meaty feasting. The very birth of the giant, his arrival in the world, is provoked by the "large quantity of tripe" ingested by Gargamelle, his mother, one "fat" Tuesday, the third day of February, which exerted such extreme pressure on the stomach that the child was pushed out. The quantity of tripe, coming from 307,014 generously fattened cows, suggests that perhaps the birth took place as the result of a challenge or eating contest.[34]

Another ironic reminder is the stomach as first "motor." Gaster, the "noble master of arts," the "belly power" god of the Gastrolastres in book 4, is led to the most noble inventions by ordinary and massive appeals of the belly: "all arts, all machines, all professions, all tools and subtleties" are initiated by it.[35] The abdomen as ultimate source of inventiveness.

Rabelais fattens his text to bursting with an accumulation of fat remarks. A simple meal makes infinite associations between words and foods: the "dozens of hams," the smoked beef tongues, the "botargo" and "chitterlings sausages" that follow "delicious meats" accompanied by drinks "without end or measure" followed by "large quantities of mustard" shoveled continuously into the giant's mouth by "four of his men."[36] This infinity of oral desire stands as a facetious counterpoint at a time when the obligation to become lighter is asserting itself more and more.

Béroalde de Verville transposes this idea to a cosmic theater a few decades later in his *How to Succeed*, magnifying a world in which everything is "fat," including "the days of Lent." There are enormous amounts of food and outrageous characters, especially "Monsieur Lent," a traditional model of thinness, who has become so big "that the fat spurted from his eyes like fleas jumping into an oven sweating from cold."[37] Verville takes pleasure to farcical extremes, thus confirming that the dream of an interminable intake of food does not disappear in the modern era.

Sancho Panza plays a very similar role in Cervantes's *Don Quixote* from the beginning of the seventeenth century. Teasing, big off-color jokes, and vulgarities are all vehicles to recall the value of some earthly realism, and especially the "reasonable" poise that comes with the enjoyment of things and a full belly. His profile is right away suggestive: "big stomach, small size, thin bowed legs"; as are his habits: constantly eating; and desire, "Let's all live and eat in peace." The story is therapeutic about food intended to "comfort the heart and the brain." As governor of his imaginary island, Sancho throws into prison a doctor who is too "reserved" about meat and drink, thus inverting the medical advice of the day.[38]

It is worth pausing, however, over a particular image that shows the persistent ambivalence about the big person.[39] The subject becomes

explicit in this first grand literary narrative. The body of the heavy peasant who is promoted to become the squire of a knight encloses a mind
that is both "obtuse" and "clever."[40] It's the mind of a tricky realist, "a little
malicious" and with "a touch of playfulness."[41] There are countless scenes
where Sancho's banal pragmatism contrasts with the strange divagations
of his master. He becomes the man of immediate pleasures, with "ever
natural simplicity,"[42] who is always eating instead of dreaming. Pushed to
the extreme of caricature, he is the round circle, the opposite of the thin
line; he embodies the grounded truth of the earth in opposition to the
flights of the imagination. "I am in no state to give an account of myself
by recounting stories. . . . My housekeeper is waiting for me. When I have
finished dinner, I will return and be ready to satisfy Your Grace and the
whole world."[43] References to the big person can be moments for praising
the bon vivant who is intuitive and imprecise, and this ambiguous blending persists over time even if a criticism of fatness is clearly dominant.

The image of the laughing fat person lingers hauntingly in a number
of pictures and stories at the beginning of our modernity. The erotic, for
example, wants to display infinities of flesh so as to transpose a tactile
and sensual absolute as something always beginning anew. Brantôme has
a talent for evoking women as "big, fat, and fleshy furnaces with big proud
stomachs," women whose total fullness equals total seductiveness. Their
flesh abounds to materialize all the better the sensual and display its force
and intensify the intimacy.[44] Sixteenth-century storytellers know how to
mix the big with the low. For example, during a difficult voyage a cart
puller in the seventh of the *Hundred New Stories* who shares the bed of
his masters becomes as "hot as a mare" from contact with the "big back-
side" of the wife.[45] One may also recall the ordinary people who stand
out the most in Brueghel's village scenes, heavyset male and female danc-
ers and harvesters displaying abundant flesh and overflowing robes.[46] Or
Dürer's village woman in a treatise on proportion from the beginning of
the sixteenth century, which opposes highly rounded lines with the thinner norms of refined effigies.[47]

Models, however, definitively change. Now the fat person is no more
than an amusing or popular touch of nostalgia to reinforce new modes and
distinctions. Even Brantôme describes the "great narrowness" of "waist
and size" as an example of realized beauty.[48] "Thinness" also becomes the
leading attribute of an old doctor in love with a fifteen-year-old servant in
a story by Giraldi Cinzio.[49] Sixteenth-century tales can clearly mark oppositions, as in the example of Gianfranco Straparola's stories from 1553.
Castorio, an upright young man, admires Sandro, the ruddy peasant from

Carignano who has become "so fat that his skin looks like lard."[50] Overcome with jealousy, Castorio asks the peasant what did he do "to become so fat." He answers with a terrible declaration that the naive young man accepts without question: by having his testicles removed by an able surgeon. After some terrible pain, the operation is a success, and Castorio fattens up "as he desired." But then comes the jest. The "poor man" is teased and doubly so, first for the abominable pain he underwent and then for the ridiculous result of his efforts.[51] The young idiot waits in vain for commiseration.

More important, it is indeed a social model that links the fat and the vulgar (*gros et grossier*) more than ever before—a model that belittles the enormous and turns it into vulgarity. This defect is most highlighted by classicism, but the sixteenth century is already pointing out the traits: big-throated "ingestions" and exaggerated drinking are for Arétin attitudes of fieldworkers and mule drivers; heavy-footed clunky gestures are, for Pierre de L'Étoile, associated with peasants and idiots.[52] They are evident in some of the king's as yet uneducated Swiss guards that amuse members of court in 1602:

Looking at these foreigners pass
With ruddy skin and big butts
I thought I was seeing a parade of Bacchuses
Coming to harvest grapes.[53]

The increase of distrust toward big sizes is a definitive marker of modernity even if limits and thresholds are still hardly ever evoked.

The Refusal of All Skinniness

At any rate, it's impossible to understand the object of the stigmatization of "the fat person" without taking into account the equally troubling vision of the "skinny" (*maigre*) and the affirmation of an obligatory "equilibrium." One may note, for example, the remark of Jean Liébault in 1572, "Obesity is more fitting to beauty than skinniness."[54] The danger of skinniness is that it removes what a "normal" amount of fat is supposed to highlight, namely, volume and a modulation of forms. Thus one gets the strongly alarmed description of skinniness as an "extreme extenuation" of the body recognizable from the "looseness of the skin, which, when pulled upwards by the fingertips, detaches easily from the flesh."[55] This explains the possibility for social sanction of this skinniness such as when Josse Clichtove is summarily dropped as "royal confessor" in 1517 for being "too skinny,"[56] or Brantôme's irony about women who are "so lacking in bodily volume that all possible pleasure and temptation about them is soon lacking too,"[57] or Aretin's dry mock about the "convent hussy" considered so "slight and graceless" that her skinniness would turn her into a "possessed figure."[58]

A diffuse fear surrounds the image of skinniness, the "mask of death" evoked in stories and treatises.[59] Skinniness is alarming—it recalls famine, the plague, and wasting away. It suggests dryness, roughness, and weakness, which in the older collective imagination are all opposed to the springs of life. It points to the inevitable, to the path of aging, and to death. "There is nothing that dries one out like aging, even if it happens slowly."[60] The parchment-like skin of an old person contrasts with a baby's moist skin.

Skinniness also contributes to impotence; for example, as an impediment to childbearing, as with Queen Louise de Vaudémont in the 1560s who was considered by the Italian ambassadors as having "a very weak complexion, rather skinny more than anything else."[61] It can even be associated with madness, as Jean Indagine asserts, noting the bloodless men at Charles V's court with "long necks extended like storks" considered by the German physiognomist as totally "senseless and stupid."[62]

Skinniness incarnates the ambiguity of melancholics whose earthly humor and dry complexion push toward weakness and tormented thoughts. The great century of melancholy, the century introduced by the meditative engraving of Dürer,[63] the century of the wars of the Renaissance fought in the name of God and of the "sicknesses of time"[64]—calamities judged all the more unbearable as the disasters of the Middle Ages seem to soften in popular memory—is also the century that witnesses the emergence of the idea of genius, the grandeur of the artist as tortured visionary: the educated class "oppressed by black bile, detaches its thoughts from the body and bodily things to unite itself with the incorporeal."[65] But black bile is what dries out the body, provoking weakness and skinniness. It endangers life. This explains the proliferation of books on melancholy in the sixteenth century with their insistence on the dangers of excessive thinness and suggestions on how to limit its effects. There are "supervised" diets for men of letters, the advice of André du Laurens at the end of the sixteenth century counseling that one surround oneself with bright, pleasant colors—red, yellow, and green—to avoid "troubles of the mind and black vapors that pass continually through the nerves, veins, and arteries between the brain and the eye."[66] There are also the suggestions of Timothy Bright who counsels ingesting quantities of liquid foods "to modify the dryness and humor of the body."[67]

The description of the thin person becomes more developed in the writings of La Bruyère, illustrating clearly how the drying out extends to something "moral" with "hollow eyes," a "hot looking face," and possible "stupidity" that is said to accompany lowness and timidity.[68] In contrast is his description of Giton, a man with a "full face," a "rich" man whose bearing is "firm and deliberate" thanks to his "broad shoulders" and "high stomach," and whose confident manner supposes thickness and density. La Bruyère emphasizes contrasts: force versus fragility, fullness versus emptiness, the unfortunate, vulnerable situation of the thin person versus the assurance and serenity of the rich person. His account would seem to recall the old ascendancy of "the big." The theme receives an original treatment, though, with new details added by the moralist. For the first time he insists on a criticism of possible pretension. Giton inaugurates a particular character: one whose discreet roundness translates an "unacceptable" power, the body transformed into redundancy, a status transformed into abuse. Moreover, his "enjoyment" is "presumption."[69] No longer the popular vulgarity, it seems, but an imperial thickness, the exuberance of the powerful. Thus one gets a reorientation of the criticism. At the same time, the theme is original for another reason that touches on the ambiguity of thresholds. Giton is thick without being explicitly fat, imposing without being an imposition. He is heavyset without falling entirely into the truly heavy. There is, however, abuse, a discreet excess, impossible to clearly evaluate, as neither measurements or precise words specify the matter. A new type of oafishness is born though not entirely defined.

Yet another form of thickness, more easily accepted even if it is rarely cited, is present in some of Saint-Simon's infinite number of descriptions, one that suggests a possible nobility emanating from a "measured" bigness. Not that of the Prince of Monaco, for example, who is also evoked by the essayist as "fat as a hogshead and unable to see the end of his stomach,"[70] but rather instead that of Monseigneur, a man of royal blood, "on the tall side, very big, but not with piles of fat, with a high and noble air with nothing rough about him." His height no doubt permits the loose appearance that makes him handsome on horseback where Monseigneur "was in his element and looking very well indeed."[71] There's an indescribable density, more a characteristic of men than of women, that eventually allows a steady bearing to impose itself. The approximation of a threshold here bespeaks the entire ambiguity of the matter. There is a way for men to affirm a martial air that blends a relative bigness with an uncontested grandeur. This underscores an insistent tendency in the mythological references to the bodies of the powerful, namely, the stakes of bigness—the sad softness of the swollen, but the indeterminate ampleness of the "strong" (forts). All these distinctions are shown more than commented upon, "practiced" more than rendered explicit.

Here at the dawn of modernity, it remains the case that, to be understood, the necessary but imprecise presence of fat that is supposed to give form to bodies requires an understanding of the concrete, threatening, and equally imprecise reality of thinness.

6. The Plural of Fat

Doctors of the sixteenth and seventeenth centuries use fat to accentuate their emphasis on a norm. Their examples become more precise. Their repertory of symptoms becomes more diverse. The observations are more numerous even though they still avoid questions about possible "stages" of bigness and their possible gradations.

There is no extensive transformation of the image of fat, which is still strictly limited to intuitive markers; but there are new attempts to specify its origin, its states, and its particularities. All arguments, statements, and even wild ideas confirm a heightened preoccupation with bigness. Hydropsy and adiposity are distinguished, plethora and apoplexy become more precisely defined. Knowledge increases, though nothing proves its usefulness, and the traditional vision and treatment of the fat person do not change.

Dramatizing the Threat

The doctors of the sixteenth century resort to alarming descriptions: intolerable weight, impeded body movement—the fat person becomes a focus of ridicule in order to better impress on the public's mind a justification of "sobriety," while a relative indifference to defining thresholds clearly continues. For example, the phlegmatic, described by Ambroise Paré as rheumatic and overflowing with thick liquid, only exists as an extremely enlarged figure with a "leaden, swollen front," "heavy, gross, and stupid" mind, a stomach emitting "froggish noises," an individual "vomiting," "spitting," "projecting excrement from the nose," with a "dog's appetite," and beset with "edemas and tumors."[1] The phlegmatic is someone with inflammations that attack the head, organs, and skin and that spread over the entire body. This maintains an ambiguity between phlegm and fat and equates misfortune with extreme heaviness. What's more, such extremism adds to the idea of a "temperamental" origin of the fat person, a "too much" that comes from the depths of one's being, with its aqueous qualities and other troubling substances; whereas at other moments one has an evocation of the "incapacity" of the gourmet and glutton and the idea that fatness results from daily behavior with its passions and "endless eating." In other words, it's difficult to distinguish between what is innate and what takes shape slowly.

The use of extreme references occurs again in the writings of Henry IV's doctor, Joseph Du Chesne, an amateur storyteller whose historical anecdotes published in 1604 offer a gallery of "models" chosen from the past that recount the ignominious end the overly fat person will face.[2] There is Pomponius whose great size requires him to carry his stomach around in a wheelbarrow; Adelbert, the bishop of Worms, who died suffocating in a body that had become "grotesque"; Denys of Heracles, the hedonist philosopher, who was subjected to leeches day and night to treat his landslide of flesh. The argument is new: invoke the "monstrous" to better disturb the public and transform "abusive" bodies of the past into "unquestionable" lessons for the present. The "vituperative" doctor intimidates. He imposes by alarming and preaches with threats without the least nuance or limit.

There remains the quasi-pedagogical evocation, this exaggerated transposition of the very big into a warning sign about the danger of all excess. The gluttonous passion is even sometimes described as the ultimate punishment: constant ingestion, endless meals, such as with the madness of the Baron Montfort related by Louis Guyon in 1614.[3] Montfort is so far gone that he renounced all sleeping in order to eat more. As though eating made everything increase: feverish feeding, infinite accumulation. It offers doctors a way to exploit fear. The accent is placed less on the sin and disorder of the gourmet than on the physical defeat and falling off of the endless eater; the point is less one of fault than of perishing, even though the doctor retains a preachy tone and is short on explanation.

The images are specifically focused on the extreme, because judged to be the most visible and striking, and tend to ignore all intermediate stages. Nothing is more difficult than explaining degrees of something. Nothing more difficult to apprehend either. This is evident in the description of Catherine de Médicis's doctors by some Italian ambassadors. These doctors express no worries until the queen becomes "enormously plump."[4] This might explain the possible enduring silence over "medium" fatness, the beginnings of becoming too big, its stages, and slow progressions.

Fear of Apoplexy

A number of symptoms related to bigness are better objectified by "modern" doctors: plethora, apoplexy, and hydropsy. A number of links between volume and symptoms become more fixed, although volume remains largely undefined. Laurent Joubert is one among those who theorize this attention to symptoms in 1578, reserving for the doctor "intelligence about many things that people do and say without knowing why."[5] Such an initiative has already been largely studied by historians, revealing the emergence of modern science, the attempt to push away folk knowledge so as to better specify new ways of knowing, though still formalist, and deepen affirmations about the palpably visible.[6] Observations seize on objects in order to specify them better.

It is filling up, the accumulation of "an abundance of all the humors," that takes on greater presence.[7] Not just simple stomach pain, for example, as evoked by Aldebrandin of Sienna or Bernard de Gordon in the thirteenth century, but an ensemble of interrelated signs. A certain Jean Fernel in 1550 notes "reddening of the eyes," "beating arteries," "lengthening of the body," "slowness of movement," "heaviness of sleep," and "suffocating heat," thus privileging concrete observation instead of the old pronouncement of diagnostic certitude.[8] The sense of "too much" becomes more refined and diversified, even if the investigation into this plethora still has trouble distinguishing between the simple presence of blood and that of fat and humors. A threat is also specified that targets "some violent and pressing symptoms"—apoplexy.[9]

This mortal accident, with its abrupt loss of consciousness and all sensation, was not "discovered" by sixteenth-century medicine. Bernard de Gordon already mentions it in the thirteenth century, claiming plethora as its "antecedent cause."[10] The risk of apoplexy had been noted for a long time. Everything changes, though, between the medieval commentary of these deaths and the modern commentary of these same "accidents." As we saw, in relation to the "drama" of 1391 involving Gaston of Foix's return from a hunt, Froissart especially insists on the immediate effect, the total surprise, and the effort to bring the count back to life by giving him "comforting things" to restore his force.[11] In that account there are no early signs, except perhaps the big meals evoked by Froissart more as ornament than as omen. One notes the necessary step taken after the accident: the attempt to "fortify" the "patient" during his loss of consciousness, the turn to food to restore force.

With another outlook comes another approach, however. In the classical France of Saint-Simon, the death of Monsieur provokes exactly the opposite gesture. Moreover, the early signs are insisted upon: the prince's large size, "worn out by debauchery, fat, no neck,"[12] the impassioned dispute with the king, his brother, some hours before the fatal accident and the "inflamed visage" that followed, and the meal where Monsieur "ate to extremes," downing "all day the patisseries, jams, and other treats that always filled the tables, cupboards, and his pockets."[13] The reference to signs targets behavior, physical features, and the skin. They imply a more mechanical and familiar representation of vessels and their saturation, tension, and possible blockages of the natural course of blood "rolling like through the tubes of a fountain."[14] Apoplexy is thus more associated with the world of the fat, to the point where Monsieur's confessor threateningly warns the prince some months before his death.[15] The only treatment in this case: bloodletting, the evacuation of the "too much" rather than its "reinforcement."

The discovery of the blood's circulation in 1628 probably played a role in the development of these fears. The massive influx and rupture of canals that are now better understood lead to a crisis that is quite different from what was described before. The earlier situation was linked to a lack of force, the later one to a visible pressure. More important, there is a new way of observing that starts in the sixteenth century, long before the discovery of blood's circulation, that gave more presence to apoplexy: redness in the face, thickening veins, and diverse feelings of lengthening or heaviness. Doctors observe differently. One notes, for example, the certitude of Jacodomus Lommius, the doctor of the princes of Orange around 1550, who points out those most exposed to this condition as being people with "short thin necks" who lead an "idle life, passing their time eating and drinking."[16] There is also Nicolas Abraham de la Framboisière, at the beginning of the seventeenth century, who points out "phlegmatics and drunkards who have short necks."[17] The image of the "short neck" recurs often among the notable signs, an indication of compression, internal constraint, of difficulty living or breathing. The image of drink also blends with these traditional, intuitive effects of "filling up."

Jean Riolan explains it even more, invoking the "large size" and "compression of the neck" (*collum breve*), where both constrict the "passages" and tend to "deprive the brain" of its blood, obstructing carotid arteries and "cephalic veins" and thus blocking nourishment to the head, resulting in an abrupt loss of consciousness caused by compression of the flesh.[18]

Apoplexy is more frequently cited in memoirs and other accounts. Pierre de L'Étoile, whose *Journal* gives a sort of inventory of sudden deaths occurring at the end of the sixteenth and beginning of the seventeenth century, describes big eaters, notes scrupulously the aqueous climate, the "humid, unhealthy" air, the "muggy, rainy" weather that all weigh on the humors, increasing the number of "apoplexies."[19] The letters of Guy Patin some decades later multiply the examples of "good, round, full, ruddy companions" dead from "apoplexy or from some suffocating inflammation."[20] Not that bigness gets any better definition here. The symptoms that are likely to accompany it, however, are more closely observed.

Fat Talk, an Abstract Discourse

This does not mean that there is better knowledge of what fat is. Confusion persists, as well as strange associations between the abundance of fat, of blood, phlegm, and other humors. Everything stems from "the combination of heavy feeding and idleness," affirms Henri de Monteux in 1559,[21] or "intemperance and idleness," writes Michael Ettmüller in the seventeenth century.[22] But this "everything" remains an opaque mixture, even if engendered by a common cause. Blood and fat, though distinguished as words, are silently confused as factors contributing to a heavy accumulation pressing on flesh and vessels. Jean Deveaux, the author of *One's Own Doctor* (*Médecin de soi-même*) at the end of the seventeenth century sees as proof the "quantity of blood" provoked by "debauchery" and immoderate practices that lead to excess materials.[23]

Fat remains an obscure substance for seventeenth-century medicine. It is a substance that, outside of all chemical knowledge, is known through intuitive references and partial observations that combine divergence and obscurity. Disagreements on the subject multiply, proving only the new interest in exaggerated thickness. About its localization, for example, Jean Riolan affirms in 1661 that fat is held together by a membrane under the skin, a sort of "tunic" that can grow in size while covering the body "like a piece of clothing."[24] Whereas in 1672 Diemerbroeck insists on the diffuse character of this "oil" that infiltrates with no precise limit.[25] In 1682, Fabrice de Haldan suggests, on the contrary, that there are balls of fat accentuating the volume of the stomach and floating freely in the abdomen like so many "autonomous" objects susceptible of being expelled like waste. This is supposedly proved to Haldan by a fat patient who abruptly becomes thinner after expelling from his anus three balls of fat covered with skin. No surprise, however, once these balls are sliced in half: the fatty envelope reveals a gelatinous pulp of silvery fat that is rather compact and milky.[26] There are disagreements about the origin of this material as well. Does fat come directly from blood, essentially its denser component that the liver supposedly badly processes, as traditionally said? Or does it come from chyle, a white, milky liquid that issues as a material from the stomach, an aqueous conversion of food before it is transformed into blood by the liver, as Michael Ettmüller believes?[27] At the beginning of the seventeenth century, Sanctorius considers fat to be the effect of a relative cooling of humors (*ex frigiditate*) that leads to a certain petrifying of material.[28] There are also disagreements about what it resembles. Is the "nutritive essence" of fat related to that of nerves, as the English anatomist Walter Charleton thinks,[29] or to that of milk, as the French physician Charles Perrault believes?[30] Finally there are disagreements about the stability of the material. For example, fat is presumed to be in movement once the circulation of blood is discovered by Harvey in 1628 and the lymphatic system is discovered by Aselli in 1647. Malpighi claims to show fat traveling and sliding as it's distributed by the abdomen to other parts of the body through "adipose canals" making improbable passageways;[31] while Claude Perrault imagines oily stocks bringing nourishment in case of necessity in a way similar to how marmots and bears in their winter dens absorb their "lard."[32] There is also the vision furthered by microscopes in the second half of the seventeenth century that orients toward unexpected descriptions discounting the localization of fat, imagining sacks, pockets, and glands as minuscule opacities the magnifying glass reveals as saturating muscles and skin.

These indications are largely formal—esoteric even—and hardly serious. They are confined to hypothesis, limited to the narrow circle of medical elites, and their effect on practice is all but nonexistent. They only testify to the increased interest among European doctors of the classical age in this fatty substance and to their relative powerlessness when it comes to explaining its creation and composition. The doctors' unquestionable curiosity and demands do not yet translate into anything truly practical or medical.

Specifying Hydropsy

It is especially concerning hydropsy that a new vision becomes established in the sixteenth and seventeenth century with a clearer opposition between the swelling of erring waters and the density of fatty flesh. Ballooning, on the one hand, and compactness, on the other, organize the differences between the hydropic and the adipose person.

More attention is paid to the effects of dispersed aqueosities. Observations are more pointed—the eye judging the possible modification of volumes according to different gravities, body bent, body prone, each with different floatings; the finger measuring the possible depression into the skin; the ear listening for the possible noises of the waters. One example, among others, is the affirmation by Ambroise Paré in 1570 that when "the patient is lying on his back the protuberance is less apparent because the water spreads here and there."[33] This explains the differences in the flaccidity of contours. One symptom dominates in descriptions of the sixteenth century, ascites and its exceptional abdominal expansion and aqueous resonance. Jacodomus Lummius shows how the swelling in this case is confined to the lower parts of the body, beginning with an invasion of the legs, followed by that of the abdomen, while leaving "the rest of the body thinner."[34] This is in marked contrast to the overall invasion in the adipose person.

The anatomists pause over these movable masses. The hundred and eighty pounds of "rotten water"[35] found in the bowels of a woman dissected by Vésale in the middle of the sixteenth century or the "great quantity of reddish water" extracted some decades later from a cadaver of a "young Utrecht girl" whose stomach had become "incredibly enormous" while the rest of her body remained "strongly emaciated."[36] These are all cases of liquid accumulation that are judged quite differently from the compactness of fat people.

Classical-age doctors also spend time developing mechanical explanations: the strain exerted by excess humors on the liver, for example, the organ "producing" blood, and how these humors crush the blood's canals to the point of obstructing the passage of liquids and serum fluids, disturbing the interstices and generalizing diffusions.[37] Or overly cold drinks that paralyze a patient's organs, as Ettmüller affirms, acting during the night and accumulating hepatic chills and excess before the exaggerated swelling of the stomach is noticed.[38] The hydropic person has a particular profile, combining thinness due to lack of "food" and engorgement due to excess water. This is precisely the description given by Jean Lhermite in 1598 of Philippe II, who died of "hydropsy": "his calves, thighs, and stomach were very swollen, while the rest of his body was so thin as to be only skin stretched over bone."[39] Other causes would seem to have been possible: urines, hemorrhoids, or retained menstrual fluid—all conditions mobilizing different humors.

The artificial opening of the stomach, however, is done more carefully. Around 1580 Ambroise Paré can still find "normal" the story of the Parisian porter named "Go-if-you-can" (*Vas-si-tu-peux*) whose enormous stomach is pierced by the knife of a companion in some kind of brawl, exuding a "quantity of rotten water,"[40] before the man recovers his strength and goes back to work. There remains the delicate problem of making an incision. In 1613 Nicolas Abraham de la Framboisière insists on the necessity of alerting "the friends of the patient that this remedy is accompanied by great danger."[41] In the middle of the seventeenth century, Lazare Rivière, after having mentioned the case of a man "opened" without feeling any pain, describes him dying "without any strength left" some hours later. The observation is clear: "Never have any of those operated on recovered."[42] The 1683 treatise of Thomas Sydenham on hydropsy confirms the inevitable failure: vital lesions, gangrened flesh.[43]

Strange beliefs persist. Lazare Rivière, for example, affirms around 1680 that hydropics with swollen legs can get rid of some fluid by cutting their toenails short to the point of bleeding.[44] The image of a bladder containing liquids like a wineskin has not been erased. Strange convictions persist as well, such as in the description by Margrave of Bayreuth of a curious malady overcoming a German princess at the start of the eighteenth century: "Her body swelled up enormously every morning and the swelling subsided every evening."[45] And there are the odd cases described by Marco Severini in the seventeenth century: anatomies deformed by immense extravasations transforming their backs into a number of extremely curved little "bellies."[46] These are mysterious, secret symptoms noted with little commentary or explanation. The novelty, let's repeat, is elsewhere, in the better definition of hydropsy, a better definition of its incidence and its aqueosities.

There are also new limits however. Obstacles to a clear definition arise from doubts about the origin of the growth, as well as from the "diversity" attributed to the malady—a disorder that is above all associated with these volumes. Thus Tommaso Campanella in 1613 cites hydropsy right away as one of the major maladies he wants to prevent among the inhabitants of his "City of the Sun."[47]

Specifying the Excess of Gout

In addition to the interminable debates about the origin of fatty or aqueous matter, there are the interminable debates about the origin of gout, also considered to be linked to "superfluities of humors."[48]

In 1550 Jean Fernel suggests an explanation that breaks with tradition: the tightening around the brain of humors then falling by gravity and infiltrating overly soft or uncontracted articulations.[49] The brain would act like a plunger, its coldness attracting humors upward before letting them fall down loaded with hard cold phlegm.[50] Whence comes the beginning of the malady: the liquid mixture, thoroughly pressed under the skull, slides into the narrowness of the joints causing irritation and impeding movement. There is also the overall image of a body traversed by humors, a sort of cycle where the vapors rise and, once condensed in the head, fall back down toward the limbs, stopping at the very bottom. Following Jean Fernel, Nicolas Abraham de la Framboisière claims confirmation of this fall by pointing to a traveling pain specific to gout patients: "one senses the pain little by little along the neck, or through the shoulders and along the elbows and hands, or along the back."[51] The pain is a disturbed distillation: the "defluxion" is all the more swollen as the malady of the brain is revealed, provoking "excrement and superfluities."[52] The description of the gout patient is complicated further, inflammations take over, obstructing spittle that is dense with condensed matter.

There remain a number of disagreements about the origin of these joint torments, all supposedly linked, however, to excess humor as well as to some eating excess. There is no doubt about the superfluities, particularly ones that fall down from the head like "a fountain of inflammations [catharres]";[53] but there is a multiplicity of hypotheses concerning the presence of other disorders, digestive troubles, unprocessed mixtures, and the lack of coction,[54] for example, the body's insufficient "cooking" of certain foods. In addition, there are impeded flows: "menstrual or hemorrhoidal,"[55] sweats and abscesses—diverse substances that are retained too long. Suggestions abound even as to the specific role played by wine, for example, in this account by Thomas Sydenham of his private experience in 1683: "Though it's true that overeating and a too large quantity of food often produces gout, it is even more often the result of excess consumption of wine whose harmful vapors corrupt the digestive bacteria, precipitating uncooked particles, and loading the blood with an abundance of excessive humors that weaken and destroy animal spirits."[56]

The sources of gout tend to diversify, even if the malady appears primarily as the "child of wealth," to the point where Paul Dubé writes in 1640 that he long hesitated about including it in his "maladies of the poor."[57] Louis XIV's doctors seize an occasion in 1697 to accuse the wine of Rivesaltes of having provoked an episode of gout so strong the king was prevented from sleeping more than "two or three hours,"[58] and another in 1698 to decry the "great meals of Fontainebleau" supposed to have produced a "swelling of the right ankle" (301) and another in 1699, when eating a "highly flavored ragout," triggers such a sharp and enduring pain that the king "cannot put weight on this foot" (304). And then there are the "strong, cold southwest winds" that occur in December of the same year that "make the gout last longer" (305). It's a serious malady that causes the king to have "shivers," "sharp pains," "weaknesses," and "dizzy spells." The "infirmity" of gout impedes walking, necessitates constant care, special equipment, and transportation such as a wheelchair that becomes necessary for the king to get around starting in the 1700s (304).

Beyond these debates about causes, the *Health Diary of Louis XIV* (*Journal de santé de Louis XIV*) shows the impossibility of identifying a gouty humor. The malady is too mobile: seizing the foot, conquering the ankle, spreading over the flesh of the leg, attacking the shoulder, turning into a cold, or alternatively deciding to move to the head (320). It is also too obscure: "It seems that no one has yet discovered exactly from whence it comes or how it flows."[59] Nothing is more difficult to master than this humor, whereas it's clear it corresponds to an "unhealthy lifestyle and too much idleness."[60] Nothing is less identifiable, even though its mechanisms appear to be close to those of the fat person.

The only suggestive parallel would be the description of the gouty person proposed by Syndenham at the end of the seventeenth century: "big head," "full, soft, humid corpulence," "strong, robust constitution."[61] Overeating is considered central, it would seem, to the mechanism that triggers it, but the consequences remain somewhat mysterious.

Despite these confused images of excess humors, their removal is prescribed with a single program: evacuating, cutting back, drying out. But slimming down is still a singularly complex problem.

7. Exploring Images, Defining Terms

Beyond the world of medicine, a new curiosity about size expresses itself in the sixteenth and seventeenth centuries through more developed iconographies and a wider array of terms for thin and fat.

Engravings and paintings attempt more than before to represent the heavy person, to give visible detail to the apparent shortening of the limbs, the squashed neck, and the flabby chin and cheeks. The associated terminology tries to suggest nuances in the absence of all quantified measurements. New words try to express degrees of profiles beyond the sorts of insults already mentioned. These gradations remain obscure and vague, however, and often of limited use. There are, at any rate, more terms available in the sixteenth and seventeenth centuries to specify levels of bigness, whereas they had been extremely rare in the medieval period, even if odd combinations persist. For example, in his *Diverses Leçons* from 1604, Louis Guyon associates thickness and tallness as characteristics of "corpulence," whereas he associates thinness and shortness with being skinny—as though for him no one could be both short and fat.[1]

Images and Realism of Features

The world of images confirms the heightened attention devoted to the subject. The iconography changes significantly during the Renaissance.[2] The curves of the "real" body as much as the "extravagances of nature" mobilize the energies of painters and engravers.[3] Physical contours adorn visual art of all kinds. Things and people take on more thickness—and strangeness. Space exists differently. A realism commented on and exemplified countless times by art historians imposes itself and alters ways of looking and interests.[4] Moreover, this renews the "science of monsters" at the end of the sixteenth century,[5] one fascinated by some sort of divine intervention. These developments confirm especially the extent to which the unexpected, the astonishing, and the excessive have become dominant.[6] And this explains the curiosity for excessive and even dissonant forms.

But it is exclusively the very big person who acquires additional characteristics. A vague lack of distinction continues about the phases that range between the "enormous" and the "normal." Hieronymus Bosch's monk, carefully represented as a ball, is a characteristic example: no neck, extremely round face and trunk, with the sitting position being itself precarious, as though the round volume were tippy and unstable.[7] The portraits of Lucas Cranach around 1520–1530 multiply the representation of massive faces atop neckless trunks, chests that extend beyond the visual frame, and ill-defined shoulders lost in the overall roundness.[8] The witches of Urs Graf, on the other hand, demonstrate their excess consumption of meat with a total collapse toward the ground.[9] The "beyond normal" focuses curiosity and questions about "the natural." The very big drowns in details and sweeps aside all preconceptions and degrees. Furthermore, a single formal possibility seems to be considered—that of generalized roundness, the disappearance of joints, a general swelling, a compact, unitary ball. The specific expansion of the belly, the local abdominal roundness, for example, is not at all studied as it will be later. What counts is overall roundness, the global glob, in other words the archaic vision of the big person. And this is so despite the fact that sixteenth-century physiognomy specialists carefully put forward two profiles: that of the "big belly" belonging to the deeply proud lover of luxury and the "soft hanging" belly belonging to the intemperate drunkard.[10]

The originality of these images in the sixteenth century, however, is not exclusively descriptive. The forms of the very big person are not only represented, they are explored. Their study becomes central with the attempt to render forms and aspects. Lucas Cranach shows this in his religious scenes where the studied academic quality of the attitudes and positions ought to have dictated all the features; whereas an abrupt realism is what wins out. His 1533 engraving of the crucifixion gives the thief on the left a body overflowing with fat, his sins thereby declared by this intense sagging: soft flesh, falling belly, knotted, rounded, short swollen thighs.[11] Cranach is in search of what will translate the total "collapse" of the body: the belly, the loins, the thighs with fatty folds, the thickness of the skin between the trunk and arms, the apparent shortening of the limbs provoked by the accumulation of "too much." The goal is nothing less than an iconographic study of excess: the redundant body of the thief on one side, the haggard body of Christ on the other. Albrecht Dürer confirms this exploration in many concise representations. For example, the ink drawing of the "fat man before the mirror" insists on the squashed neck, the infinite folds of flesh, and the rounded features of the legs and arms.[12] The drawing of women bathing depicts one of them as immobile, sagging, with no neck, and a square trunk as wide as it is high.[13] Every trait seems to focus on the "too much." There is, however, only a single formal possibility: the perfectly round sphere.

Albrecht Dürer wanted to systematize the study of the very big person by exploring in his book on proportions the differences between skinny and fat: double chin for the latter, the bend of the belly, swollen legs, and a tipping forward of a profile that cannot be offset by amply large and displayed buttocks. The static or dynamic quality or the physical forces contributing to the posture are not being studied, rather the description remains one of forms, the traits simply "seen." The bodily shape of the Renaissance is not one of levers. This is a first explicit attempt to transform the lines of the "excessively" fat into an object for pictural study, an ensemble of global, totalized traits.

The Choice of Rubens

In the seventeenth century the theme takes on new importance. In the middle of the century Charles Mellin does not hesitate to portray the Toscan general Alessandro del Borro[14] between two monumental columns in order to better underline the amplitude of his contours: the "immense" belly largely extending beyond and thus partly covering over one of the two vertical lines which becomes itself the quasi-geometrical indicator of his fatness.[15]

Rubens is one of those who, in the seventeenth century, carried this exploration of the overflow of flesh the furthest. *The Fall of the Damned* (1621) in the Pinakothek in Munich illustrates it most simply, as can be seen in the *Preparatory Studies* from 1617 that show an accumulation of bodies with exaggerated amounts of flesh, deforming heads and necks, swelling bellies and limbs, squashing each dimension in folds of fat.[16] René de Piles, the biographer and contemporary of Rubens, sees only "the damned" victims of their "loose laziness and insatiable gluttony" delivered to the "cruel stings of infernal beasts" all falling in bunches into Satan's fires.[17] Along the same lines, he sees only "the deplorable state to which are reduced those who misuse wine" in *The Drunken Silenus* painted in 1615,[18] which shows the mythological old man stumbling under the influence of excess alcohol and weight.[19]

There is also the systematic exploration of the collapse of the flesh. Rubens undertakes a precise study of undone envelopes with the spongy skin and the flocked and falling flesh of the Silenus or Bacchus.[20] Also of interest is overall swelling, the spherical, balloon kind being the only one explored—archaic balls and exaggerated traits. Rubens questions, researches, and plays with the descriptions. The big person is the center of an iconographic research project, thus confirming his status as an object of curiosity. He is probably also the example of a kind of extreme profusion of life,[21] of a reconnection with the mythological—the ambivalence of the theme, the secret fascination with drunkenness, and "liberty and abandonment"[22] are revealed in the image of a transgressing Orphic Silenus as painted by Rubens, who was always quick to declare his own restraint, his refusal of all strong drink, and his will to follow the injunction engraved on a wall of his house in Anvers, "Mens sana in corpore sano."[23]

The originality of Rubens derives from his anatomical exploration of this falling off, the pictorial representation of fat that becomes paralyzing as its infiltration becomes total. This conquering fat, crackling the flesh, is intensely observed and minutely studied. This makes the size given by the painter to "normal" forms seem less noteworthy, the thickness of flanks, buttocks, and arms. Without a doubt, Rubens has a tendency to do up "everything larger than life."[24] He accentuates, varying the gnarled physiques and stressing roundness and folds. For Philippe Muray, he paints with bursts of "vasodilatation."[25] This is most in evidence in the naiads of the big paintings in the Médici Gallery.[26] This also provokes disagreements among his contemporaries. André Félibien, among others, in his widely circulated *Dialogues,* sees all this roundness as only "an illstudied manner."[27]

But although the painter tends to affirm a personal taste in this area, he keeps this same dilatation out of the "real" portraits. Hélène Fourmet, in *The Garden of Love* from 1630, exhibits a fineness of clothes and features,[28] while the young girl in the Rotterdam museum, drawn in the same year,[29] remains strongly tied down with a corseted waist, a profile that also occurs in the painting of Isabelle Brant, his first wife, done in 1609.[30] Rubens marks an obscure and personal taste for the luxuriance of flesh while recalling, as we have said, the neoclassic will for thinness.[31] However, even if it is exclusively limited to overall spherical impression, his studies of fat figures, especially his Bacchus and Silenus, testify more than anything else to a new curiosity about specific circumstances of excessive expansions, fallen flesh, and redundancies disfiguring the body to the point of deformity. A curiosity that still ignores accentuations, stages, and degrees of fatness.

Groups of figures positioned by classical engravers also confirm this apparent "negligence." The world of Abraham Bosse, for example, with his countless genre scenes such as *Wedding in the Country*, *Wedding in the City*, *The Cobbler*, *The Pastry Shop*, *The Prosecutor's Study*, and *Gallery of the Palace*, shows hardly any attention paid to the possible spectrum of physical volumes, their extent, or their diversity.[32] Questions of thickness and gradations remain in the shadows, except when it comes to the very fat, who are occasionally represented.[33] The result is a relative absence of precision about the beginnings of excessive volumes.

The Power and Powerlessness of Words

Starting in the sixteenth century, the world of images confirms the new curiosity in modern culture for the most massive forms. Interest is in the "biggest" just as the medical remarks concentrate on the most remarkable signs.

And yet there are changes in language happening at that time. Attempts are beginning. Some words are coined that suggest very slight degrees, beyond the images that remain "silent." These are indecisive borders, always allusive, between the slightly big and the very big. It is on the basis of these approximations that stories during the Renaissance invent terms. *Rondelet*, for example, in the middle of the sixteenth century, to designate a moderate, entirely "natural" roundness,[34] or the roundness of a young woman from Basel mentioned by Platter around 1530 as "filled with gentleness," or the more sensual roundness of the young girl (*jeune pucelette*) evoked by Ronsard in 1584,[35] or the words evoking fat such as *grasselet* and *grasset* that abound in sixteenth-century love songs, with their diminutive intent, or the word for rounded, *dodu*, that accompanies at the same time references to softness (*douillet*), or "belly potent" (*ventripotent*),[36] another of Rabelais's creations, to specify the ballooning and heft of the belly, and even *embonpoint*, literally "in a good state," which became current around 1550 to designate a medium corpulence that is neither too little nor too much.[37] Antoine Furetière includes in his seventeenth century *Dictionnaire* the words *grassouillet*, *pansard*, and *ventru*, thus enriching the intuitive panoply around roundness. These are first attempts to evoke size while suggesting *less* and *least*, *very* and *more*, in other words, the inscription of a gradation in words, even though allusive and approximate given the absence of actual numbers.

The concentration on change and the theme of a "passage" are also present in the sixteenth and seventeenth centuries. The attention to a covering layer that is different at different places of the body, notably the breasts, which indicate most clearly the early weight gain of Madame de Champré in the *Historiettes* of Tallemant de Réaux: "She looked well and except for her breasts was not too big at that time."[38] Comparison can also help with the description. "The Prince of Soubise is a little taller and fatter than Monsieur de Coëtquin," says Madame de Maintenon when she describes the wedding of the former in a letter to Madame des Ursins.[39] A whole array of suggestions and words tries for the first time to capture progressions and degrees, even though with inevitable and very evident approximation.

The interest is carried over to groups, collectives, and the entire population and its contours as a body. Martin Lister, a London doctor visiting Paris in the second half of the seventeenth century, claims to observe an overall fattening of Parisians over the period of a few years. "The thin and skinny became fat and corpulent." Strong liqueurs are said to be the cause.[40] Guy Patin makes the same observation in the middle of the century, attributing it to other causes. "Ordinarily, our Parisians exercise little, drink and eat a lot, and are becoming strongly plethoric."[41] The same remark is made by René de Piles at the beginning of the eighteenth century about bodies lacking their former "finesse" because given over to drink and savory foods.[42] The explanation relies on the idea of "too much" consumption. For the first time there is a verifiable claim about human groups, even though it remains a rather distant, summary description.

The affirmation could probably have been quite "real." The increased presence of butter in kitchens at the time, as well as the increased and varied use of sugar, which suddenly became more available as an American import, along with the invention of liqueurs and other distilled products may have all had an impact on bodily contours and favored their thickening.[43] The increased use of sugar, especially, sweeps aside traditional habits. Moyse Charas, noting the greater diversity of compotes and syrups, affirms in his *Royal Pharmacopia* from 1670 that "if one wanted to stock all such preparations, the stores wouldn't be big enough to display them all."[44] Jean Delumeau speaks of a "plumped up silhouette between the years 1450 and 1600."[45] And Jean-Louis Flandrin also describes the advent of an entirely new larger envelope of the body at the end of the Renaissance.[46] He attributes it to the revolution caused by sugar, a phenomenon that goes as far as modifying the criteria of beauty. Even though probable, these changes are difficult to verify in the absence of all quantifiable physical measurements. What remains more noteworthy is the new attention at the time to observed changes of contours and to their possible progression. The observations are so keen that they probably accentuate the degree of change. This is, however, a noticeable step in the refinement of the Western gaze at the forms of the body.

The words are nevertheless imprecise and the nuances difficult to get a hold on. The term *embonpoint* that was still new in the sixteenth century is the best example. How can it be defined without numerical precision or an implicit reference to such precision? The expression translates the idea of a "balance," a medium size between fatness and thinness, such as in the young woman in the Saint-Omer abbey described in the *Hundred New Stories* as totally "gente et belle," thanks to her proper *embonpoint*,[47] or that of the female laborer in the county of Saint-Pol who is esteemed beautiful and whose size is "so right" (*en si 'grand point'*) that the village pastor falls in love with her.[48] Adjectives add nuances without objective content, as one discovers with the prosecutor's female friend who receives gifts and other generous attentions in the *Joyous Estimates* of Bonaventure Des Périers such that she became "more full-figured every day."[49] There is the same difficulty with "well made" and "poorly made," which the classic descriptions overuse. The Count of Montalban, for example, has a "very well-made figure," we read in a story by Regnault de Segrais in 1656, while his rival Érignac is "quite badly made," and Orton, a second rival of the first two is "not badly made."[50] These are imprecise nuances, to say the least, insofar as they suggest more than they specify while at the same time awakening visual attention.

The ambiguity persists when some decades later Madame de Sévigné regrets in letter after letter the skinniness of her daughter. "Your skinniness kills me,"[51] "The idea of your skinniness is something my heart cannot put up with,"[52] "God do I so hate your skinniness,"[53] "I'm overwhelmed by how thin you've become."[54] The marquise worries, takes action, consults Fagon, the king's doctor, alerts her friends Corbinelli and Jean-Baptiste Grignan, while hoping for a fuller figure that she does not define. She threatens: "You ought always to fear drying out."[55] She wants her daughter to be "fleshy" (*grasse*),[56] but not fat, pregnant, or corpulent. She is insistent about her advice to her daughter to "fatten up." However, it's just the opposite when she speaks about herself as having to constantly combat any increase in size. "My whole fear is to gain weight."[57] "I'm nothing but a flattened fatty" (*une grosse crevée*).[58] "I fear fattening back up again, that is what I worry about."[59] "I'm skinny and feel good about it."[60] There are but few hints as to what the marquise means by skinny when writing about her daughter: "a weak voice, a melted face, a beautiful but unrecognizable throat,"[61] whereas she's outspoken about her own skinniness and proud of it. As a result, the words get mixed up. The generous bust—the sign of proper equilibrium between thin and fat—is immediately evident along with the other physical traits, more so than they are translated into terms and expressions. The vocabulary reveals its own limited precision, even though it did contribute some nuances to discussions of fatness in the sixteenth and seventeenth centuries.

The sticking point is the word *grasse*, which for the marquise designates the plumpness (*embonpoint*) expected in her daughter, the proper equilibrium between skinny and fat. In other words a very paradoxical way of nuancing the idea of "thin" (*mince*). The latter is a decisive term, it denotes curves, defines a certain density, and suggests round more than big—and definitely not "fat." Furthermore, it describes a minimal "layer" whose presence is not a consequence of muscle but of "flesh," in other words, an "oily" aspect to the skin, for example, whose specific smoothness sets off forms in full relief. The result is an inevitable ambiguity: the thin, in these older representations, cannot exist without the fat or, put another way, the balance cannot be struck except by a portion of discreet luxuriance of a certain consistency and liquidity. There is no muscle invoked here to designate "normal" or "beautiful." A woman's arms, for example, are to be "white, delicate, and gentle," while men's arms must be "strong, powerful, quick, and muscled."[62]

One form dominates all designations of the fat person, or, rather, the *very* fat person, in both words and images; namely, the globe. This ball shape is infinitely repeated to reproduce this or that body part and assimilate various traits to the logic of the circle. This adds further figurative associations. Curves multiply and illustrate by their very multiplicity the clear excess of their carrier. The round person is conceived with inevitable, empirical uniformity, as is clear in these teasing words of Cyrano de Bergerac to Montfleury: "Your legs and your head are so united as extensions of the roundness of your globe that you are nothing but a ball."[63] Furetière also uses the globe or sphere to designate the roundness of the fat bourgeois.[64] Mother nature, he says, "had given him in width what she had taken from him in height." The spherical torso, the close proximity of the limbs around that globe, and the shortening of the neck taken together compose a single mental image, a simple circular form that coheres with the idea of overflowing flesh. This is the teasing idea that Molière seeks to get across in the *Impromptu of Versailles*: the figure of a vast, stuffed circumference is posited to represent the total inverse of what the king ought to be.[65]

8. Constraining the Flesh

In the sixteenth and seventeenth centuries, original treatments that also lead to more systematic and better categorized actions occur. There are the very first steps toward an evaluation of weight based on physical signs: the tightness of clothes provoked by fatness and the tightness of rings and various other points of tension. The "feeling" of fat and its quasi-internal perception is supplemented now and then by an evocation of the empirical, even though the words are missing to express it. There are also diets, now more frequently mentioned in letters, customs, and stories, with their simple recommendation of the smallest nutritive quantities and drying substances all designed to restrain bigness, a condition still principally viewed as one of excess liquid. Then there are the imagined drying agents: vinegars, lemons, and chalks that are thought to tighten the skin by dissolving the fatty waters. Finally there are "compression" techniques: circles, belts, and corsets whose use becomes more systematic in the sixteenth and seventeenth centuries, and their deployment is pursued with the particular certainty of exerting a direct physical constraint so as to better "mold" forms and features with the expectation that they conform to the desired shape.

The Beginning of an Evaluation

Some concrete, objective assessments of bigness become established in the sixteenth and seventeenth centuries without words or numbers.

In the middle of the sixteenth century, Girolamo Cardan, a mathematician and multitalented writer, records a long description of his physical appearance in his memoirs. He notes his "medium height," his "slightly narrow chest," and his "long, thin neck." He also notes his facial features.[1] However, he hardly says anything about the center of his body. His stomach and legs resist description. But he observes himself, finds particular markers, and notes them down. It is an exceptional testimony, which, for the first time, shows an individual evaluating his form and describing his profile. Cardan also says he is watching over his volume; he is mindful of becoming neither fat nor skinny. The evaluation is entirely indirect, based on the state of his rings, their pressure, and his feeling they "have not changed."[2] Cardan does not weigh himself or rely on numbers of any sort. He does not study his reflection, "full-length" mirrors still being unheard of in the sixteenth century. He does not evaluate his fleshiness in relation to the fit of his clothes or the state of his contours. He simply trusts in the tension of his rings as an indicator of the state of his "volume." This confirms a dual concern for his profile and for sticking to an approximation— an indeterminate watchfulness with relatively low precision compared to the criteria of today. It is a fundamental observation that uses few tools.

Other indicators inevitably become important, such as the pressure exerted by clothes. This is spoken of by Baldassar Castiglione in 1528 in his address to the "lady of the palace." The "calculation" is perceptual, and empirical judgment remains uppermost. The idea is to judge "if she is a little too fat or thin than reasonable" and "make use of her clothes" to compensate for any lack or excess.[3] The evaluation relies on how clothes fit, and the response is to adjust the clothes. This is the method employed by the jokers in a seventeenth-century text by Tallemant des Réaux. It tells of a practical joke played on an "oaf" to make him think he has suddenly become fat from gorging himself on mushrooms, an airy, puffy food. The man becomes alarmed and believes he has "swelled up" when he feels his clothes are suddenly tighter, but in fact they had only been cinched up by a scheming valet.[4] The example seems minor, yet it confirms the role clothes played in some spontaneous evaluations. The same indicator is used in 1560 when Élisabeth de Valois, who became queen of Spain at age fifteen, is required to change her wardrobe due to the enlargement of her body. Her dresses "need to be four fingers larger than when she arrived."[5] Madame de Sévigné uses the same method when she discusses her attempts to lose weight at age fifty. "I no longer throw myself at food and am so far from popping that I was able to take in a skirt by a half-finger on each side."[6] Finger and half-finger widths constitute a genuinely handy, effective measurement.

At the end of the seventeenth century Elizabeth Charlotte, Princess Palatine evokes quasi-internal sensations of swelling. "My body is swelling. I have colic and must get myself bled."[7] She localizes the problem in the spleen and attempts to assess its progress. "My left side is swollen like the head of a baby."[8] These observations are rare and new, and suggest a "listening" to one's body, however partial. The focus is on more or less local changes rather than an overall evaluation of volumes and densities.

Even rarer, however, are statistical measurements of the traits themselves. The lone specification in 1638 by Pierre du Moulin, who describes a chest as being twice the size of the neck, is as contrived as it is rare. "Twice the neck size equals the chest size at the level of the diaphragm. I am speaking of a well-proportioned body, not of one that is swollen and weighed down with fat."[9]

Rarer still are indications of bodily weight in daily life. The remarks of Samuel Pepys about bets placed during a dinner party in the seventeenth century are an exception: "to Mr. Lucy's, a merchant, where much good company, and there drank a great deal of wine, and in discourse fell to talk of the weight of people, which did occasion some wagers, and where, among others, I won half a piece to be spent."[10] The process suggests first a "theoretical" affirmation of weight, and then an "objective" verification on a scale. This is an action that the *Diary* and other stories hardly suggest was ordinary.[11] The fact is that intuitive contours are the benchmark in the seventeenth century more than measured weight, as the scale is generally never mentioned. The visible continues to be what counts as a guide to perceptions. The modified form trumps modifications of weight.

This is confirmed by the equally exceptional testimony of Matthäus Schwarz, a rich sixteenth-century Augsburg banker and a friend of Fugger who is overcome by an autobiographical passion that leads him to commission an annual painting of himself "to represent my own clothes" and "to see what will have happened in five, ten or more years."[12] Ornament is the focus of the images, and luxury the focus of this practice. There remains a particularity that is as precious as it is remarkable. Matthäus, who claims to have become "replete and fat" in 1526, has himself painted naked twice, front and back, at "twenty-nine years, four months, and eight days" as a double record of his thickened size. However no traits are commented upon, no numbers are given. There is only the fixed, heavy, "mute" contour—a testimony to a new but still "blind" attention to size.

In general, there is no tradition of measuring the weight of the body, not even for animals at the time of sale. The price of animals is calculated by head, by skin color, by hair type, by age, or by pedigree (descending from this or that mother, in the case of a cow, for example). This gives rise to very specific descriptions of animal transactions: "two-and-a-half-year-old, black-haired, pedigreed cow" sold for thirty Tours pounds (*livres tournois*) in Orléans in 1606; "red-haired cow sold with calf" for fifty-four Tours pounds in 1640 in Orléans.[13] Volume is probably a factor and imposes by its immediate presence, but remains an intuitive bargaining point.

In the seventeenth century new observations are made about the human body, but all are limited to cases that are bizarre and extreme. It's still mostly only the very fat person that matters at this time. In 1635 Daniel Sennert records two characteristic examples: a thirty-six-year-old woman from Strasbourg who weighs 480 pounds and can barely move at all, and another 400-pound man who "appears in public" despite great difficulties moving. An additional particularity of this man, says the doctor, is how "nature," pressed by the mass and weight, tried to evacuate the serus humor through the navel."[14] This confirms the ambiguity that persists about the excess materials: liquids, fats, and serous fluids. In addition, there are a few "extreme" statistics cited here and there in the seventeenth century: a 200-pound child of ten mentioned by Thomas Bartholin in 1638; the 30 pounds of fat "falling to the knees" of a woman mentioned by Domenico Panarolo in 1637;[15] and the 600-pound man incapable of movement noted by Michael Ettmüller in 1691.[16] These extreme statistics demonstrate the very slow establishment of excess fat within the category of maladies. It further shows the extent to which medical texts concentrated for a long time on particular cases such as "gigantism" and the "uncommon" collapse that led to unbearable deformities.

However a banal evaluation based on weight still does not exist.

Only the "High" Size

Practical treatises, however, signal some new types of watchfulness. Beauty manuals from the Renaissance are the first to develop the theme of contours, in contrast to their medieval equivalents, which had only concerned themselves with the care of the face. One notes, for example, discussions of a woman's stomach after a pregnancy. The focus is on childbirth, an "anatomically" targeted vision despite the dominance of the general impression of the bodily sphere. In his *Decoration of Human Nature* from 1542 André Le Fournier considers ways to avoid a flabby stomach after childbirth,[17] as does Jean Liébault in his *Beautification and Ornament of the Human Body* from 1582.[18] At the beginning of the sixteenth century, Louis Guyon extends the discussion to ways to correct the many "deformities" of this type of stomach, its sagging and size, its "swallowing" and thinness, its cracks, as well as the "displacement of the hips" and the "distended skin."[19]

The subject is very focused and leaves aside the legs, for example, whose size and possible deformities are rarely of concern since they are hidden, "covered by clothes,"[20] and not susceptible to "correction." This is underlined with insistence in an exchange between mother and daughter at the end of the sixteenth century: "What good is taking care of one's legs since they are not to be seen?"[21] This is said even though the principle of a body made of humors, especially the female body where phlegm multiplies liquidness, favors a weighing downward and an inexorable expansion of hips and thighs. But how exactly can one worry about something that remains hidden? This is brought out by Giambattista della Porta's female nude from 1586 illustrating physiognomy, with its oval shape accentuating the thickness of the thighs and the slenderness of the shoulders, while the lightness of the bust and neck contrasts with the ample buttocks down to the knee.[22] The Italian translation of this text and its engraving from 1644 are even more striking: the strongly cone-shaped thighs of the woman contrast with the distinctly cylindrical thighs of the man drawn here as a winged Mercury.[23] The feminine aesthetic remains for a long time an upper body aesthetic: the head is privileged, as is the rectitude of the chest and the tightening of the belt, while the lower part of the body is effaced under an indistinct mass of cloth and folds. This is a manifestation of prudery, no doubt, and a masking of fat buildup too, as much as a wish to accentuate the spirituality of the higher regions.[24]

A gaze susceptible to noticing or avoiding the stomach and lower limbs remains socially determined. Olivier de Serres in his *Théâtre d'agriculture* from 1600 illustrates this with formulations meant to embellish country women while specifically limiting his consideration to oils and creams, the cheeks, lips, and hands.[25] The stomachs and silhouettes of these villagers do not appear, though they are present in the more precise counsels of Jean Liébault. The anonymous secret *Receipes* also make the point in their own way. These recommendations intended for popular audiences confine themselves to facial care, whereas the more "noble" advice books can venture onto other parts of the body.[26]

Diets and "Modern" Restraints

Socially distinguished slimming techniques are also developed and implemented outside the medical world, of course, and these practices are described. Montaigne explicitly states his wish to conserve his own appearance and stop becoming fatter. He admits "skipping a few meals" to heal his stomach, to avoid feeling overfull, and especially to ward off having the profile of Bacchus, that "little undigestible burping god, swollen with smoke and liqueur."[27] The aim is to limit food intake so as to fend off the unwanted image of the god of wine and roundness. Thus a watchfulness is encouraged that inevitably involves the estimation of volumes and traits. There is a certain eagerness about it too. Montaigne admits to a hunger impulse that leads him to bite his tongue and fingers. And finally there is an approximate account of contours. Montaigne does not relate the starting sizes that motivate his behavior, but instead the redundant size of the classical wine-soaked god.

Some letters from the Renaissance confirm this restraint. For example, in 1537 L'Arétin says he wants to lose weight and follow a "half-diet." He admits his frustration, not because his body resists or opposes such efforts—the theme of possibly being a failure when it comes to dieting does not appear in the Renaissance—but because life in his home city of Rome keeps him from getting much exercise. Whence the fattening up that he regrets and the "state of permanent rage" provoked by this failure.[28] It takes a profound sadness, such as the "loss of a woman once mine and today someone else's,"[29] or some moral suffering, for true skinniness to set in—a slimming that men and women in older European times associated with "the claws of the plague and famine."[30] There is then another outrage: skinniness and its excesses.

Slimming down is not always the objective of restrictions. Luigi Cornaro, a mid-sixteenth century Venetian nobleman who offers his thoughts on sobriety, seeks to "listen" to the reactions of his own body to the foods he consumes. His goal is simple: to reconsider these foods and select them in a way that erases the "infirmities" that a "disorderly life" provokes.[31] This diet is entirely empirical, moreover, as Luigi Cornaro searches out those foods that he supposes agree with him because they cause no trouble or tension. There is no question of physical appearance in this case. An identical project is pursued by Léonard Lessius a few decades later when he dispenses "advice for living long." In 1613 this Jesuit elaborates with erudition on how to accede more directly to "spiritual functions" by consuming "an appropriate measure of food and drink."[32]

What can be said then of the interminable enterprise undertaken by Sanctorius at the beginning of the seventeenth century? And what of the "chair scale" where the Venetian doctor sits for hours while working, eating, and doing other activities? The instrument is so large and complex that it reaches to the ceiling. His goal is precise: to verify the loss and gain of body weight throughout the day and over many days. An unusual experiment, certainly, but not a calculation aimed at slimness or the size of volumes. He is interested in the temporary loss of weight caused by "imperceptible perspiration," the invisible sweat that evaporates hour after hour, which Sanctorius was the first to study scientifically. He also pursues maintaining weight equilibrium and considers it a sign of good health, the idea being to block all superfluous humors that might corrupt and harm the body. A proof of the similarity and difference of these attitudes to those of today is that the use of the scale (*la balance*) is not a means for exploring appearance or contours. In fact, fat is never mentioned. What matters are the humors, those impalpable, infiltrating liquids. This totally unprecedented use of a scale, however, is decisive, even if its use is not yet in the service of evaluating bodily contours.

Diets proposed in the sixteenth and seventeenth centuries are focused on reducing food intake: cutting down on "light meats,"[33] for example, as a bishop says to a visiting priest about his diet in a story by Bonaventure Des Périers from the sixteenth century, or a Toulouse woman's elimination of the "habit of a late supper" (*souper*) in another of those stories.[34] These diets are also focused on calculation and even weighing the food consumed. In Florence at the beginning of the sixteenth century, Jacopo da Pontormo, Leonardo da Vinci's student, is one of the first to measure each of the foods he eats in ounces.[35] Luigi Cornaro makes identical calculations, specifying the number of ounces retained and their imperceptible disappearance.[36] At the beginning of the seventeenth century, Héroard, the doctor of the future Louis XIII, also notes scrupulously day by day the exact weight of every food consumed by the prince.[37] The measurement has more to do with evaluating the food than it does with body weight.

Dieting at this time is also concerned with the qualities of food; for example, the necessity, among others, to favor meats that dry out or dry up,[38] those judged "nonexcrement-producing" and "cleansing," as was said.[39] The idea of dryness is all important. The origin of fat is still linked to liquids and the characteristics of the body are still associated with humors. Sixteenth- and seventeenth-century knowledge continues on with the convictions of previous times, adding details here and there to principles that remain unchanged. Thus there is a focus on the danger of animals associated with "foggy" environments or humid climates, those that may have lived near stagnant waters such as ducks, scoters, or teal taken from muddy ponds, or animals considered too old with overly dense humors, or those that are "over boiled," raised on too much fatty food such as pigs who are allowed to roam gluttonously, and those that are too hot and lascivious such as male goats with a "strong bad odor."[40] Thus there is a tendency to read danger at the slightest sign of goo or grease. Lamb, for example, "especially the very young lambs still nursing under their mothers are too viscous and humid to be easily digestible."[41] And various kinds of fish have flesh that is "massive, viscous, heavy"[42]—especially those species that live in waters with no waves or lively current.[43] The liquid of some vegetables, citrus fruits, and other overly juicy fruits can also be worrisome.[44] There is also the danger posed by foods that provoke "air" such as "chestnuts, cabbages, peas, fava beans, and the like,"[45] which provoke swelling and dilation in the body; whereas what is healthy are "all sorts of mountain birds" and their smelly, "airy" flesh "that contains little water."[46] A continuum of wet to dry, on which there is either balance or imbalance, is what separates healthy from unhealthy, digestible from indigestible, thin from fat.

Along with this attention to diet, there is the importance accorded to bleedings and purges, which are cited frequently in medical manuals of the day. Among the special foods are the "musk rose" for "purging serosities and other humors," rhames roots (*racines de rhames*), rhubarb, and thistle seeds to "overcome obstructions and gently purge the viscous humors."[47] A shared conviction underlies these practices; namely, that the fat person poses no major therapeutic challenge, the volumes have only to be diluted, liberated, and oriented toward the most ordinary exits. Consequently, fatness, in addition to the awkward oafishness that accompanies it, could be taken as a sign of a resistant will or stubbornness over an evacuation that necessitated merely submitting to technical gestures that were "legitimate and profitable" and "removed from the body what was harmful either because the wrong substance or because present in the wrong amount."[48]

Drying Out

Diet, finally, is related to exercise: drying out as a function of warming up. This is confirmed by a few precise examples from treatises where it is mentioned more than in accounts of daily life. The case recounted by Italian ambassadors about Catherine de Médicis combating her fatness is notable. "The queen mother is very fond of the pleasures of life. She is disorderly and eats a lot; but afterwards she seeks remedies through large amounts of bodily exercise. She likes walking and horseback riding and never stays in one place. The most amazing thing is that she even goes hunting."[49]

In the same way, the handball players in Rabelais's Thélème gather before a fire with large towels and rub themselves to evacuate excess humors.[50] And in the seventeenth century, the Palatine Princess speaks of pacing in her room a half hour to aid her digestion.[51]

The general idea is one of exercise undertaken to counter something. It's an opposite, the inverse of immobility, reversing little by little the pairing of the lazy and heavy life. Everything here is a matter of varied movements and effervescence, no matter how unsystematic. There is no allusion to gymnastics of any sort. The evacuation is thought to be achieved by the simple movement of the body parts in action, their heating up, and the vapor thus given off. This explains the particular importance of the maxim to "never rest at ease,"[52] which appears in Antoine de Bandole's long panegyric to Henri IV in 1609, and the insistence, which increases in the seventeenth century, about the slimming effect of all physical labor: "laborers are rarely beefy or beer-bellied. . . . They demonstrate how vigorous and frequent exercise slims the body."[53] Exercise receives little commentary and is considered less as a system than as simple agitation: "the rubbing of parts" favors the evacuation of superfluities.[54] One can note the observations of Madame de Caylus around 1680 concerning the future queen, the Duchess of Bourgogne, whose "tendency to fatten up" at age twelve is responded to with a multiplication of movements and deliberate agitations of the body.[55]

The relationship of food and exercise, but also a concern for the local air and atmosphere as well as the substances that might penetrate the body are all preoccupations of Prosper Alpino in his explanations for the size of Egyptians noted during his travels at the end of the sixteenth century.[56] Everything about the environment of the inhabitants of Cairo, for example, should make them thin—especially the dryness of their climate. Everything in their lifestyle, however, makes them fat, overwhelmed by a variety of excess humors. Prosper Alpino lists the causes of this swelling: constant lasciviousness and abandon of all sorts, watery foods, frequent intake of liquids, repeated baths, and continuous inhaling of stagnant vapors. The Venetian doctor insists on the waters and overly thick air infiltrating the bodies there. The body of the sixteenth and seventeenth century remains traversed by its environment; it's a porous envelope openly vulnerable to the four winds. The heat of women's baths, in particular, distends the skin and penetrates into the body with excessive humidity. Only a dry climate can induce slimming in this case. This is noted in the seventeenth century as well by Madame de Sévigné, who contrasts the dry air of Grignan, which favors slimness, to the humid air of Bourbilly, which provokes fatness: "One needs only to breath the air of Bourbilly to get fat."[57]

Vinegar and Chalk

In Western countries at this time one notes an increasing amount of attention given over to female slimming. There is, for example, this entirely "natural" observation by Fabio Glissenti in 1609 about the Venetian and Neapolitan women and their diets: "The first [the Venetians] obtain Indian walnuts, almonds, pistachios, pine nuts, melon seeds, and the flesh of partridges and capons. They mash them together with a little sugar to form a sort of paste, and each morning they eat a certain quantity of this and then drink a glass of Cyprus wine."[58]

The Neapolitains use instead rice, barley, sesame, fava beans, and other southern plants believed to air out the humors. Even simpler, and as widely followed apparently, was a recipe from a "treatise of secrets" from the seventeenth century "to keep from getting fat": "Break cherry pits, make them into hard candy with sugar, and suck on them in the morning and evening."[59]

However, the anecdotes of Jean Liébault in the second half of the sixteenth century indicate how tough these practices could sometimes be: "abstain from eating" and even substitute "pulverized chalk or clay"[60]—a recourse to rough substances to reduce the hated humidities with dryness. Jean Liébault lingers over descriptions, such as of "many well-born older and younger women" who are all expecting to have the desired result from such practices; namely, "to have a thin body."[61] Vinegar, lemons, and other acids are considered "astringent" thinning agents.[62] This is borne out by the action of the Compte de Lude around 1660 related by Bussy-Rabutin. "Born to be very fat," the compte conserved a "goodly waist" with "diet and vinegar," but "ruined" his stomach.[63] Then there is Madame de Gondran, a salt tax collector's daughter mentioned by Tallemant des Réaux around 1650. She thought herself "already quite fat" and decided all of a sudden to try and lose weight. Her decision to drink "pure wine" brings a change: her waist is "prettier than before."[64] When she becomes a widow, her old habits take over and she becomes fat again; and again she resorts to the same methods, but even more harshly, consuming larger quantities of "vinegar, lemons, and other terrible things." She becomes thin again, "but is hardly ever healthy."[65] Tallemant des Réaux teases, of course, and makes wisecracks about her overdoing it; but he himself is convinced of the effectiveness of the acids and judges their action decisive in the case of Maréchal de Saint-Germain, among others, who was able to go from fat to thin "thanks to drinking vinegar."[66] This attitude conforms to the belief of pharmacists in neoclassic times in France who attributed to vinegar the power to "cut and attenuate fatty material."[67]

More deeply, a slow but steady change in the status of women leads to a new era of weight watching in the modern West. The first focus is on the "lady of the palace" whose place becomes more aesthetically structured with the developments of court life. "There is no court, no matter how big, that can possess beauty, splendor, or liveliness without women," insists Baldassare Castiglione.[68] And Brantôme adds, even more directly, "a court's entire decoration was its women."[69] Catherine de Medici is a notable example from the middle of the sixteenth century. The growth of the queen's residence, explicit investment in beauty, and constant watchfulness of appearances and their upkeep lead to the punishment of any and all negligence of aesthetic matters and tight regulation of Catherine's court: "The deliberate order to these women and girls to adorn themselves . . . so that they appear as goddesses. . . . Otherwise they were harshly scolded and punished."[70] This attitude no doubt intensifies the whole business of maintenance and the necessity of further refining appearances and habits.

The way forward is based on symbols and underlines the stakes of a feminine beauty that is increasingly a "décor beauty," and parallel to that the equally specific punishments it could provoke. There is an orientation, in other words, of feminine appearance toward welcoming, to the "inside," as the "ornament" of homes and apartments; whereas masculine appearance would be for the "outside" and for facing people and things. These differences are reinforced without ambiguity in the beauty treatises of the Renaissance: force for man, beauty for women; for one "work in the city and fields,"[71] for the other "the cover of the house."[72] To which is added, of course, the criteria of the "thin" waist and the "firm and solid belly without wrinkles or lines."[73] The manuals on dress from the same era go in the same direction, whether it's insisting on the thin, tight cut of the cloth such as with the young ladies of Ferrare, for example, praised for their "svelte waists," or the women of Anvers whose "corsages over the lower dress, round and well-fitted, gives the whole bust a gracious, svelte form."[74]

Belts, Blades, and Corsets

The theme of strangulating clothes and the constant adjustment of clothes becomes central in the sixteenth and seventeenth centuries. Out goes the simple cloth belt, for example, which encircled the waists of women at the tournaments of King René in the fifteenth century, and in comes recourse to intense tightening in the case of overly noticeable girth. Linen straps, says André Le Fournier,[75] straps of animal skin with laces, says Jean Liébault[76]—both provide powerful compression in response to the possibly abundant belly. This decisive method of constriction confirms a double goal: an attempt to limit fatness and a belief in the effects of mechanical constraint. A new era that imposes the hope of directly obliging bodily forms to "shape up" begins. These new types of harnesses can also be used on very big men. There is a new prestige, probably, that comes with these mechanical tools, which are adjustable and articulated.

In 1592 Pierre de l'Étoile is hardly surprised by the case of the Spanish legate "strapped like a mule" and wrapped up with belts after his meals to prevent possible deformations of his belly.[77] The examples of such strappings become commonplace over the next decades. Montfleury, known as "big René," who acted in plays by Corneille in the 1650s and was teased by Cyrano for his fatness, wears a special belt called a *cerclage* made of wide and rigid iron that was designed to press against the abdomen.[78] In the 1630s Gros Guillaume, the actor of the hôtel de Bourgogne, supports his belly with two strong belts, one just below his chest, the other below his navel, thus transforming his fatness into a spectacle and also drawing attention to the restraining device of these straps.[79]

More important, these methods diversify and are aimed at other parts of the body, including the upper body. At the end of the sixteenth century, Jean Liébault proposes a device conceived to prevent women in childbirth from experiencing any enlargement of their "mammaries."[80] The metal becomes a mold: a steel blade suspended from the neck supports the two breasts while "two little pieces of cork" placed under the armpits exert a lateral pressure. There is no indication of the frequency of its use nor of how widespread that use was. Liébault's book, however, as well as a *Treasury of Secret Remedies for Female Maladies*, which repeats these recommendations, had wide circulation and was republished several times.[81] The idea of an "elementary" appliance imposed as an aid to failing or falling bodies becomes standard—a machine to sculpt forms and anatomies. The development of fat could now be explicitly prevented or corrected by the rigidity of plates of steel.

The invention of the corset is really only the extension of such initiatives. The mold become sheath, a practice reserved for women, adds to the expectation of slimness. Queen Margaret of Navarre is an example from the end of the sixteenth century. Having "become horribly fat,"[82] she turns to steel to retain her flesh: "she had white steel placed on both sides of her body."[83] In the last decades of the sixteenth century, the practice becomes standardized among upper-class women who all seek to have a "tight waist."[84] The most ubiquitous tool employs rigid flat metal or whale baleen as "boning" stitched in place onto a cloth framework. This stitched framework is the compressive device remarked by Lippomano, the Venetian ambassador traveling through France in 1577, which indicates its social diffusion: "They have a corset or camisole that they call 'corps piqué' that makes their waists light and svelte. It is attached at the back which makes the form of the breasts even more attractive."[85] It is a triumph of instrumentation and toolmaking.

The payoff is clear: an apparent slimming of the contour equals an apparent lightening of the body. The types of sheath can very, but the tightening involved is central. Montaigne offers one of the briefest accounts. Solid hooks that impose narrowness, but the constraint is extreme: "To have a slim body [bien espagnolé], what will they not put up with? Girdled and strapped with big hooks on the sides that press against the skin, sometimes to the point of dying."[86] Cesare Vercellio cites another Spanish example in 1590: "The corseting is so tight on the sides that one has difficulty believing that there's a body inside."[87] The device becomes more widespread in the seventeenth century, to the point where a guild of tailors for women's and infants' bodies is formed.[88] There are eight such tailors in Paris at the end of the seventeenth century with very precise fabrication rules designed to prevent all "escaping" of the belly: "place the strongest and thickest baleen more at the rear and the front than on the sides."[89] The focus is on "holding" the belly. The remark of Madame de Maintenon speaking to the pupils at Saint-Cyr says it all: "Never be without your corset and flee from all excesses that have now become ordinary."[90] Fatness has found a treatment, and molding the body its tools.

However, one cannot forget the fatalism of Madame de Sévigné's friend Coulanges who upon returning from a journey remarks on her excessive fatness: "Ladies, I fear that you will find me enormously fat, but what can I do?"[91]

PART 3

FROM OAFISHNESS TO POWERLESSNESS

The Enlightenment and Sensibility

Body volumes become more individualized during the Age of Enlightenment. A disorderly agitation becomes possible. The notion of size supposes many sizes and diversity supposes degrees of difference, even if they are more sketched than studied. Procedures for measuring emerge modestly but insistently.

These slow but steady changes permit formerly latent distinctions to come into view. For example, the profile of a man where a certain roundness is acceptable versus the profile of a woman where such tolerance is absent. There are also social differences where here a certain visible ampleness might carry value but not there. This training of the gaze transforms perceptions, creating warning signs and attention to sizes that formerly did not exist, displacing worries, and making for a general sharpening of attention.

Another more direct change concerns the representation of excess. The old idea about an invasion of the body by watery matter becomes more complicated. The noticeable bodily collapse is no longer merely a question of weight, but has to do with a loss of reactivity and nervous dysfunction. Instead of questioning the body as if it were like any ordinary object with its "sacks" and "canals," the body is now considered to have a special organic life spring susceptible to irritation and other sensitivities. Thus criticisms of the fat person are reoriented to underline powerlessness and sterility, focusing especially on a lack of vitality. For the first time these criticisms can extend to a stigmatization of too much civilization, too much artifice and agitation that has become redundant and useless. There begins a denunciation of what this new era tends to strongly deplore: a loss of sensibility. Fat people become powerless people, and their stigmatization is inseparable from the times.

Unprecedented practices favoring the well-toned body can thus be invented such as excitement with cold baths or even, in some cases, the laborious use of electric stimulus—all practices guaranteed to succeed in activating and enlivening the body.

9. Inventing Nuance

The judgment of contours is the first thing that changes in the Age of Enlightenment. Numerical measuring of weight appears here and there in the medical literature, and a ranking of volumes also appears in the most ordinary circumstances. The social milieu depicted in engravings and paintings is signified and even ranked by, among other things, different physical "thicknesses," even if the associated vocabulary that would explicitly define traits comes late and remains imprecise. The history of the fat person is the history of this slowly arriving consciousness of the variety of forms and their possible progressions, while, at the same time, the will to weigh less is not necessarily intense. The culture of the Enlightenment is more attentive to the individual and therefore also to the individualization of size.

"Tireless" Measuring and "Fruitless" Measuring

The *Spectator*, one of the early inventors of the chronicle of social mores, evokes a strange example of weighing in an issue from 1711. A long letter from a reader communicates the details. The man declares himself to be "one of that sickly tribe, who are commonly known by the name of Valetudinarians" and describes turning for help to the ancient practice of Sanctorius; namely, maintaining an equilibrium between the weight of his food intake and his outgoing wastes. He built a massive instrument to best record all oscillations in weight, a gigantic Roman scale with a chair and table incorporated that was similar to the apparatus used a century earlier by the doctor in Padua. He used it rigorously, weighing himself for three years, noting his ingestions and excretions, comparing them day to day, tracking every excess humor that might compromise the interior of his body. He admits his disappointment. His physical state is unchanged, he remains "sick" and his condition "languishing." What's more, the constant measuring nearly did him in. The *Spectator* agrees, remarking humorously on the gentleman's obedience to "the prescriptions of his chair" with "a short fable" to demonstrate that one who "tempers his health by ounces and by scruples" may end up ruining himself.[1]

Then there are the accounts of different foods, though focused mostly on quantity. And the presence of calculation, notably the scale, and the insistence on taking frequent readings. This procedure is particularly observable in England from 1720 to 1730, during which time doctors attempt readings over an extended duration.[2] Bryan Robinson and John Lining's texts offer a series of tables recording the various weights of the body, foodstuffs, and wastes.[3] John Floyer of London compares the statistics concerning his barely perceptible perspiration to those recorded by Sanctorius to assert a difference between England and Italy: the intensity of imperceptible perspiration is less under the skies of London, which are cooler and more humid due to the fog.[4] Similar calculations are made by Thomas Secker of Leyde and George Rye of Dublin.[5] It is conquest by numbers. Apparently this attitude becomes so present in the medical world that in 1726 Jacob Leupold sets out to reinvent Sanctorius's scale and posits a model so subtly reduced in size as to be transportable and more widely used from then on.[6]

There is no doubt, however, that neither the notion of fat nor that of slimming is central to these practices. The focus is a vision of healthiness. What's of interest is not fat but perspiration, not physical volumes but vapors, humors, and water. Moreover, it is a masculine vision and a medical vision in search of functionality. All that counts is the daily maintenance of the body, a numerical balance between ingestion and excretion. Mastery over contours counts less than mastery over this imperceptible evaporation. Excretion is judged essential to avoiding all internal corruptions. The goal is obviously not the study of weight loss as it will be later. And then there is the complex use of instruments, which discourages ordinary initiatives.

The presence of numbers, however, must be strongly emphasized, even if they are very far from being used to evaluate the fat person. Their presence constitutes a remarkable first premise: the gradual emergence of a principle about weighing bodily "things," repeating the gesture, and comparing results. The premise is all the more important since what's at stake is maintaining the body's weight.

Waist or Weight?

The new consciousness, however, comes slowly. This is clear from the short reply made by the lieutenant general of the Paris police to a request by "Sieur Desbordes" in 1725. Desbordes asks permission to install an instrument of his invention in public places that will allow all people to be weighed. It is a suspended chair equipped with a balancing arm and weights. Desbordes sees it as an "innocent amusement," a game consciously limited to the "superficial." The reaction of the police lieutenant is more characteristically short and sharp: "We see no need or usefulness in installing scales to weigh people." Besides the lack of interest in weight, there is the fear of provoking disorderly assemblies, tumults of people gathering "to dare and bet."[7] Public authorities in 1725 remain indifferent to all acts of weighing. Recording one's weight is considered a ridiculous pastime, a vain curiosity.

On the other hand, measuring the length of belts and thus the circumference of the waist they encircle introduces a new precision about size into Enlightenment culture. Voltaire does not neglect to provide the exact dimensions of his character Micromégas in 1752: 120 thousand royal feet in height, 50 thousand feet around the waist; whereas Jonathan Swift had not given any such measurements of his Gulliver and the strange people of Lilliput and Laputa in 1722.[8] Similarly, the editors of the *Journal de médecine* writing an inventory of extreme cases in the middle of the century include precise figures for some surprisingly big "perimeters": a six-foot waistline (182.88 cm) for the parish priest of Saint-Eusèbe cited in 1757, and eight feet for the bailiff in Sens (243.84 cm) cited in 1760.[9] And there is the estimate linked to a bet in the case of Edward Bright of Essex, whose prodigious volume turned him into a curiosity: seven men supposedly were able to wrap themselves in his coat without bursting the buttons. There is no daily attention to figures, it should be noted. Numerical curiosity is centered on the exceptional while it simultaneously introduces the possibility of a new marker.

The testimony of Élie de Beaumont from the second half of the eighteenth century is very revealing for the self-evaluation it contains, which confirms this markedly new sensibility.[10] From 1760 to 1770 Jean-Baptiste Élie de Beaumont, a lawyer practicing in Paris since 1752, a friend of Voltaire's, and a defender of notable causes, consults Antoine Petit and Samuel Tissot for a condition he describes as "extreme fatness."[11] His letters detail the lawyer's dismay. They also tell of his quite particular way of arriving at his diagnosis. He notes a visual judgment of forms and their changes that is both "modern" and "dated"—the waistline once again rather than weight, extreme size rather than attention to degrees. A numerical figure is obtained with the help of a string sent to the doctor to better convey the "evil"—a number that increases over time, going from "three feet" in 1767 to "three feet, eleven and two-thirds inches" in 1776 (i.e., from 97.45 cm to 129.02 cm). However, this number is given without a corresponding measurement of height and thus lacks precision.[12] An unprecedented concern is present though; namely, this will to measure the waist in regular units of *pouces* and *lignes* and note its inexorable progression over months and years. Moreover, an additional desire for accuracy leads Élie de Beaumont to measure himself before each meal "in the morning on an empty stomach after going twice to my dressing room" so as not to "falsify" the result.[13] And there is another innovation here: for the first time the measurements are taken as part of an orientation of consultating with his doctors.

Inventing the Means

Now far from an intuitive vision based on direct apprehension, the string transformed the body's volume into an "object," while the marker of weight takes hold more slowly. The case of George Cheyne directly centered on weight was for long highly exceptional. This English doctor notes the results of weighing himself at the very beginning of the eighteenth century when he had regrets about having stopped a diet some years earlier. He records a weight of thirty-two stone (180 kilos).[14] He considers the "enormity" of it. He is alarmed and returns to his diet, which he applies rigorously. But he neglects to record his subsequent weight gain or loss, which gives an indirect sign of the relatively modest importance of the first notation.

Some additional examples, though still rare, occur in the years 1760–1770. They coincide with the invention of a new instrument. In the middle of the century, John Wyatt invents a balance scale whose wide horizontal platform can support the weight of a person or animal.[15] There are some notable weighings that follow in the wake of this innovation. In 1760 Malcolm Flemyng, for example, reports the loss of 28 pounds (14 kilos) in one month, thanks to a treatment with diuretics and soapy water by a patient initially weighing 291 pounds (130–140 kilos).[16] The measurements are undertaken very occasionally, however, which is a sign of the persistent lack of interest in weight's progressive steps. More important, and more suggestive as well, is the remark by Buffon in a supplement to his *Natural History* from 1777 that evokes a numerical figure for weight correlated with a figure for height. With Buffon there is no confirmation of a general increase in weighing, but he makes use of a relationship that had already been intuitively grasped and silently perceived but not calculated; namely, that the girth of a tall man and a small man is not the same, and the weight of a giant could not be the same as the weight of a dwarf. From this follows the totally new presentation of rule-governed correlations. "Normal" weight and "excessive" weight are determined in relation to a fixed marker of a body of identical height. The new idea is to posit diverse gradations of weight for a given height, with numbers assigned from low through intermediate to high. What's innovative too is this attempt to name them. Buffon established a series of four levels, but gives only one example. The weight of a man measuring "5 pieds, 6 pouces" (1.81 m) should be between 160 and 180 pounds (80–90 kilos). He is "already fat" if he weighs 200 pounds (100 kilos), "too fat" if he weights 230 pounds (115 kilos), and "much too thick if he weighs 250 pounds [125 kilos] and above."[17] For the first time, these numbers are true "statistics" since they designate an average, even if Buffon hardly speaks at all about this method of calculation. Nevertheless, the practice is totally original, even though it is completely isolated.

Buffon's hypotheses roughly coincide with other number-based questions being asked about proportions of body fat to body weight. Curious about adipose proportions, the Montpellier anatomist Boissier de Sauvages asks, What should the weight of fat be relative to the body's weight? He gives a numerical answer: "In moderately fat subjects, I found the weight of the fat to be half the weight of the whole body."[18] In 1783 the Parisian doctor Jacques Tenon, in a study of the inhabitants of Passy where he had a country house, posits a number for "maximum," "minimum," and "medium" weights. The project has a clear goal: to weigh sixty men and women between the ages of twenty-five and forty. The results are reported in ranked order. Among the men, 83.307 kilos is the maximum, 51.398 kilos is the minimum, and the average is 62.071 kilos. Among the women, 74.038 kilos is the maximum, 36.805 kilos the minimum, and 54.916 kilos the average.[19] But the correlation with height is missing. Averages and extremes, however, are explored and the differences between men and women are specified. Enlightenment culture definitely cares about what constitutes an average body.

The numbers are important. First those of Tenon. His curiosity is almost anthropological. The weight is an indicator of the "physique" of a given population, the state of its flesh, while passing over the question of the "too thin" or "too fat." Nevertheless, these results record a looming issue: the precise location of a group on a continuum of more and less, most and least. Buffon's numbers are different—more programmatic and "modern" too. They are directed at individuals and constitute a graduated scale that establishes for each person the excess or lack of weight he or she has compared to an average weight for people of the same height. These numbers contribute more to establishing cohorts of humans, the ranked representation of a population via tables, and the oppositional confrontation of the "less fat" and the "more fat." Buffon establishes a way of thinking the collectivity and of making comparisons that will display in orderly fashion the ratios of big and small bodies within a single population. Actual tables are left to the imagination, of course, and weights are only related to one height ("5 pieds 6 pouces"). Nor is the information actually applied in any way, but it does alter the mental profile of a society's physique. In theory this technique could be extended to numbering and comparing the average physique of different populations. The article on "Probabilité" in the *Encyclopédie*, a text prepared by Buffon, in fact, reveals an attraction for calculations and points in the direction of a new genre of public administration—one that would process a wide array of data about temperature, age, measurements, and illnesses so as to "determine over time and over an extended set of events those which come about one way and those which happen another way."[20] It is the beginning of a social physics in the service of a centralized state. Buffon's calculations do not extend much beyond a vision or thought experiment; however they do suggest the emergence, modestly and for the first time, of a statistical scale of fat people.

The First Specifications of Forms

This new sensitivity to gradations is also observable in literary contexts. For example, in the middle of the century, Marivaux succeeds in adroitly combining forms and words, as well as the accompanying dynamics and gestures to represent a "fatness" which is not really fatness while yet retaining notice of it. It is a particular sort of game playing on borderlines and excesses. "I saw a fat woman of medium height. She had one of the most curious throats I've ever seen. . . . She did not move with the heaviness that one associates with women who are too fat. She was not burdened by her bust or her throat. One saw this mass move about with a vigor that substituted for lightness . . . and the freshness that comes with a good temperament."[21] Here movement and vivacity are said to modify one's spontaneous impression of the fat person, adding nuances and suggesting degrees. This is Marivaux's deliberate way to specify discrete differences and above all to attempt to indicate thresholds. It is also an exploration of language and the play of paradox, an examination of limits that texts of the preceding century were far from going into with the same conviction. A similar situation occurs in another Marivaux description that pushes as far as possible the double meanings of words in order to more closely unite the lesser and greater extremes of the physical traits being referred to. "The woman was about fifty years old, perhaps sixty, and was a bit buxom. . . . She was still graceful; her allures were aged but not wilted, fading but not faded. . . . Her only wrong was being a little too tight in her clothes."[22] The goal is to stretch the language to better bring out a nuance and even impose one, to laboriously go beyond the signifiers of the language of previous centuries, which was limited to words such as *embonpoint, grasset, grasselet, rondelet,* and to list new examples and traits.

Engravings in the Enlightenment era and the universe of images in general turn even more and better toward graduated scales that display the new demand to mark degrees of inflection. Those who draw in the eighteenth century have sharpened their eyes to explore different types of fatness. The illustrations of physiognomists, for example, note specific "stages," display side by side different sorts of heaviness, and juxtapose images of the progressive fattening up of the chin or neck, bags under the eyes, and the sag of cheeks.[23] They also note the slow bending of the head under the growing weight of flesh. These drawings proceed feature by feature to display gradual differences that, up until then, had been ignored. Around 1780 Gaspar Lavatar is also interested in silhouettes: "physical attitudes, gaits, and postures,"[24]—the overall allure and no longer simply the face—as personalized markers. There is thus an investigation of various profiles in various positions. The image alone could be said to be the witness here, claiming to communicate better than words can. For the first time it "knows" how to inventively reveal nuances and degrees—

dichotomies that Marivaux, as we've said, tried to bring together and that Buffon attempted to tabulate. The gaze has definitely sharpened.

The series of military men drawn by Daniel Chodowiecki to illustrate Lavatar's physiognomy treatise (1772) juxtaposes the rotund belly of the general, the more retrained waistline of the officer, and the skinny soldier. The series of ecclesiastics in the same work shows the different volumes that are supposed to distinguish the various leaders within the Church hierarchy, accentuating the widths according to the prestige of the prelate.[25] Chodowiecki's intention is explicitly physiognomic: to "study" physical attitudes just as the face had long been studied, to interpret postures and positions as signs of personality and morals. The study of weighted flesh, long confined to representations of Silenus and Bacchus, opens up to the universe of degrees and diversities.

The first change is that the canonical image of bigness is no longer solely a question of degrees of roundness. The old spherical accumulations that had been the determining feature up until then are no longer the only factor. The theorization of caricature by William Hogarth and Francis Grosse at this time also opened up different varieties.[26] The principle of alteration that was explicitly laid out by the caricaturists leads to a fruitful way to point through deforming. It shows a way to reinvent the particularity of a subject through extreme emphasis of a specific trait of the person that singles it out for ridicule. This procedure also heightens the importance of the individual qua individual. The caricature promotes that higher status by harping on a singularity. At the end of the eighteenth century, there is a felt need for "more freedom to be granted to a humoristic art, a liberation from inhibitions" to allow the wide satiric potential of the fat person to be systematically explored.[27] Plurality then becomes the order of the day. Franz von Goez stresses the point in the title of his study from 1784, *Imaginative Exercises of Different Human Characteristics and Forms.*[28] Throughout, the expression of different physical sizes is keyed to different social and moral "types": "the magnificent," "appetite," "the heavy-eating gourmet," "the financier," "contemptuous," "important," "after libertinage," "the drunkard," etc. In each case the excess contour differs. Each one evokes an attitude or state: the exhausted roundness of the heavy-eating gourmet, the affirmative belly of the financier, the weighty stiffness of the important person, etc. Most are fat, but each in a different way. Individuality wins out in the eighteenth century both in its appearances and affirmations. The leaders of the Enlightenment favor emancipation and diversity. Drawings of the body are a prime example. These values give rise to the unprecedented habit of noticing and underlining singular types and paying attention to what defines and differentiates volumes.[29]

The second change is that degrees of bigness are more systematically pointed out and studied. This scrutiny is evident in the *Monument du costume* (1773) of Jean-Michel Moreau the Younger.[30] Here each character is attributed a specific profile such that an almost visible graduated scale is suggested. The intensity of the profiling of the oval belly changes from one scene to another, and curves are accentuated according to the character being featured. For example, the preening man in *La grande toilette*, one of the major engravings of the series, has contours that are bent enough to push far forward the arc of the jacket even though he's only moderately fat. At least he's less fat than the spectator drawn in the background with a belly hanging prominently over his belt. Less fat also than an innkeeper depicted in another scene holding a hot drink out above his massive abdomen such that the saucer practically rests on it like a shelf. In these three examples the belly advances to different degrees. In each the engraver seems to be exploring gradations of bigness, although there are few words to convey the nuances. The images recall the progress put forward by Buffon, even if there is no way to prove a connection. Nevertheless, there is clearly a new cultural sensitivity to degrees, whether highly or weakly explicit. The silhouette has taken on importance with its nuances and graduated rankings. These are clear signs of a categorizing gaze, even if slimming techniques have not changed as yet.

Masculine "Gravity" and Social "Gravity"

These images also display an accentuation of cultural and social changes. There is, for example, the heightened differentiation between male volumes and female volumes. Two adipose cultures are more distinct than before, especially two thresholds of "acceptable" bigness. *The Gallery of Fashion* published around 1780 emphasizes the intense strangulation of the female waist and the greater freedom of the man's waist—thus opposing the visual lightness of the former to the density of the latter. The engraving of close-fitting Brandenburg jackets accentuates the man's belly carried out front, smoothly rounding the silk shirt and thus the ball-like volume into something more "normal" and even desirable; whereas the female figure, in contrast, has her bust darkly magnified.[31] Similarly, the scene of a ball imagined by Duclos in 1770 opposes a wide range of men's bellies to the strictly uniform thin waists of the women.[32] There is no sluggish heaviness in the male case, but rather a certitude speaking through the body and translating self-assurance via the accentuation of contours. It is a clear way for the man to carry his belly as a badge of opulence and dignity.

The difference between the corseted waist of the female effigies and the freer waist of the male effigies further clarifies the opposition of former times that had long been rarely named or discussed but instead intuitively felt and silently accepted. The eighteenth century makes it more explicit and worked over as the consciousness of profiles becomes more refined—as can be seen from the very coinage of the term *silhouette* and the fashion of cutout shadow portraits in profile that focus attention on contours more than ever.[33] The engraver's stylus meditates on the silent varieties of the male belly, and each is scrupulously represented in its own profile.

These changes are translated into society, thanks in particular to the sharpening effect of a new theatralization of social conditions. For example, there is the stronger ascendancy of the formally dressed man in the eighteenth century, be it the financier, the merchant, or the bourgeois. The prominent chest of the man of finance announcing his opulence in a 1776 evocation of "the different clothes and states of the kingdom" is part of a vast iconographic enterprise.[34] His weight incarnates his status, valorizes the sedentariness of banks, business, and officialdom, and insists on the importance and successfulness of office work. The men drawn by Moreau the Younger in the middle of the eighteenth century do not have the same traits as those drawn by Abraham Bosse one hundred years earlier. What's more, they do not represent the same public worlds. The discreet extra weight of the merchant is far from the forced slenderness of the courtier. The office worker is not the man on horseback. The goal is no longer "good graces,"[35] and even less the classical dexterity in the manipulation of various arms,[36] but instead a noticeability that plays on imposing, on weighing in—to which corresponds an apt effigy that speaks of accumulations made in private and long hours spent at desks and behind counters. This figure bears no relation to the medieval fat person and the early notions of imbalanced forces giving rise to redundant debilitating masses. Now plumpness means a satisfied full envelope of flesh, a placid contentment with additional pounds. The best examples are Daniel Chodowiecki's silhouette studies, which display social ascendancy via a tranquil, medium-sized thickness of body that's far from the excess heaviness of the fat person and also far from the exact slenderness of women.[37]

Miller's engraving of the interior of a London merchant in 1766 is another example. It clearly underlines the nearly invisible, medium-sized stomach of the servants, the moderately larger envelope of attentive assistants and salesmen, and the yet weightier abdomen of the master of the house commanding those about him from a seat in the middle of the scene.[38] The scale of social conditions is exhibited from "least" to "most" in a clear, rule-governed way that's very different from former oppositions between popular fatness and elite thinness, which were often oversimplified in fact and more frequently assumed than verified. Crossing into the realm of nuances probably facilitated this new type of praise, which was formerly less noticed or hardly drawn at all. Attention to nuances made it more explicitly visible. Here now a "big" person is capable of garnering prestige, which is all the more favorably remarked and judged as attention becomes particularly attuned to the discrete and relative.

The practical representation of these degrees of difference is evident in an anecdote from the *Memories of the Old Court* that tells of Louis XV's visit in Arras in 1745. The king receives a "crowd of inhabitants" in a small, overpacked room. A local counselor thinks he will extract some advantageous priority thanks to his "thick and wide corpulence," but the Swiss guards rebuff him: "Stay there. Before we can let you enter, three have to exit."[39]

Of course this shows once again the ambiguity of all sizes. The conquest of nuances changes the way tolerance and rejection will play out. The "enormous" silhouette is refused as firmly as the "full" silhouette is accepted.

Finally, there is the new and decisive iconographic subtlety that comes when Berry de Nogent sets out to record the portrait of *The Beautiful Flemish Woman* and *The Beautiful German Woman* in 1761.[40] The drawings retain the classic strangulation of the waist, reinforced by the armor of the corset as a major marker of allure and poise.[41] However, he adds an ever so slight thickening of the chin, a minuscule line to suggest the wealth of flesh that supposedly characterized northern women. Of course the nuance is perfectly deliberate and perfectly achieved.

10. Stigmatizing Powerlessness

The possible prestige accorded to certain types of thickness that are relatively moderate and very culturally embedded has no effect on the rejection of the very heavy, whose condition is practically assimilated to an infirmity. Besides the heightened attention paid to degrees of bigness, the contribution of the Enlightenment era is surely a more acute stigmatization of "excesses." Already their organic significance is turned upside down. Eighteenth-century culture is sensitive to excitements and reactions and worried about their possibly being crushed under too great a heaviness. This new culture has a different vision of the body that is focused less on liquid humors and more on solid fibers, less on vapors and more on the tone and vibrancy of nerves. It wonders more about the origins of life force[1] and has an unprecedented interest in muscle and nerve tensions and in the causes that might lead to softening or relaxation of fibers.[2] A concern for lines and their interlacing displaces the earlier concern for liquids and sacks. In addition to the traditional focus on the compression of blood vessels by fat, there is now a similar alertness to the possible compression of the nerves. The new goals in Tissot's study of nervous maladies from 1770 is evidence of this. "Excess fat, despite being soft, will produce a compression strong enough to bother the nerves and produce regular swelling."[3] And conversely, a softening of fibers is said to favor the buildup of fat in tissues. There is one failing that weakens enormous bodies, namely, loss of "vibrancy,"[4] an absence of "tonic force,"[5] a major deficit of reactivity.[6] Powerlessness, in the end, is the fate of the weighted down anatomy. This explains the focus at this time on what is most feared, namely, loss of reproductive faculties and loss of the faculty of reaction.

Introducing a New Word, *Obesity*

Enlightenment thinkers posit a new vision of primary organic matter, promoting in a symbolic mode what the eye, with the help of microscopes, suspected when looking at the masses of filaments they revealed. This new vision singles out fibrous tissue and its reactive force and liveliness as the major emblem of animate bodily flesh. A body afflicted by some insufficiency that manifests itself as slackened tissues tends to favor the accumulation of fat and not simply a swollen body. It is this weakness that will orient both criticisms and remedies. Soft fiber causes the body to be invaded. It is a condition particularly common in "subjects who are nonchalant, puffy, and pituitary."[7]

The observations of Charles de Peysonnel, for example, at the end of the eighteenth century, renew the evocation of Dutch heaviness, stigmatizing the "awful dampness of the country that slackens fibers, the cheese and other dairy products that multiply cases of serosity, and the consumption of beer that attacks the nerves."[8] The observations of Louis Le Pecq de la Clôture around 1770 renew the evocation of fat rural folks; in this case people he encountered across the Norman countryside in woods and villages where he had set out to measure the effects of winds, marshes, mud, and fog. Here again were the old Hippocratic notions targeting particular "airs and spaces," but now updated and deepened by passing them through a prism of references to fiber and principles of reactivity.[9] Le Pecq compares the physical allure of populations alongside comparisons of geographical features, assimilating silhouettes and landscapes in a vast amalgamation of animals, vegetables, and minerals. He scrutinizes the body's contours as the sum of effects of location and climate. One example among others compares the inhabitants of Rouen and those of Caen eighty miles away. The first, exposed to "generally mild temperatures and dampness," and tending to consume too much "cream, milk, butter, and sugar," acquire "a delicate, weak tissue" and are "early on considerably stout" such that they become "doddering, thick, and heavy."[10] The second, living in drier conditions with "less fog," have "more frugal" habits and conserve their "natural vigor," avoiding all "extra layers."[11] The central distinction is that "the greatest cause of obstructions" provoking internal problems of thickness and swelling resides in the "solids" of the body, which leads to a softening of fibers and nerves.[12]

This theme of weakness subtly brings general fatness to be classified as a malady. The emerging use of the new word *obesity* in the eighteenth century—instead of *corpulence*—is proof of this. Antoine Furetière uses the term in the second edition of his *Dictionnaire* in 1701, whereas it did not appear in the first edition of 1690. "Medical term. State of a person carrying too much fat or flesh."[13] This word was not a totally new coinage, but now its use becomes more open, systematic, and scientific.[14] This is clear from the commentaries on the subject in chapters from medical treatises. Fatness is no longer a simple quantitative excess that calls for sobering moderation, it is a disorder, an internal degradation with its locations and progressions. It is an imbalance that supposes developments, accelerations, and failures. It has its particularities and therefore its own name. The *Encyclopédie* of the 1760s also associates obesity with *médecine*: "excessive stoutness," "a malady related to stagnation."[15] For the first time big size is a particular infirmity, a disorder that cannot be overcome by simple addition or subtraction.

A new insistence on the pathological arises. A few cases here and there were cited by doctors in the previous century, but such documentation becomes more systematic in the Enlightenment era. In 1755, for example, the *Journal de médecine* reports the death from "excessive stoutness" of a three-year-old child whose waist measurement exceeded her height.[16] The inevitable question is, How can a fat disorder invade such young flesh? In 1760 the same publication reports several extreme cases, citing waistline measurements, and asking with astonishment about the "agility" of some of these excessively stout beings. This reveals the extent to which eighteenth-century medicine remained exclusively interested in gigantic sizes when considering obesity.

More important, a general pathology that would lump together very different symptoms comes to be designated with the expression *slack tissue*. William Cullen describes the Dutch living in "flat, muddy, watery lands" as uniformly obese or hydropic.[17] The old distinction between hydropsy and corpulence does not disappear, however. For a long time the first remains linked to effusions of water, the second to effusions of fat. Enlightenment-era doctors are interested in these differences between fat, blood, and water. But their way of grouping symptoms under the heading "slackness" shows how much the evils of corpulence and hydropsy are never able to be totally distinguished and thus continue to belong to the same world for them. Louis Le Pecq de la Clôture's writings illustrate this, as when, for example, he evokes in the same description various degrees of stoutness as well as "swellings, wastings [*cachexies*], edemas, and other hydropsies" all provoked by dampness or abuses.[18] This explains the more frequent references to all types of bigness now considered as a symptom of weakness of both "fat people" and "humid people" who are exposed to "all manner of indispositions."[19]

Also a part of this theme of grouping is the will to class maladies into pathological "families" that can be subdivided into genres, classes, orders, and suborders, as Linnaeus did for plants in his *Systema naturae* (1735).[20] Enlightenment era medicine seeks a more structural rationality. Thus it is no longer the location in the body, in analogy with topography, that primarily dictates the inventory of illnesses. It was a long-standing tradition to speak of headache, neck pain, shoulder pain, chest pain, stomachache, sore legs, etc. But now classification is pursued according to general principles of dysfunction by "type" of pathology: fever, weakness, inflammation, spasms, pain, irregularity, etc. It is now symptoms, visible disorders, that reveal illnesses. In this approach, hydropsy, plethora, and fattening are inevitably grouped around an increase in body volume now considered as "intumescences": "overabundant fluids accumulated unnaturally."[21] They therefore resemble each other, even if resulting from different liquids. In the nosography of Boissier de Sauvages they belong to the ninth category of illnesses that group together those involving additions and secretions. Their proximity is such that a number of eighteenth-century doctors do not abandon the certitude of identifying the hydropic person as "a big eater and drinker."[22] The Enlightenment thinkers had not really overcome the confusion of different kinds of bigness due to attributing different types of source material to a common cause. Thus different kinds of puffiness were lumped together and all linked to "slackening." This is a holdover of the traditional vision of the fat person as a mysterious mixture and of intuitive reasoning and a relative absence of verification.

This confused imprecision is evident in an account of the dissection of the body of a woman who "died of hydropsy" told by Alexander Monroe in 1745. The Scottish doctor discovers in the abdomen of the cadaver a "big vesicular body" covered by a "black membrane" mixed with fat—a substance so curious that Monroe, believing he may be onto a discovery, thinks it best to bring the object home for closer examination. The interior of this "belly" supposedly consists of fat and water as well as some unknown, opaque, semisolid matter.[23]

The Bad Symptom: Insensitivity

The even greater originality is that the ballooning up of the obese person is explained differently, insisting on an absence of reactive feeling, whereas Enlightenment empiricism had made the acuity of the senses into the leading sign of a being's acuity in general. George Cheyne is one of the first to write of this particular deficit in the obese in a long confession from around 1730 that mixes thoughts about fatness and thoughts about insensitivity. He had the impression of "getting a bit fatter every day" and of losing all reactivity to the point of being entirely "lethargic and listless."[24] This English doctor, one of the first to totally refuse turning to the old discourse of humors, transposes the collapse of tissue into a mental collapse: the extinction of all stimulus, boredom, loss of desire and interest, and absence of pleasure and will.[25] He also reports an impression of vertigo mixed with anxiety that he simply names "melancholy."[26] Attention has shifted from oafishness to powerlessness, from awkwardness to zero affect; i.e., to the interior effect of a specific personal lack. This shift is made possible because a quasi-psychological attention to interiors has developed.

Here again the testimony of Élie de Beaumont is striking. The lawyer is introspective. He describes and judges himself beyond just numbers, revealing the slow but steady advance of self-perception in the eighteenth century. First the external appearance: his vision of his belly, its rounded curve, like "the arc of a circle," so prominent that it hides "totally from view the lower body."[27] Then he notes his fatigue and his lack of breath climbing any set of stairs. Then he notes the diminishment of his senses. "Nothing moves him, nothing excites him, not the sight of a beautiful woman, not an opera performance, not stimulating books, nothing in fact that normally flatters and animates the senses" (56). His body, he says, is nothing but a "baked pumpkin in the snow" (61), an envelope devoid of reaction, organs with no "appetite." Finally, on sexual matters, he notes, "no erection, not even desire for one." The obese person is "a wet rag," the Paris lawyer insists, a being in lack and "lethargy" (61).

This account corresponds to a particular moment in the personal history of the lawyer—the time in 1775 when Élie de Beaumont says he would like to have a second son though his wife is already forty-three. It also corresponds to a specific cultural moment, namely, the time when Enlightenment thinkers are drawing attention to everything relating to the senses, especially to the "reproductive faculty" (60). There is a focus on the life spring of the family and the physical force of populations generally. A preoccupation with "demographics" and "regeneration" increased in the second half of the eighteenth century, inflamed by a vague impression of a downturn in the birthrate and by "disastrous secrets penetrating into the countryside" about *coitus interruptus* that spread with the heightened solicitude accorded to children and attempts to limit the child-rearing burden and promiscuity.[28] The new image is that of a fecundity of symbolic significance, of the health of an individual being passed to his descendants, and of the vigor of a nation depending on the numbers of the able bodied. Power is considered reproductive power and also a function of sanitation—a key to abundance and wealth, as the first grand census-taking projects at the end of the eighteenth century will assert.[29] Fecundity is thought to depend on both force and sensitivity—the quality of one's descendants in the presence of excitements. And it's precisely the extinction of those two resources that the lawyer deplores. His general sensitivity is lost as well as the "spring" of the "lower parts."[30] Here fatness is lived like never before as a downfall.

Diderot's novel *The Indiscreet Jewels* (1748) gives a bawdy representation of these ideas. A magic ring given to Mangogul by a capricious genius plays the role of truth teller. Its jewel, which is supposed to make the intimate organs of those it is pointed at "talkative," encounters only nonsense when directed at overly fat people. One of them is the spherical woman, crushed by fat, says Diderot, to the point of "resembling a Chinese maggot or a giant, deformed embryo."[31] Incapable of answering the ring's questions, she can only convey her sensibility through some cold utterances about geometry—no vibration, no excitement. Fat has stifled in her all possibility of direct experience.

The rejection of excessively fat people intersects with what eighteenth-century culture fears most: loss of sensitivity.

The Criticism of the Affluent

So there are new markers exploited by a new type of social critique in the eighteenth century. The fat person is no longer simply an uncultivated, incapable oaf; he is now a "useless," "unproductive" character. He is at the intersection of two negative lines of thinking that criticisms of affluence latch on to more than ever: loss of power and gluttony. The argument is aimed against privilege. Fatness is linked to fortunes, and vindictive attention turns to those who "fatten themselves on the substance taken from the widow and the orphan" while "the people perish from misery and hunger."[32] Those who "abuse" are, in effect, displaying their own uselessness.

This is a striking moment of our modernity when the former critique of popular fatness gets partly inverted. Heaviness can be unlinked from simple vulgarity and instead symbolize another social milieu when coupled with a seizing grasp and gain. It can literally embody profit, advantage, and "surplus" to the point of figuring the fraudulent swindler. This can only emerge, of course, under new social and economic borderlines, now no longer primarily religious, that expose and maintain collectivities. There is a new social and quasi-political indignation against "cheaters" and "abusers" that is very different from the sort that had been voiced until then against blasphemers and negators of God. This new feeling requires sharpening the image of the disadvantaged as contrasted with the privileged. Incessant repetitions of "slavery" versus "despotism" attempt a sweeping condemnation of businessmen, government officials, local leaders, and law enforcement.[33] Many studies have demonstrated the centrality of criticism within Enlightenment culture, especially criticism that affirms the "progress of the sciences, mores, and the human spirit" and that "questions former social relations" or the criticism originating in England concerning "constitutional debates."[34] These criticisms have iconographic translations, as it were, in visual form, and the fat person, incarnating powerlessness and insensitivity, played a major role.

William Hogarth's stuffed magistrates offer a leading example, with their vacant, drooping eyes, lowered heads, and slumped postures crushed under folds of clothing and flesh.[35] Their ascendancy within the propertied class has changed them into swollen, deformed men. Here satire has been constructed far from the religious themes of earlier times. Courtiers, magistrates, and country landlords are stigmatized in popular songs of the eighteenth century as "the famous fat," "the heavy gluttons," "the big swindlers" in part to deride them for being unproductive and powerless.[36] The Revolution-era caricaturists in France develop the theme further. One finds, for example, the wine press—a gigantic machine with its monumental levers and gears—being used to symbolize the action to be taken against the privileged. Abbots and country priests, represented with enormous swollen bodies, are forcefully led to the machine to have their "sacred fat" and "stolen assets" pressed off.[37] There is also the engraving of the "Parade of the Landlord" whose immense belly becomes the focal point of the image as it spills out from a robe—exaggeratedly swollen, gigantic—while grotesque, fallen companions follow behind.[38] The fat person here is a prop to orient the criticism. His presence shows above all the extent to which his significance mattered for this culture at that time.

The Big Bad Husband

The theme is given further symbolic significance in representations of the king at the end of the eighteenth century.[39] The denigration of his physical body shows the relative freedom to criticize at the time, evidence by then of the desacralization of the royal figure.

For a long time thin and even svelte,[40] Louis gets fatter "by the second" in the first years of his reign, according to the *Secret Correspondence*.[41] The doctors are worried in 1778, judging his "stoutness excessive and dangerous."[42] They try to reduce the amount of food eaten by the twenty-four-year-old king, get him to take walks, and recommend drinking Vichy water. But none of this has any effect; his appearance hardly changes and is weighted down even more by the heavy countenance of the king himself.[43] There are thus occasions for humor, such as in the observation of Frédéric d'Hézecques, a court page in the 1780s, who describes a particular moment when the king returns at night after hunting and feasting at Rambouillet, and he reveals his fatigue in front of silent witnesses. "Arriving half asleep, his legs swollen, and overwhelmed by the light and torches, he had difficulty climbing the stairs. The valets who saw him, already convinced of his debauchery, believed he was totally drunk."[44]

Such interpretations of deviance are largely independent from the "true" personality of the king.[45]

Suspicions of weakness intensify over the seven years that follow his marriage in 1770, during which time an heir was impatiently hoped for. "Everyone asks privately, Can the king do *it* or not?"[46] The theme expands to encompass his political power with its attendant decisions, accidents, and the people involved—all of which regularly add more doubts:

Maurepas returns triumphant
Here's what it means to be powerless
Says the king as he embraces him.
When two are alike
They should live together.[47]

The arrest of the king in 1791 gives further sway to all the negative judgments. Powerlessness and fatness are systematically linked, and the image of the "baby doll" (*poupon*) is used endlessly.[48] The king is nothing but a "fat animal," a "royal cuckold," a "king of clubs," a wimpy grass eater; whereas the strict antimonarchy logic depicted him as a Vulcan, blacksmith of the world, a master of iron and a man-eater.

> Alas, my powerlessness
> Reduces me to a sad fate.
> For my Venus I am dead
> A Vulcan of high birth
> But as my great misfortune
> I go from man-eater
> To clover-eater. O woe,
> This is my true fall.[49]

These images have often been studied in recent accounts. Especially that of the "pig" considered to wallow in its stoutness. Powerlessness and fatness become all the more striking in this symbol, which stresses the defeat, in the eyes of royalists, of any and all royal hold. This exaggeratedly swollen and useless body as well as the "passivity" of this being reduced to powerlessness become clear to everyone. The queen has the last word in a remark that underlines the degeneration of obesity into lack of sense, sensibility, and sensation and a loss of dignity that signals a caste's capitulation to debility and inertia: "My pig is an immense mass of flesh that eats and drinks but can't get it up."[50]

11. Toning Up

Treatments for the fat person change direction considerably in the Enlightenment era. The image of powerlessness and the theme of a collapse that favors fat buildup are central to the orientation of new slimming programs. An illness explained as a slackening of tissues logically calls for a remedy based on their reinforcement. This causes anti-obesity recipes to become an arsenal of toning formulas and stimulants all designed to "fortify" the flesh in order to better eliminate all excess. This leads to a diversification of practices that give greater importance to exercise and elevate the discovery of electricity and the promise of it improving the tone of limbs and skin. Diet now becomes the focus of numerous debates. Questions arise, for example, about the consumption of light, delicate, and juicy (*de bon suc*) meat. It is considered a tonic by some, but "dangerous" by others. Choices multiply and options compete with each other. There are arguments with a "qualitative" approach to diet before modern chemistry will eventually make them more "objective."

The Virtue of "Tonics"

The tone and springiness of solid volumes becomes uppermost, though the theme of evacuation remains, and formulas for "lightening," "purges," and "dissolving" soaps have an insistent place on pharmacy shelves. At any rate, the food of the obese person is not supposed to "stay"—it must evaporate, traverse the body without "occupying it," dilute, and "pass" without adding more burden. Thus, one finds "soap pills," "big Venice soaps,"[1] and "aloe emollient pills" generously prescribed to Élie de Beaumont by his two doctors.[2] These recommendations are repeated often, since the soaps themselves would be absorbed or simply dissolve rapidly.[3] There were also "scillitic vinegars" used by Antoine Baumé to "divide thick viscous humors" in the case of hydropsies, which were still confused somewhat indiscriminately with obesity.[4]

Toning up, however, becomes central as a result of the fear of slackening and of the collapse and insensitivity of bodily envelopes. Prescriptions make tone into the number one goal, and thus tonics are the major active ingredient for a "return to vigor."[5] In 1760 the journal *L'Avant-Coureur* recommends the virtues of "Russian pine nuts" to fight "against low tone" of tissues.[6] In 1776 Georges-Frédéric Bacher invents a mixture he claims is the best tonic. He names it after himself, markets it, and writes about it in an authoritative work on hydropsy. It is a mixture of "black hellebore," myrrh, and "holy thistle." He reports where he collects these ingredients, how he combines them, and specifies the dosage and duration of use.[7] This type of prescription is decisive, since, despite the tacit blending of hydropsy and obesity, the use of tonics becomes the answer at the first sight of the fat person's fleshy profusions, and these are immediately linked now to his powerlessness and lethargy.

Tonics containing iron, tartar, cinnamon, oxymel scillitic are central to Pinkstan's mid-century recommendations for a seventy-two-year-old retired navy captain who had become "prodigiously swollen."[8] Antoine Petit and Samiel Tissot make massive use of tonics to treat the "frank" obesity of Élie de Beaumont—unperturbed by the lawyer's laments and recriminations. Creams of tartar, pills of *asafoetida*, Commander's balm, Balaruc water (judged wonderful for the stomach by the *Encyclopédie*), balsamic formulas meant to increase "movement of the blood" and "resolve obstructions,"[9] and "mint lozenges," especially English ones (judged "comforting and good for the nerves"),[10] were all prescribed to better "excite" the patient. In addition, there were aphrodisiacs—discussed and criticized at length—and a choice of stimulating "softening powders" as well as recommendations about how best to position one's body to favor the union required for one's "conjugal duty." "One is to stand, the wife lying back on the edge of the bed with thighs raised and resting against the arms of the husband with the legs hanging over the shoulders."[11] Powerlessness is indeed a "global" evil. And the doctor's answer will also concern itself with the "venereal act."

The Virtue of "Excitants"

Tonics are not alone in promising vigor. Exercises are also promoted, now with new explanations. Movement is said to strengthen less by drying out than by firming up. It works on the filaments, enlivening while hardening them. Exercise "reanimates fibers and maintains the suppleness and spring of muscles."[12] It's the inverse of a baby's overly tender flesh that total absence of movement would render "fat and swollen."[13] Reinforcement depends on contractions, shocks, shakes, and convulsions, even if provoked from the exterior. This is what Montesquieu intends to concretely bring about with horseback riding. "Each step of horse provokes a pulse in the diaphragm, and over a league that amounts to about four thousand pulsations one would otherwise not have."[14] The same reasoning is behind the invention of the "mechanical armchair," the "mechanical horse," and the "horseback stool" described in the *Encyclopédie* and the journal *Posters, Announcements, and Diverse Opinions*.[15] A curved rocking chair base and other special handles allow oneself or a servant to induce regular movement and thus permit exercise "in one's own room."[16]

"Continuous work, travel, and business" are what Antoine Petit and Samuel Tissot recommend to their patients.[17] Their vision of exercise is based on agitation and tension. William Cullen sees these practices as the "only effective way" to combat obesity.[18] Élie de Beaumont yields docilely to the recommendations. He specifies the types of movements he performs, their duration, and the precautions for each, noting the mix of firming up and cleaning out that goes on. He walks through Paris for one hour in a warm overcoat. He does this either in the morning at 6:30 or in the early afternoon between 1 and 2. He then returns home sweating profusely. He has servants rub him with a dry towel, then a wet one, then with a "stiff" brush, before donning a "slightly warmed shirt."[19] This shows the continued importance of friction and perspiration.

Élie de Beaumont hardly loses any weight despite all this effervescence. On the contrary, he gets fatter. This is what convinces him that he has a real illness, and it is why he feels so disappointed by the many and sometimes contradictory prescriptions of his doctors. "One is against tea, the other is for it; one says to cut back on mental work, the other sees nothing wrong with it."[20] More than ever, obesity can seem like a disorder that resists treatment. An obstacle for doctors and a source of disillusion for patients now provokes new forceful feelings of bitterness. All the more since heaviness hardly facilitates physical movement. Certain exercises are sometimes impossible to perform.[21] A whole new dark side to obesity begins to emerge when the body does not "obey" efforts to control the evil that may arise. However, there is no medical response to this obscure inertia and unchanging state despite close supervision and restrictions.

Baths further multiply the panoply of treatments. The cold bath, of course, with its provocation of tension and tightening is associated with cold air, wind, exertions, and other methods for toning up tissues. The arsenal of hardening agents grows, inverting traditional practices and multiplying the aims and explanations. Baths are a vast topic that extends well beyond slimming programs to the general maintenance of health and hygiene. In the 1760s Poittevin opens his thermal boat on a bank of the Seine to offer the stimulation of cold baths.[22] These particular baths become a focal point of Pierre-Marie de Saint-Ursin's beauty and health treatment at the end of the century.[23]

Many of these baths are aimed specifically at slimming. All those, for example, that induce a particular compression and an evacuating effect, "attenuating the blood to make it more fluid and runny."[24] Also those of Madame du Barry, which link regular cold baths to the firmness of her bust. She proudly displayed the results to Dufort de Cheverny, who paid her a visit in the 1780s and had the surprise of being invited to feel for himself under her clothes.[25] There is also the case of Pomme's patients who stay in the water for hours hoping for a retightening of their organs that will eliminate their "obstructions" and "engorgements."[26]

Electric Dreams

Another excitant turned to is electricity. This "fluid" and its commotions and shocks were experimented with by amateurs and savants starting around 1750. Schwilgué proposed a cold bath with electric current that he expected to produce retightening and secretions.[27] The Abbé Nollet recommended direct electrification and provided statistical evidence of its success. An electrified cat became seventy grains lighter, a pigeon thirty-five to thirty-seven grains, a sparrow six-seven grains.[28] These figures may seem silly, but they testify to the intense interest in weight loss and its numerical verification. The calculations are more tentative, however, when it comes to human weight loss. "After being electrified for five full hours, a man and woman of between twenty and thirty years lost several ounces of weight."[29] Becoming "lighter" is equated with greater liveliness. Pierre Bertholon offers many explanations about stiffened fibers and about the material effects of the electric current. He comments

on the types of heaviness susceptible to treatment and speaks indiffer-
ently about hydropsy and obesity. "As for universal intumescences, those
related to corpulence (polysarcia), where the human body is disfigured by
a too great quantity of fat, those related to swelling and to leucophleg-
macy which are emphisematic or edemic intumescences, electric commo-
tion and strong electric current directed against certain excesses of long
duration and intensity appear to be appropriate remedies for these types
of cachexia."[30]

Pierre Bertholon cites the case of "too fat" people who lose "a part of
their excess" weight after the application of "a great number of commotions."[31] All constitutions are "eager to receive electricity," in the words of
Noël Retz in 1785, and are lightened thanks to the flow of current.[32] This
practice, however, is not the most usual, nor without its critics. Its popularity depends on the new idea of body parts susceptible to being "excited"
and made more slender thanks to a particular tension—a state in which
the fibers dominate over the watery substances.

The Nerve Regimen

Finally there are the regimens or "diets" designed to act positively on
the fibers. They oppose contracting foods to slackening foods, "aromatic
plants" to rough ones, and exciting effects to softening effects. A double
action is systematically pursued to combat obesity: a *tension* that permits
the evacuation and a *stimulation* that permits the restoration of forces
by exaltation. William Buchan orients in this dual direction with all the
foods and liquids he prescribes to hydropics, sedentary artisans, and literary types in his *Domestic Medicine*, a work published eighteen times
in English and ten times in French between 1770 and 1803.[33] There is an
insistence on dry foods, "stimulating" plants,[34] and on eating small quantities of meat that will "fortify the fibers of the stomach"[35]—thrush and
partridge being the best examples. There is also an emphasis on choosing
the right liquids, such as liqueurs known as "spirits" that will "fortify the
spring of body masses."[36] Certain other practices are also said to favor
excitation, such as inhaling the smoke of burning partridge feathers,
which supposedly "strengthens the nerves." This is mentioned within a
long inventory of good foods and other health products by an English
doctor around 1750.[37]

When looked at closely, however, the content of these diets hardly
changes at all during the eighteenth century. Perhaps due to a lack of

chemistry knowledge, thoughts about food remain as intuitive as they are dogmatic. The light, the heavy, the dry, the watery, and the fat remain primary reference points, with the "sticky" and the "rough" motivating a rejection, as though the sensual and especially visible qualities of ingested foods determined their slimming or fattening potential. A number of rejected items continue to be shunned. These include animals believed "to live off garbage such as ducks and pigs,"[38] animals from stagnant waters ("bogs and ponds"),[39] "bitter and airy" plants,[40] "viscous" meats, and "oily fish." The danger of these foods is they might form "a tenacious doughy mass" inside the body or provoke wind and bloating.[41] And all of them tend to soften instead of tighten. All favor obstruction instead of transit. One is reminded of the slow, difficult setting aside of references to the simplified explanatory model of the humors.

The originality at this time is a new way of talking about diets and the solemn prestige accorded them in letters, memoirs, and other autobiographical writings. "Healthy simple" foods are mentioned regularly by the Prince de Ligne during his visits to Bailleul;[42] "bowls of hot wine," "spicy roasts and wines," and "cups of tea or coffee" are regularly cited by James Boswell in his daily diary as things to make him "feel well";[43] and "the regimen of the English farmer,"[44] based on sober, light broths, is mentioned in letter after letter by Horace Walpole, who was afflicted by a case of gout he couldn't overcome.[45]

George Cheyne inaugurates this detailed attention in the first half of the eighteenth century—linking diet to the body's form, and noting every single thing consumed and its effect day by day. He is so insistent that he sees it necessary to justify his pioneering ways:

> I know how indecent and shocking egotism is, and for an author to make himself the subject of his words or works, especially in so tedious and circumstantiated a detail. But so various and contradictory have been the reports of and sneers on my regimen, case, and sentiments, that I thought thus much was due to truth, and necessary for my own vindication. And perhaps it may not be quite useless to some low, desponding, valetudinary, overgrown person whose case may have some resemblance to mine.[46]

Diet becomes a topic of conversation and commentary among the Enlightenment's cultivated classes. It is worried over and inventoried to the smallest detail and always with the constant certitude of giving healthy advice to the one addressed.

More generally, beginning at the end of the seventeenth century there is a heightened importance accorded to tastes and a development of a "more refined, more delicate" type of cooking that condemns the heavy eater more than the gourmet.[47] The "light suppers" of aristocratic households in the eighteenth century favor attention to quality. Stephen Mennell refers to it as a "civilizing of the appetite."[48] The heavy use of spices decreases and that of vegetables, light fresh meats, and fruits increases at the same time that growing methods and transportation possibilities improve. The daily cuisine of the elite favors delicacy over sheer abundance; a new quality over the old priority of quantity. This is evident in a passionate description by Pietro Verri in 1764.

> The table is filled with the most delicate foods possible. All the nutriments are healthful and easy to digest. There is not overabundance or exaggeration, simply what is strictly necessary and pleasing. Heavy, viscous meats, garlic, onions, strong liqueurs, salted foods, truffles, and other things poisonous to humans are totally prohibited from this table. One finds essentially chicken and other bird meat, herbs, and oranges and their juice. The tastes are exquisite but not strong. . . . This is our meal and we complete it with an excellent cup of coffee. One feels satisfied, full, but not stuffed or sleepy as one would from eating rough heavy foods.[49]

Plants or Meats?

The new custom of serving meat on a regular basis contributes to the striking originality of the eighteenth century. For Antoine Le Camus and his doctor Abdeker,[50] there is no doubt that meats that will keep the trunk from becoming too stout are to be chosen on the basis of the manifestly slender physiques of carnivorous animals.[51] George Cheyne is also sure of himself as he surveys what foods he eats at the beginning of the eighteenth century. The only vegetables he includes in his diet are exclusively those that provoke the hefty, heavy feeling of meat. A clear contradiction, which shows certitude carries the day over debate or doubt.

A debate intensifies however around a cultural matter that has been studied at length, namely, the criticism of luxury and artifice, urban fashions and excess refinement, and the "softening" that eating too much meat is said to contribute to.[52] Rousseau adds to these criticisms in the 1760s with the themes of "asphyxiation in cities," clothing constraints, and the evil of sedentariness. The threat of a collective "perishing" is here put forward in a way markedly different from the old fears about moral backsliding and loss of religious faith. The worry now is about physical diminution from attacks on the organs that are the presumed consequences of certain practices as well as a certain preciousness. The concern is how to prevent an evil from halting progress and converting modernity into weakness, and the means include altering public health, now spoken of collectively for the first time. The menace is a declining slope where "races perish or degenerate within a few generations."[53] Enlightened humanism condemns the mass killing of animals, the "massacres," people's "voraciousness," and the construction of "vast butcheries" throughout the world.[54] At the end of the century, Françis Mundy even denounces the cruelty of those who hunt hares and shoot birds.[55] Consuming animals comes to be considered as both noxious and a sign of insensitivity. Eating plants, however, is an entirely different matter. Plants are life affirming and valued for quickening the reflexes, restoring one's old vigor and "forces," and warding off indolence and blindness.

Obviously vegetarianism does not receive unanimous backing. Voltaire includes an amused look at the interdiction of meat in an entry within his *Philosophical Dictionary* (1764).[56] A number of health specialists maintain a favorable opinion about eating "healthy, juicy" meat.[57] Buffon, who seems to have had reservations about total vegetarianism, recommends mixing and matching "the food regimes of different peoples" and taking inspiration from the best of these, whatever the choices may be.[58] The very existence of so many alternatives testifies to the adoption of new considerations, notably Enlightenment culture's increasing awareness about the two-edged sword of "progress" and its elaboration of philosophies of food where the stakes are significantly more spelled out than in former times.

The Chemistry Revolution

An entirely unprecedented dimension of the new food culture would be added with the chemistry revolution, which got started at the end of the eighteenth century. It is not that all the interests of the Parisian chemist Lavoisier, for example, converged a priori with the concerns of digestion physiologists. Nor is it the case that the early questions of Lavoisier even took up the physical economy of animals. The manipulations of air, water, metals, and the inquiry into elementary bodies dubbed "simple" are not aimed at nutritive substances and their combinations. Nor were their sealed chambers, balls, and retorts made with the purpose of analyzing foodstuffs. It was the discovery of oxygen and its role in the respiratory system that allowed new ways of thinking to develop, notably a totally revised conception of foods within the alimentary canal and their effects.

The experiments carried out in 1778 on people placed in sealed chambers entirely change the way people think about the organic. The analysis of the air breathed inside the chamber revealed that oxygen had been absorbed and carbon dioxide expelled. The inevitable conclusion was that respiration is a form of combustion.[59] The act is therefore to be reinterpreted. Its function is entirely different: breathing is no longer about helping the heart contract or refreshing and refining the blood, as doctors and scientists had always thought, but instead plays a vital role in maintaining animal heat, and more generally life, by means of some sort of invisible furnace. A flame exists for which the presence of oxygen must be a necessary condition. Some combustible "material" must also exist, like a candle's wax or the coal of a stove. Food must be this "aliment," and one of its "transformations" is explained by this contribution to the act of combustion.

Some completely new lines of thinking begin, even if they are not present in Lavoisier's writings. For example, the attempt to distinguish foods based on their combustive properties and on their presence or absence in the combustive process. There is also a new interest in defining principles of a "balanced" diet that assimilate excess weight to a pathology analogous to the insufficiency or inefficiency of a process of "burning." Lavoisier himself turns the scale into a judge's verdict. "The same individual, after increasing in weight by the combined amount of all that he has ingested, returns at the end of each twenty-four-hour cycle to the same weight he had before; and if this does not take place, the individual is suffering from something or ill."[60]

The reasoning is not yet expressed in terms of calories and calorie counting. A revolution has started, though, in which "slack tissue" is no longer the heart of the matter, and instead balance takes on a role it had never had and combustive power transforms all representations. This revolution will fully assert itself during the nineteenth century.

1. Ancient miniatures did not distinguish different profiles. In 1311 the glutton consuming food is not shown in his presumed actual size. *Sobriety and Gluttony*, ms. 6329, folio 200v, Bibliothèque de l'Arsenal, Laurent d'Orléans, "La Somme le Roi," Picardie, 1311. *Bibliothèque nationale de France*

2. *The Marriage of the Virgin*, 12th century. No difference yet is represented between the contours of the bodies. French MS. *Rue de Archives*

3. *The Marriage of the Virgin*, 15th century. The first representation of the fat, awkward "oaf" who understands he has no chance of marrying Mary. His size (*grosseur*) is synonymous with gauche vulgarity (*grossièreté*). Jean Fouquet, "The Hours of Étienne Chevalier," ms. 71, folio 24, Condé Museum, Chantilly. *Bridgeman Giraudon*

4. Hydropsy, the spread of liquid throughout the body, for a long time, is poorly distinguished from the spread of fat throughout the body. *Head and Face of a Hydropic Man*, a drawing attributed to Hans Holbein the Elder, late 15th century, Louvre Museum, Paris. *Réunion des Musées Nationaux*

5. Albrecht Dürer is one of the first to explore the traits of extreme fatness: the sunken neck, the spherical appearance of limbs, a diffuse rigidity, and a proliferation of folds of the skin. The drawing *Women Bathing* that inspired the engraving dates from 1496. Kunsthalle Museum, Bremen. *Bridgeman Giraudon*

6. Rubens explores extreme fatness like no one before, exposing cracked and collapsed flesh. Pierre Paul Rubens, drawing for *The Fall of the Damned* (1621). British Museum, London. *Réunion des Musées Nationaux*

7. Rubens is sensitive to "generous" flesh when treating mythological subjects; but he also knows how to depict in everyday paintings the formal requirements of his time: narrow waists and tight belts. Pierre Paul Rubens, *Portrait of a Young Woman*, early 17th century or 1630. Uffizi Gallery, Florence. *Leemage*

8. During the Enlightenment come the first comparative explorations of differences in possible degrees of body size. Here the volume of the merchant's belly is accentuated, the clerk's volume is less pronounced, the domestic servants are thinner still, and the female figures show the obligatory tight waists. Mill, *The Household of the English Merchant*, 18th century. *Bibliothéque nationale de France*

9. Other early Enlightenment-era explorations into the different possible forms of bigness take into account individual variations. Obesity can manifest itself in a variety of curves. James Gillray, *Two-Penny Whist*, 1796. *Bridgeman Giraudon*

10. A heightened interest in obesity in the eighteenth century can be seen in the search for "phenomenal" cases that are represented and exhibited. These extreme figures both challenge and reinforce norms, limits, and thresholds. John Fairburn, *Separate Portraits of Daniel Lambert (1770–1809) and Edward Bright (1720–1750), 50 Stone and 44 Stone, Respectively*, engraving, 1806. Wellcome Library, London.

(Upper-right hand corner)

The representation of the fat person began to have a specifically social and political dimension in the eighteenth century as an abuser, profiteer, exploiter—a swollen, obtuse spirit. The fat person is a "possessor" of ill-gotten gains, the fat male being the character specifically targeted. *Wellcome Library, London*

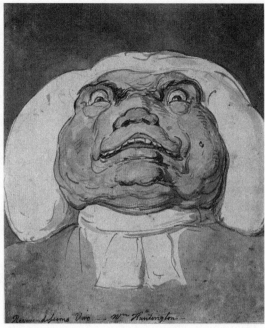

11. Joseph François Götz, *The Financier*, in *Imaginative Exercises in Inventing, Painting, and Drawing Different Characters and Human Forms*, Augsberg, 1783–1784. *Réunion des Musées Nationaux*

12. *Reverendissimo Viro – V. H. Huntington*, an ink drawing by Thomas Rowlandson (1756–1827). *Bridgeman Giraudon*

13. *The Patriotic Weight-Loss Machine*, "Patience, Monseigneur, your turn will come." Engraving, late 18th century, Carnavalet Museum, Paris. *Leemage*

14. The invention of the pear-shaped effigy in the 1830s. The bourgeois figure is reduced to his digestive functions with the focus on lower-body collapse and a gradual widening from face to abdomen. Honoré Daumier, *The Pear*, a caricature of Louis-Philippe in response to an "insult" addressed to the artist. Archive for Art and History, Berlin. *AKG*

15. Two opposing profiles: the bourgeois "reassured" by his belly versus the dandy exhibiting his stout chest and narrow waist. In the 1830s social success is generally judged to belong to the former. Jean-Igance Grandville, *All That Glitters Is Not Gold*, in *Cent Proverbes* (Paris, 1844). *Kharbine-Tapabor*

16. The "heavily freighted" image. England's Edward VII (1841–1910), a particularly fat king, is ridiculed here for his colonial ambitions, despite apparently good relations with France at the beginning of the twentieth century. Jean Veber, *Caricature du roi Édouard VII d'Angleterre, Le Foudre de guerre*, an illustration from *L'Assiette au Beurre* (The butter plate), September 28, 1901.

The enduring belief in the possibility of molding the body's contours with a rigid sheath is behind the very long history of a slowly evolving garment: the corset. From metal frames to those made of various fabrics, from strapping down the bust to encasing the hips, from a generic look to more individualized ones. *Rue de Archives*

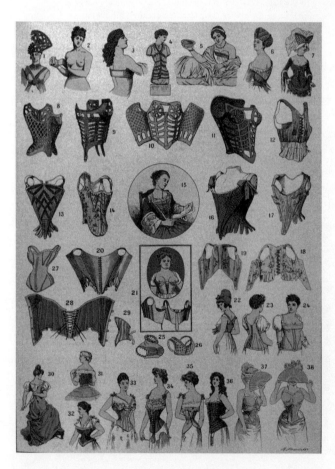

17. The evolution of the corset and women's lingerie over time. Illustration, 19th century. *Leemage*

18. *The Marvelous Effect of Lacing . . . a View of the Pretty Miller's Wife*, print, 1792–1803. Bibliothéque nationale de France

19. For a very long time, an approximate rough idea of bigness gets by with practically no use of scales whatsoever. At the beginning of the seventeenth century, Sanctorius installs a heavy and complex balance scale suspended from the ceiling to conduct his precise experiments about weight gain, weight loss, and the effects of perspiration. Santorio Santori, *De statica medicina* (Lipsiae [Leipzig], 1624). *Leemage*

20. The popularity of spas and thermal baths led to increased use of human scales in the middle of the nineteenth century. The Thermal Weighing Machine, Vichy, France around 1900. *AKG*

21. Two innovations appear in anti-obesity advertising at the beginning of the twentieth century: an insistence on the "inelegance" of male obesity and the standard recourse to a personal scale with a raised dial at eye level. Advertisement, 1920s. "Obesity makes one ridiculous. Men with big bellies, get rid of the silhouette that makes you look disgraceful by wearing the Franck-Braun belt." *Kharbine-Tapabor*

22. The revolution of the female silhouette at the beginning of the twentieth century: abandonment of the corset, lengthening of the body, and a relative disappearance of the hips. What's now grotesque are the fat, mocking men. *The New Game*, a caricature by Charles Léandre. *L'Illustration* (1897), Bibliothèque des Arts décoratifs, Paris. *Bridgeman Giraudon*

LE NOUVEAU JEU

23. The insistence on "skinniness" rather than "obesity" at the beginning of the twentieth century is accompanied by an imperative to slim down in response to the earliest signs of the slightest weight gain. An advertisement for "Clark's Slimming Bath Salts" in *Les Dimanches de la femme* (A woman's Sundays), 1924. *Kharbine-Tapabor*

24. New instruments and new standards in the 1920s: an appliance designed to "passively" sculpt the silhouette, a massage rolling pin, headgear designed to "passively" sculpt the face, and a portable personal scale—all for a person whose fat deposits are not yet visible. Photograph, 1920s. *Viollet*

PART 4

THE BOURGEOIS BELLY

Businessmen, financiers, and civic leaders of the Enlightenment era succeeded in making a prominent belly into a mark of prestige, even if the
strict requirement for women was to remain thin. Yet this celebration of
masculine volume is ambiguous, since eighteenth-century social criticism
strongly denounces the physiques of those judged to be "profiteering" for
themselves and "starving" others. This equivocation about the bourgeois
remains identical during the Restoration (1815–1830) and the July Monarchy (1830–1848). His physical thickness may be persuasive, even while
satires that mock the pear-shaped belly of certain authority figures multiply. The denunciation increases in tandem with the profusion of descriptive details. With the refinement of nuances about the fat person, fatness
gains in notoriety.

A new precision appears on the scene as well with the slow but steady
entry of numerical evaluations of morphologies. The gaze becomes a measuring instrument used on people just as it can be used to size up things
in business and industry. Figures are increasingly used to measure the
perimeter of limbs, the densities of fat at different locations in the body,
and the ratios of height to weight. More deeply, the image of organic function changes. The body is now an energy apparatus, a furnace, an engine
that allows for the calculation of the quantity of heat introduced and the
quantity of work produced. Thus evaluations of efficiency and output
become important, as does a quantified vision of possible improvements
thanks to variations in the amount of "combustibles" and adjustments

in their exploitation. These ideas are far from the old models of humors, fibers, and nerves. Chemical analysis that for the first time links fat to an insufficient organic combustion extends the calculations even further into discussions about changing diets, eliminating seemingly "innocent" foods, sugars and starches, and evaluating combustive potentials, supervising caloric outputs and wasted energy. These are huge changes that amount to a new way of looking at and taking care of the body including stigmatizing its weaknesses and possible inferiorities.

12. The Weight of Figures

The increasing importance of figures merits attention. It is not weight that first becomes significant, but rather circumferences and visible volumes and contours. It is sight that first seeks the supplement of figures to judge the physical envelope, whereas weight relates to a more complex set of references. Nevertheless, in the wake of industrialization this culture relies more on measuring instruments. Figures are the center of the sudden explosion in statistical publications at the beginning of the nineteenth century that scrupulously record quantities of production, results, etc.[1] Numbers change the way people think.

The Presence of Numbers

By the beginning of the nineteenth century, treatises on obesity had become common, although they continued to be strongly focused on extreme cases. Only the biggest bodies are truly "studied." The presentation of these cases, however, includes something new—a flurry of numbers accompanies them as though suddenly all measurements were now considered useful. In 1810, for example, Ange Maccary insists on his wish to take measurements when he learns of someone's very big size.[2] When he hears of a new case, he seeks the person out and records the measurements he wants. The exceptional cases hold out the promise of new knowledge. He's expecting some new revelation from these "excessive" anatomies—

the discovery in them of a secret. The idea is to record in numbers what had up until then never been recorded and first of all what could be seen, the surfaces that are immediately apparent. First circumferences, of arms, thighs, calves, necks, waists, bellies. Fat thickness is also recorded after having been measured for the first time by Guillaume Dupuytren in 1806 on the body of a woman who "died from suffocation" under the weight of her flesh, a woman so exaggeratedly swollen that this surgeon at the Hôtel-Dieu decides to make a mold of her body and put it on exhibit.

There is nothing more formally carried out than the numerical calculations of Guillaume Dupuytren who explores the presence of fat right down to the ears, eyelids, and fingers. His measurements silently offer a topography of fat. The four inches in the pubic region contrast with the one inch at the abdomen, while the four inches in the hip area contrasts with the one inch at the shoulders—all clues that suggest heaviness is more concentrated at lower levels.[3]

Another frequent measurement one finds in treatises on obesity at the beginning of the nineteenth century, even if not the dominant one, is the numerical pairing of height and weight. Ange Maccary notes the measurements of a deformed child in his 1810 study as follows: 240 pounds, 5 feet 1 inch tall, and 5 feet in circumference. By including the perimeter, the numbers alone give a clear image of this unusual body where the height and circumference are represented by the same figure.[4] One finds the same correlation of height and width when Brillat-Savarin mentions a friend in his *Physiology of Taste* (1826) who is 5 foot 7 and weighs 245 kilos.[5] Giving these numerical values of width and height together suggests a will to make a topography of the body.

Figuring the Waist-Weight Relation

Everything changes, however, around 1832 when these paired observations are submitted to statistical analysis. First, measuring weight takes on more importance. Second, this importance is magnified by its being given in the form of a key relationship that coordinates a scale of weights and a scale of waist measurements. In 1832 Adolphe Quetelet is the first to construct grids and tables that go far beyond the rough initiatives of Buffon by including the variables of sex and age.[6] For each height a "normal" weight is statistically established. Based on a wide sample space, the height of 1.6 m, for example, is said to correspond on average to a weight of 57.15 kilos for men and 56.73 kilos for women; a height of 1.7 m corresponds to a weight of 65.20 kilos for men and 63.28 kilos for women.[7] Quetelet also establishes quotients that allow one to calculate the degree of discrepancy between a given thin or fat individual and the abstract statistical average. This is the beginning of the establishment of norms and their abuse, all entirely derived from manipulating numbers. It is not the normality of an ideal, but of reality. Man is defining himself based on what he lives more than on his judgments or wishes.[8] It's important not to read these numbers with today's reference points. None of them seems intended to guide any individual's slimming program. These numerical comparisons with progressive, graduated scales of the human body are nevertheless unprecedented benchmarks.

New types of investigation guided Quetelet's practices. Beginning at the end of the eighteenth century, there are studies launched by the scientific community and public administrators that make use of the laws of large numbers, facts calculated en masse such as crimes, births, and deaths, which are all related via averages that report increases or decreases over time.[9] These projects were greatly expanded by scientists and administrators in industry during the period 1810–1820. Certain democratic aims also transformed expectations that now extended to evaluating the procedures of government—their efficiency, for example—and more generally the physical and moral state of populations. The variables chosen are concrete and have a social aim: greater knowledge about the organic foundation of human groups via an exploration of the "flesh" of states. Administrators have the feeling that a new tool is in their hands: a technique for assessing "corporeal quantities" and their distribution. It is a "limited" project, however, once one hears the words used by Quetelet to justify his calculations: to better know the burden that "certain constructions" can stand,[10] to better know the "personal weight" of man so as to better organize his work, to better know various weights according to age and sex so as to better help forensic specialists identify corpses and other bodies. These are pragmatic tasks and activities. And their realization and efficiency necessitates a technical vision. Beauty is not mentioned.

One is struck by the importance of numerical measurements, the production of tables and their role in shaping thinking.

The Question of Self-Weighing

The scale and weighing oneself are not yet commonplace in the first decade of the nineteenth century. A look at French and English recruitment history of that time clearly shows that measuring fatness or thinness was not even mentioned in the documents laying out military recruitment rules. Moreover, the label "weak constitution,"[11] applied to 280 of the 2,180 recruits in the records of the Upper-Rhine region for 1826 and to 431 of 6,307 recruits in the North region for 1841,[12] is never explicitly backed up with a reference to weight.[13] According to the *Physiology of the Conscript* (1846), the waist is the only "true object" of concern for the recruitment board at that time.[14]

There does, however, seem to have been an inexorable, subtle development within the mores of the nineteenth century of a new vision when it comes to physical measurements. Literary descriptions provide evidence of this. There is the allure of Balzac's Grandet with his "five foot waist," short and squat with calves twelve inches in circumference.[15] There is also the unfortunate priest from Tours who, becoming painfully skinny, notices one morning while putting on his "blue mottled stockings" that his calves had "lost over an inch in circumference" (*8 lignes*).[16] There are also testimonies in memoirs such as the Countess de Boigne's observations about Louis XVIII, who suffered from gout, and her surprise in 1826 that in a few short months "the black velvet gaiters that covered his calves had doubled in size."[17] There exist also the writings of tailors such as a certain Barde who insists for the first time in 1830 on using a "corpimeter," a device for calculating diameters with a sort of compass instead of the usual strips of paper that up until then had been used to "calculate" cloth measurements. "Only the diameters of the body indicate on what side the protuberances whose circumference is to be clothed are located."[18] The eye and hand of the tailor have changed. The evaluation of volumes becomes all-important. Indicators of fatness and thinness are clearly explored, and each is recorded as a numbered circle according to the graduated spacings of the compass.

References to weight are rarer, more specific, and yet also striking. Weight is infrequently mentioned in daily affairs except when talking about extreme cases like the Englishman encountered by Alexandre Dumas around 1820 whose weight is estimated at 350 pounds.[19] Weight does come up more often in discussions of slimming techniques. Brillat-Savarin makes it a rule in his *Physiology of Taste*. "The first rule is to weigh oneself at the beginning and end of the treatment in order to have a mathematical base and verify results."[20] Baron Louis Greffulhe, who is "seriously on the verge of obesity," comes to ask for his advice and accepts weighing himself regularly each month. At the beginning of the century, Lord Byron also reports trying a slimming regimen that he speaks of with numbers—going from 100 kilos to 70 kilos, for example, and the mention of specific amounts of weight loss such as "two pounds" after leaving a circle of friends in 1807 whose negative influence he feared.[21]

Popular theatre productions in the 1830s also refer to bodyweight which reveals the notion's penetration into broader segments of society. Performances of Adolphe d'Ennery's *bouffonerie* about "the fat and the thin" at the Théâtre du Palais-Royal in 1838 is the best example.[22] Chapotin, an obscure bigwig in a provincial town, deplores his daughter's fondness for a distant cousin. He considers the young man to be too thin and weak. He sets out to fatten him up and later decides to find out his exact weight. Disaster! The young man has become thinner instead of fatter. The audience laughs. But the important thing here is that for the first time a scale imposes a public verdict. Size is now identified with weight that is measured and announced.

One distinctive image reveals the presence as much as the rarity of the scale in ordinary everyday life. In an issue of the magazine *Charivari* from 1844 a woman with an enormously round body is shown enthroned on an armchair-scale in the middle of a minuscule fair stall, listening attentively as her weight is read out from the meter above her.[23] "Well, honey bun, you've lost weight since last year. You only weigh 326." In other words, she is teased about her size via a supplementary dig at the sublimity of mathematics with the expression of her weight as a power of three—2,541,865,828,329 kilos! This example also says something about the roundabout access to scales and being weighed. The scale exists, but as an exceptional curiosity. A fair, with its temporary stands and stalls, seems to be the select space where the public can weigh itself. The presence now of a reference to weight, even if mostly mental, is nevertheless decisive. It entirely reorients ways of looking and judging.

13. Typology Fever

The presence of numbers is not the only factor contributing to the new evaluation of silhouettes at the beginning of the nineteenth century. There are also social factors, especially the stir-up that the Revolution is said to have introduced into the codes of physical appearance. Travelers and observers in the years 1820–1830 report being suddenly confronted with a more confusing world. "Castes" are said to have disappeared. The old borders erased. Resemblances multiply once the society of orders is abolished.

This gives rise to the desire to "look" with greater precision, inventory more, single out specific looks and their maintenance, and fix "physiognomies, poses, gestures, and grimaces."[1] And also posit categories. This gives rise to a publishing enterprise of a new sort: *The English Depicted By Themselves*, *The French Depicted by Themselves*, *The Parisian Museum*, etc., all inventory the society in pictures.[2] Balzac's *The Human Comedy* stands as the supreme example of such enterprises.[3]

There is no scientific sociology going on in these investigations, dominated by subjective observation. No overarching general vision either. What one observes is a new way of identifying physiques—their profiles, their possible original particularities—and this involves new evocations of the "fat person," including new sharper techniques of self-description.[4]

"Gastrophoric" Men, Adipose Women

Descriptive attention undergoes a revolution at the beginning of the nineteenth century. It becomes more important in literature, influences social studies of mores, and positively invades the world of engravings and illustrations.[5] Progressions of weight are more exactingly divided up. "Deformations" are analyzed inch by inch. Noting degrees of this or that happens much more than ever before. Especially in democratic and industrial societies such as Great Britain. For example, the weight gain of Tracy Tupman, Pickwick's friend in Charles Dickens's first novel from 1836, happens in slow stages that are each described in precise detail. "Time and feeding had expanded that once romantic form; the black silk waistcoat had become more and more developed; inch by inch had the gold watch-chain disappeared from within the range of Tupman's vision; and gradually had the capacious chin encroached upon the borders of the white cravat."[6]

There are also frequent allusions to age, which self-descriptions may speak of as the thickening that comes with maturity. The active man, for example, "notices one morning while clipping his beard that his waist is rounder and his hair thinner and whiter."[7] Or the mother who "ended up monumentally fat with lots of children and grandchildren."[8] One notes changes that have become sources of "unpleasantness," such as the negative assessments that are scrutinized by the caricaturists in the *Philipon Museum*.[9] The man turning forty with the thickening silhouette of one whose favorite reading material has become restaurant menus.[10] Or the bitter declaration of mothers over thirty who lament "having cursed life while young because we were thin as nails, and now at thirty-six we're so fat we can't kiss our children."[11]

What matters now are progressions. Ages become stages, time converts into a "morphology." Another factor, perhaps, is the gradual lengthening of life expectancies during these first decades of the nineteenth century. The numbers of moderately thicker people increase, and their fat forms stick around longer into old age. The "slow decline of death" needs to be taken into account, even if its impact does not increase significantly among adults until the end of the nineteenth century.[12] These observations about becoming fatter do not intensify slimming practices, however; they are simply passing remarks of curiosity and fatality.

The more important nuances are being articulated elsewhere in the elaboration of a classification of morphologies that establishes a typology of sizes and transforms the public gaze. It is no longer a question of degrees and diversities as in the Enlightenment era, but of categories that divide sizes into genres. For example, in 1826 Brillat-Savarin is the first to categorize strictly abdominal excess into a specifically male symptom. "There is a type of obesity that is confined to the belly. I have never seen it in women. As the latter have generally softer tissues, when obesity attacks them, no part of the body is spared. The male condition I call 'gastrophoria' and 'gastrophores' those who have it."[13]

This remark is repeated in medical treatises from the middle of the century, in the literature on mores, and in the art world by engravers such as Daumier who gives a prime example with his 1830 series of big-bellied, skinny-legged gentlemen: M. Prunelle, Benjamin Dudessert, Félix Barthe, M. Harlé, etc.[14] There are also specially tailored frock coats that have been developed to accommodate the outsized protuberance of men's bellies.[15] This is in evidence in Bertall's "bourgeois" couple. His *A Sunday in Paris*, among other works from 1845, systematically contrasts the well-advanced belly of the man to the overall plumpness of the woman.[16] The image takes hold, and the male with stick legs and a large circular belly becomes a stock representation in the years 1830–1840. The drawings of Henri Monnier even make it into a symbol. His Braulard, the greedy spectator who appears in *Lost Illusions*, is none other than a faithful visual transcription of the textual description in Balzac, with his oversized belt and large oval pant legs that gather together narrowly at the ankle.[17] It's not the total body ball as had been depicted in earlier times, but the belly ball alone. There is no explanation for what in our day is called "android obesity," but there is an attempt to specify sexually distinct forms of bigness that had formerly not been so categorized.[18] Brillat-Savarin had a different way of looking and developed other classifications.

These bellies, manifestly, do not all suggest a collapse. In the case of many of these stout bourgeois gentlemen, all signs point to a rather "measured" adiposity. There is an imperfect yet intact physical ease, a forthright pose, and an alert eye that is very unlike the heavy banker Nucingen in Balzac's *Scenes of Parisian Life*. This character, "a square-shaped man,"[19] "a cube," "heavy as a sack,"[20] is referred to by his wife as "the fat Alsatian stump"[21] and by his servants as "the big elephant."[22] The "gastrophore" who is more discreet, as, for example, Sir Walter Murph in Eugène Sue's *Mysteries of Paris*, can be "alert and robust" despite being stout.[23] He can be combative and almost a fighter, which accounts for his possible prestige. Baron Nucingen, on the other hand, has lost all value through weight gain. Different kinds of fatness entail different levels of activeness. The belly has its degrees and its categories, which are invented and inventoried now for the first time.

There are also inevitable references to the sometimes agreeable or pleasing profile of the full-bellied look—exclusively male again and usually of the middling classes. One thinks here of the centuries-old ambiguity of the bon vivant, the amusing rotund figure, and the jolly "good man" of popular culture. The traveling salesman in *The Illustrious Gaudissart* (1832) from *The Human Comedy* series incarnates this type in every detail, mixing malice and suavity, clumsiness and cleverness. The man is a good storyteller, a good companion, "ribald" even,[24] and plays on his lumpish looks and heaviness worsened by "travel in coaches."[25] A certain volubility and street smarts carry him along as well as easy banter, jokes, and an engaging manner where everything is big yet measured. He's fleshy but not obese, bloated but not collapsed. His heavy ease becomes a form of sociability. "Jokes, belly laughs, a monkish figure, and cobbler's face over a Rabelaisian body—his clothes, body, spirit, and pose united to make for hilarity and joking throughout his person. . . . Gaudissart [could also become] the finest and most able of ambassadors."[26]

There is an undeniable ambivalence, of course, that allows the fat person to sometimes be both seductive and repulsive. A double judgment exists in the mythology of the fat person, even a contradiction that is hardly explicit. It takes popular vivacity and a coating of fat that is not hanging heavily.

Then there is the veritable ball, of course, the "pot-bellied joker" (*ventrigoulard*),[27] the amply diffuse figure, that also tends to be exclusively masculine, among the endless variations on roundness of generalized obesity. Honoré Daumier produced multiple examples with his policemen, deputies, and other squat grandees.[28] The deputy Boulay is a prime example from the 1848 *Comic Review* in which one finds combined both physical and lexical excess: "This adorable ball is Boulay . . . in the voting box every ballot was a little Boulay ball."[29]

Rounded curves are more specifically feminine, however, according to the new classifications at the beginning of the nineteenth century. The advance of the globular is accelerated by inaction, a "flaw" judged typically "feminine." The low wench (*poissarde*) in *The French Depicted by Themselves*, for example, triggers "laughter" by "the fearfully large proportions of her body and especially the nearly monstrous development of her waist."[30] The "old maid" in *The Human Comedy* has had a "tranquil, orderly life" that accounts for her "triple chin" and fixed mass that has "melted into one piece."[31] Here again is a social vision where for the first time fat figures are divided up according to their geographical location (town/country) and social status (collective/individual). The new gaze stigmatizes groups, divides up affiliations, and highlights city neighborhoods. The stoutness of prostitutes, for example, often remarked on, becomes the focus of a statistical study by Alexandre Parent-Duchâtelet, the first investigation of its kind, in 1836.[32] This Parisian doctor, truly a sociologist *avant la lettre*, explains their large size as due to the "many hot baths" they take, to their "constant" eating due to their irregular schedules, and most certainly the result of an entirely "inactive" lifestyle noted for nonchalance and absence of movement.[33] Their lives are almost "animal,"[34] in other words, and similar to those of "adipose courtesans fattened by idleness" and women confined in narrow spaces,[35] such as sales ladies in tiny stands or young girls who become sedentary "petites bourgeoises by age thirty-five" and "turn deplorably toward obesity."[36]

One thing is certain: man, not woman, can get away with an "acceptable" roundness, even if the ideal of a tight belt is beginning to assert itself for him too.

The Bourgeois and the Avowed Belly

The gastrophore seems to possess an identity—that of the bourgeois. This character took on a specific rounded shape that has fluctuated since the days of the financiers and merchants of the old regime. With the oval belly, his figure seems to have taken on a stability that clearly confers "respectability."

This suggests a first model: affirmation through looks. Consider, for example, the coachmaster in *The French Depicted by Themselves,* whose "pronounced stoutness" gives him "a certain aplomb that is rather dashing,"[37] or the "bourgeois from Sologne,"[38] in the same series, who dominates peasants and villagers with his hand on his "grave abdomen" and "advances belly first into society." Bigness is confined to the belly, however, while the lower body remains thinner and active—"a dry lower leg" is Brillat-Savarin's expression to indicate ease of movement.[39] Bigness is "acceptable" so long as it can stand for a person's importance and seriousness.

The strong tummy of the bourgeois invites the contrast with the weak silhouette and more tubby tummy of others such as the Sologne peasant—his poor, vegetable diet condemns him to acquire swollen viscera and "the belly of a ruminant."[40] The differentiation is without a doubt crude but firm in asserting as never before a social specter around the fat person—between the strong, pot-bellied bourgeois and the weak, pot-bellied peasant and between the firm flesh of the former and the latter's flabby flesh resulting from abusive consumption of apparently crude and unhealthy foods. In this regard the peasants of the Auge region are cited for their "stoutness degenerating promptly into obesity."[41] The categories multiply as they try to distinguish among "gastrophores," contrasting the "strong" and the "wilted." Alongside these divisions there emerge other new distinctions to satisfy the curious during the 1830s, such as the distinction of physical height—people are found to be taller in the city than in the country—or between mortality rates—people are said to die younger in the country than in the city.[42] These claims at the beginning of the nineteenth century reinforce the bourgeois transposition of a big firm belly into a possible sign of authority.

Another aspect of this "contentment of bourgeois happiness" is the coldness and even distance of this figure as the result of his general corpulence. Here too the descriptions and their details are highly pointed. The notary in *The French Depicted by Themselves* hides his insensitivity "under a thick layer of fat and well-being,"[43] a "fat and short" man, whose self-assurance is translated by a "nearly always starched" look. There is also a notary in Balzac's *The Thirty Year Old Woman* (1834) who is also "big and fat" and always "screwed onto his chair" in a position of perfect imperturbability due to his weight.[44]

This heaviness can only be appreciated so long as it's masculine. For a long time it gets by as "a corpulent stature where muscle and fat are one."[45] It implies resources for its "maintenance" and incarnates a certain status.[46]

The Bourgeois and the Lampooned Belly

Consequently there is an unstable ambiguity because a profile that uses the belly to symbolize power may provoke ironic reversal. An ironic derision, more striking than straight criticism, flows more freely during the years 1830–1840. Largely present in mass-produced magazine engravings, this derision inverts the affirmative images of the bourgeoisie converting the round belly into a weakness and feelings of pride into fatuousness.

Balzac had already noted the anatomic "disproportions" of these particular morphologies when they went beyond a certain point—a lower body a bit too "frail," a too heavy abdomen, a rickety foundation implying imbalance. Maître Mathias, the notary in *The Marriage Contract*, is a prime example: "His puny little thighs seem to bend under the weight of a round belly and a torso developed like the chests of many office workers."[47] Then there's the disproportion of trousers such as those of the notary in *Scenes of Provincial Life* whose waist belt attained "an ampleness that would have merited an epic description by Sterne."[48] From now on these are no longer imposing forms but objects of disgrace and dejection.

More deeply, criticism of the day unites with its culture and time. The denunciation of the belly, even if far from extreme obesity, is a denunciation of a certain world—a society in which a number of expectations promised by civic leaders seem forgotten, in which contentment seems superficial, and the "satisfied" look of bigwigs means a refusal of all change despite manifest imperfections. The exposure, in other words, of an "area of social pathology ruining the dominant morality."[49] This is the message of the first engraving of Charles Philipon's first periodical, *La Caricature* (1833), where the organizer of the "new system," the bourgeois, has a belly as big as the eighteenth-century nobleman who ruled over the "old system."[50] The illustrator has given priority to emphasizing the two profiles—translation: the "abuses" have not changed.[51]

The insistence on the bourgeois belly suggests yet another vindictive effort. It is not only a criticism of disparities or exposure of abuses and profits. It has a more intimate target, namely, the denunciation of broken promises and an ascendancy turned into vanity. This inversion that converts the fatty physical "coating" into "pretension" is central to an episode in *Scenes of the Public and Private Life of Animals*, a romantic work illustrated by J. J. Grandville in 1842 that plays on animal allegories. A female "English cat" wants to marry "Puff"—a cat made famous by his imposing body. Indeed, his prestige is so striking that he has been given a peerage. Disillusion comes, however, with a feeling of trickery. "I noticed then that age and excesses at table had given the English peer that false and forced gravity which in England is called *respectability*. His stoutness, which men admired, hindered his movements. This was the true reason for his not answering to my gentle advances. He remained resting calm and cold on his unnamable, moving his whiskers, watching me and sometimes closing his eyes. . . . Leave off with this droll old Puff who sleeps like a peer in the English Parliament."[52]

Thus the criticism here adds to the themes of the previous century about abusively fattened bigwigs a more subtle, psychological denunciation of the abusively self-assured and pretentious. The moral space is more elaborate, deeper—inverting the will for grandeur, sniffing out false appearances, playing on poses to better reveal their smallness and even "infamy." The opposition between high and low is also more specified, changing the allure of the belly into a lure, recasting the full abdomen as vulgarity. The result is a comedy of reversal with the belly attributed inverted values.

A determining graphic invention deepens this criticism in the second third of the century: the "pear" image and symbol—a drawing that transposes from the plant world to the human world an infinitely repeated curvature. The ample waist now tips from imposing into obscenity. The major example is the caricature of Louis-Philippe, the bourgeois king par excellence, modeled on the fruit,[53] stacking face and body and exaggerating the digestive reference with excessive development of the jaws and abdomen into "hyperbolic exaggeration."[54] The lower body carries him invisibly, thus definitively fixing a profile that Grandissart, Balzac's commercial traveler, inaugurated within literature—"a protuberant belly that resembled a pear" and short thin legs capable of some agility.[55]

It is very much a graphic invention, a recombination of traits that focuses on the digestive system. The originality of this arrangement is made all the more striking by the fact that anatomical excellence and its models are transformed simultaneously. Physiological discoveries are largely responsible. The identification of oxygen by Lavoisier in 1778, the new importance this gives to the chest and its expansion, the slow maturation of this image, and the new role accorded to breathing all gradually displaced morphological polarities. This new dynamic figure gives to bourgeois initiative the sort of drive that's rather different from the staid authority of the belly.

Romantically Thin?

In contrast to the pear, this model of the generous bust—chest out, waist in, pants tight—is put forward by leading engravers of the day. The men in the magazines *Parisian Fashion* and *Tailors Journal* in the years 1830–1840 all have convex torsos and ample outsized coats that accentuate a generous layer of extra padding and big cuffs.[56] New words are invented to describe these men, such as "strangled waist" and "pinched waist,"[57] and new wardrobe instruments are discussed, such as the best buckles for belts and the vest as "masterpiece" of the wardrobe for its role in accentuating the bust's prominence. "Show me a man's vest and I'll tell you who he is."[58] Balzac's dandy wears a frock coat that "elegantly holds the waist," as with Maxime, or "pinches the waist,"[59] as with Charles Grandet. Eugène Sue's 1842 hero has an identical silhouette: "a svelte thin waist" joined to "muscles of steel."[60]

Another antagonism besides the opposition between the good "rich" bigness and "poor" skinniness or "bad" bigness also intervenes to oppose different volumes during the July monarchy years; namely, youth versus maturity, socioeconomic instability versus the established. Émilie, the heroine of Balzac's *The Ball at Sceaux*, refuses to marry a man the least bit overweight. For her thinness is the sign of elegance and firmness of character. However, her "opinion" can become "an object of mockery."[61] Is not the "achieved," "sure" man someone of a certain thickness? And isn't a bit of extra padding the natural companion of power and notoriety? This ambiguity is at the heart of Théophile Gautier's bitterness: "the man of genius must be fat."[62] And Alfred de Vigny's vexation: "What did me the most wrong in life was having blond hair and a thin waist."[63] The clerk Doutremer in Henri Monnier's *Scenes of Office Life* also expresses irritation at being "dry and thin." This "spanking clean person," who is attentive about his clothes and takes special care of his hands and nails, has to deal with superiors that are mostly "moderately stout," with some "very fat."[64] Contrasting silhouettes incarnate the difference between generations and hierarchies of power.

The problem is quite different among women for whom thinness and "fragility" are obligatory traits. As usual, all female bigness is depreciated. The bust, however, is displayed more than before, as in the "Scottish cambric dress" described in the *Journal for Young People* in 1835.[65] Its shoulders and waist form a sort of inverted isosceles triangle with flared cloth to allow the wearer to breath freely.

Descriptions multiply like never before, to the point of giving rise to some paradoxical types of thinness that, while not belonging to bigness, are no longer examples of the earlier slenderness either. Balzac's Anastasie de Restaud, for example, has "full round forms" and yet cannot be accused of being "too plump."[66] And the sylph Fanny O'Brien, "a fine elegant beauty," is described as having become "slightly plump," yet "her delicate hips and svelte waist haven't suffered in the least."[67] Balzac insists on the "roundness," making the skin "pulpy and nourished" and thus having the woman as blossom without falling into "fat."[68] The demands are precise, and the limits as well. The waist, for example, must remain "delicate" like that of Anastasie de Restaud, who has "one of the prettiest waists in Paris"[69]; their curves cannot be too round, as in the case of Camille in *Béatrix*, whose neck has lost its sinuous lankiness;[70] the skin must not have the least "wrinkle" like Rose's in *The Old Maid*;[71] and the gait must know how to "rustle the cloth" so as to better communicate one's lightness, evidence, and secret.[72] "Roundness" is unthinkable without a certain delicateness and slenderness intermixed.

14. From Chemistry to Energy

Numbers and measurements accentuated a more precise reckoning of fatness at the beginning of the nineteenth century. Categories are established. Differences in size carry social consequences often defined through tolerances or rejections. Heavy profiles, male of course, may have a positive value that confirms ascendancy, but may also be "deflated" with irony.

Alongside this social dimension, the scientific work on pathologies, material identifications, and chemical changes leads to a body of knowledge about fat that is increasingly distant from the spontaneous popular notions of earlier times. Thoroughly revised thinking about physiological mechanisms starts at the beginning of the nineteenth century. These new ideas lead in turn to very different ways of thinking about the causes and prevention of fatness. A turning point is clearly established once the mechanism of organic combustion begins to be understood. Once the body is considered like a fire-powered engine, the source of fat is reconceived as "unburned" fuel. In time this redefinition entirely shakes up ideas about obesity as well as about its treatment, including slimming programs whose logic seems irrefutable.

The Aqueous and the Adipose: New Distinctions

A first change at the beginning of the century is the end of old confusions between fat and water. It is now admitted that volumes may resemble each other, but have distinct sources. The chemical analysis of liquids and the pathologist's scrutiny of anatomy's organs change everything. The old ideas of slackened fibers and their excitation also lose much of their sense.

In 1836 a certain Monsieur Rollin, age sixty-eight, presents himself at the Charité hospital complaining of a dull pain in the lumbar region.[1] The doctors note the prominence of his belly, his swollen limbs, and the presence of skin edemas typically associated with hydropsy. There is only one explanation in the eyes of the patient: years of living in a damp room and bad eating habits—a diagnosis that was standard a few decades earlier.

When Rollin dies some weeks later, the doctors claim to verify a very different hypothesis thanks to chemistry. In 1825 the English physician Richard Bright discovered how to chemically analyze the urine of hydropics, showed the presence of albumen in many cases, and deduced the presence of foodstuffs untransformed into uria. This was the case with Rollin. These hydropics suffered from a form of "nephritis"—kidney dysfunction that led to impaired filtering or even "failure." The problem was not conceived as excessive secretion but inadequate filtering. The autopsy of Rollin confirmed this. His kidneys were enlarged, misshapen, partially decomposed, and were releasing various liquids into the body cavity. A new hypothesis inevitably forms: the dysfunction of a specific organ may explain hydropsy.

Jean-Baptiste Bouillaud adds, at the same time, another cause: possible internal compressions that may adversely affect parts of the body. He offers many examples. The death at fifty-five of Anne Villard, for example, whose body had retained much water and when dissected revealed her ovaries enlarged such that they pressed "with all their mass on the major veins of the lower body," or the death of Guillaume Caillet at sixty-eight, whose dilated abdomen revealed upon dissection a vena cava "obliterated by a mushy, breakable fibrous material mixed with coagulated blood."[2] In the words of Jean-Baptiste Bouillaud, these "dams" explain the infiltrations and abnormal volumes, and their diversity "entirely destroys the earlier doctrine."[3]

The old amalgam that favored a confusion between internal materials simply collapsed. Hydropsy is reported more rarely, but the cases are also more harmful and often fatal, as the obstructions rapidly put the patient's life in danger. Therefore it has a discreet place in medical indexes. Retrospectively, one can reasonably imagine that a number of diagnoses of "hydropsy" in earlier times would have been diagnosed as obesity in 1850 due to the radical changes brought about by more modern medical investigations.

Fat and Fire

The most original development at the beginning of the nineteenth century is the revised explanation of what fat is. "Modern" chemistry totally changes the image of the body. Gone are the humor and nerve models. The body is now a total machine whose "unique force" comes from combustion,[4] and this has inevitable consequences for how diet, size, and health are viewed.

Lavoisier's entirely new vocabulary—"carbon, hydrogen, oxygen, etc."—has the effect of aging the traditional words and concepts.[5] The quasi-poetic references to animal fattening that speak of "pastures," "tender succulent grass," and "fine and savory grass"[6] are displaced by concise descriptions that detail the chemical "elements" only.[7] For all intents and purposes, fat has become a new object once it is considered in this new way as a composite of simpler bodies.

Next comes a radical transformation of the image of food. In 1778 Lavoisier established oxygen as the combustive agent of organic fire.[8] Food is the other agent that will be analyzed more closely in the nineteenth century. "Foods are for the animal body what fuel is for the stove."[9] In the 1840s Liebig advanced the most "realistic" theories based on this new orientation, namely, the division of food into two categories: those that contributed to renewing the organs and those that contributed to keeping the organic fire going. The first he called "plastic foods," the second "respiratory foods." The first have more nitrogen, which explains their association with flesh and the body; whereas the second contain more carbon and are thus associated with fire. In the first category are animal meats, albumin, casein, and plant fibrin and in the second "fat, starch, gum, sugar, pectin, bassorine, wine, brandy."[10]

A few key experiments determine the origin of fat. Respiratory foods play a central role. It is noted that pigs fed large quantities of plastic foods become more meaty, while pigs fed large quantities of respiratory foods become fatter. Cows that are made to walk and are nourished in pastures, thus "burning" fuel, furnish milk that is high in caseum—a nonfatty material, while cows that move less and are nourished in stables, thus burning less fuel, furnish milk that is high in butter content—the very symbol of fat. Women who are relatively sedentary and consume large amounts of starches, a leading example of respiratory food, produce milk with a higher "proportion of butter."[11] An "excess" amount of these respiratory foods, their "deposit," in other words, either by more eating or less exercise of the lungs, seems to provoke fat. The chemical analysis of these substances would seem to confirm this hypothesis when its revealed that the proportions of carbon and hydrogen are the same in fat and in respiratory foods, but the proportions of oxygen are not. It is thus concluded that there must be a "simple" change in the respiratory foods that turns them into fat, namely, the loss of a certain amount of oxygen. The carbon-containing substances thus become adipose substances, accumulating in the case of noncombustion, but disappearing in the case of intense respiratory activity. Liebig is more declamatory than descriptive about these internal mechanisms, noting the changes, but with few details. There is this decisive affirmation: sugars, starches, and gums can directly give rise to adipose material. This affirmation is "surprising" as well since it challenges common sense and traditional thinking. It goes against one's immediate sense experience by associating two things that, on the surface, seem so dissimilar: sugar and fat. These new ideas challenge the old thinking and entirely change the world of obesity. "When carbon accumulates in the body and is not used for the renewal of some organ, this excess is deposited in the cells in the form of fat and oil."[12]

The unburned carbon becomes a fatty reserve, a sort of failure pile due to lack of heating. By creating fat, this "failure" underlines the full importance of the burning mechanism, to the point of turning it into the body's central function. This mechanism regulates powers and activities, maintains balances, and slows or accelerates life. It also profoundly revises the whole idea of the organic to the point of making it seem like an invisible steam engine—"the burner of Papin and Watt," as Jean-Baptiste Dumas and Jean-Baptiste Boussingault put it in 1844.[13] The analogy is further amplified by a major discovery by Sadi Carnot in 1824, namely, the mechanical equivalent of heat expressed as caloric at work.[14] Heat engines that activated wheels, cranks, and levers in new factories were the symbol: the level of combustion in the furnace had a corresponding effect on the dynamic intensity of the machine's force and efficiency. A precise consumption of heat translates into a precise amount of work produced, which can be expressed as the machine's level of efficiency.

Unused heat, on the other hand, is stocked in the body. An explanation takes hold that is easy to grasp: fat comes from an excess of unburned material. The two causes of the latter are overeating and underexercising. This tidy description conveniently leaves all complexity behind.

Fat and "Morbid Imminence"

As fat comes to be explained differently at the beginning of the century, its effects also begin to be explored differently.

At the beginning of the nineteenth century, anatomy invented a new approach for itself. It proposed no longer looking only at the state of organs, but at their "material lesions" and possible "deconstruction."[15] This created a new object: an atlas of disorders that mapped material "dysfunctions." The notion of membranes and tissue contributed to this innovation by providing the idea of distinct sorts of envelopes that remained identical in different locations in the body.[16] These "structures" separately traversed the organs, limbs, and flesh.[17] This created the possibility of conditions that were rigorously similar across different "parts" of a single organism. The specific symptoms that characterize mucous membranes, for example, are distinct from those that characterize serous or fibrous membranes.[18] Every condition would have its rules and system. Thus an ordering of lesions becomes possible like any other. A "morbid organization" that compromises the health of tissues would have its own logic exactly like a "normal organization" that maintains those same tissues. This underscores the fundamental importance of anatomical pathology. With it comes a reinvention of the task of observation. The goal is no longer, as it was in the past, an inventory of "external" symptoms of disorders that are immediately visible, but instead to precisely identity the location and rules of suspected internal alterations as well. This ambitious project is described with grandiloquence by Jean Cruveilhier, the president of the Anatomy Society. "It will be a grand and beautiful science of first importance that will give an account of the vast domain of morbid lesions of all organisms from plants to man—a science that will show the analogies and differences among the lesions occurring in such different species, as well as their occurrence across different organs and functions."[19]

The cadavers of obese patients begin to be examined differently. The condition of their tissues is recorded differently. The evaluation is no longer simply focused on the place of fat deposits and their form and size, but extends to take into account internal deformations, the comparative volume of organs, and any compression, swelling, or crushing they may have undergone. Latent conditions and hidden disorders are evaluated differently as well. The list of Michel Lévy that maps an organic geography of the obese person characterizes this malady as "sneaky"—a multiform danger secretly occurring here or there in various tissues and flesh.

The thorax is mashed and diminished in height due to the expansion of the abdomen; the compressed lungs have less volume than in thin subjects; the heart, enveloped by solid deposits of fat, is in general less large; the liver, enlarged in every dimension and under pressure, secretes a fatty fluid mixed with clear bile; the gallbladder is dilated by the nearly clear fluid it contains; the capacity of the stomach is enlarged and its muscular covering highly developed; the pancreas is enlarged and covered with fat, the mesentery is overloaded with fat, the kidneys are small and buried in fat, the bladder is small and shrunken.[20]

The effects of fatness have become a catalogue. The "deformations" are considered in terms of their anatomical materiality as well as their physiological consequences. The same holds for the new weight charts that now take into account the internal organs. John Hutchinson, for example, shows in the middle of the century that when a given body weight exceeds by 10 percent the average weight calculated for that body's height, respiratory capacity is lower.[21] These observations are numerically calculated and tabulated with gradations. The amount of this diminution—newly verifiable thanks to the *spiromètre,* which can measure breathing capacity—is proportional to the amount of weight gain. Hutchinson records it in units of cubic centimeters of lost thorax volume as a function of kilograms gained. In other words, lung space decreases in proportion to increased presence of fat. The result is an objective description of a precise and variable condition; for the first time, a malfunction is measured and placed in parallel to a chart of big sizes.

The logic of gradations is extended and alters the vision of the entire organism. The new term *morbid imminence* emerges at the beginning of the century to differentiate perfect health and "limited" health.[22] When faced with illness, certain organisms are more fragile than others. Some are more vulnerable, and their membranes more easily altered. It is this "imminence," among other traits, that doctors around 1830 identify with obesity. It is their name for what the doctors notice in the organs whose tissues are progressively attacked inside.

These new details about the phases of this negative condition also underscore more clearly its dangerous progression. The worry becomes more precise as the threat becomes more finely gradated.

15. From Energy to Diets

Numbers, knowledge, and ideas about the organic are significantly revised at the beginning of the nineteenth century. The obese body is now viewed as a body more sensitive to morbidities. And the organic is now conceived as an energy-producing machine, an "appliance" whose inputs, outputs, and surpluses can all be measured. In this context fat takes on a new meaning, when linked for the first time to an account of efficiency and yield, as a product of unconsumed energy. This in turn reorients the diet for the obese person that now rules out many foods long considered ordinary staples, notably bread, sugars, and starches. The response varies from indifference to tense resistance. No issue opposes tradition and modernity in a clearer confrontation at this time than debates about size.

The Consequences of Energy

The material cards are reshuffled, as it were, once the foods destined for combustion are identified. The "tonics" that were praised a century earlier in the *Encyclopédie* for combating obesity lose their meaning. Sugars, for example, that were for long considered effective stimulants, and starches, that had been considered comforting products, become suddenly ambiguous foods. Biscuits and cookies whose refined delicacy seemed a guarantee of lightness are suddenly suspected of invisible dangers. Even bread loses its innocence as its various flours come to be viewed as possible sources of heaviness. Brillat-Savarin describes the situation in the 1820s in his *Physiology of Taste*, a work that subtly combines an inventory of substances in all their chemical detail with that of their effects. "My God! you will all exclaim, my dear readers. My God, but he's a perfect barbarian this professor! Look at how in one blow he eliminates everything that we love—the oh so white bread of Limet, the Achard biscuits, the cookies—all the good things made with butter and flour, flour and sugar, sugar and eggs! He pardons neither the potato nor macaroni! Could we have expected such things from a food-lover who seemed so good?"[1]

Brillat-Savarin's mature thoughtful study of food was carried out independently from his activities as a lawyer and member of parliament. It underscores new divides that are the outcome of both true knowledge of the new science of chemistry and bourgeois satisfaction. He definitively condemns sugars, gums, and starches in terms that stigmatize foods that until then had been considered suspect but not strongly denounced. He redefines meats, underlining in the "thin" tissue of certain fish the presence of "a fair amount of phosphorus and hydrogen"[2] that signal them as either "heat producing" or "heft producing." These are not isolated remarks moreover. Several contemporary treatises on hygiene come to the same conclusions. However, the author of the *Physiology of Taste* does something totally new when he pursues the pleasure of eating despite calls for vigilance. He insists on the necessity of a particular diet while simultaneously sharpening its "erotic" dimension.[3] Setting aside the interdictions, the regimen he recommends for "avoiding or curing obesity" leaves room for roasts, salads and vegetables artfully prepared, as well as "jellies with alcohol, orange, and the like" and well-chosen jams.[4] Pleasure gains legitimacy in a society whose thinking is becoming more liberal—a society where "the goal of Modern man [becomes] the security to pursue private pleasures"[5] and where "individual interest" is defended and deepened with new thinking that garners newfound respect.[6]

More generally, the project consists in claiming to utilize the most recently developed sciences to institute a "gastronomy"; in other words, "a reasoned knowledge of all that relates to human nourishment."[7] As the "intelligence" of the stomach, this gastronomy claims a magisterial vocation. The scientific and cultural ambition asserts itself like never before to effect this conversion of the bourgeoisie and the scientific community by demonstrating mastery over the digestive process and over all the fine details of taste. Brillat-Savarin's regimen concords with a new overall vision of cuisine at the beginning of the nineteenth century that abandons the old-style aristocratic tables in favor of new bourgeois restaurant spaces founded on the idea of combining science and pleasure.

> Gastronomy is indebted to natural history which provides a classification of all foodstuffs; to physics which provides the tools to examine their composition and qualities; to chemistry which aids one in preparing meals and making them agreeable to the taste; to business that lets one buy what one wishes to consume at the lowest price and sell most advantageously what one has to offer; and finally to political economy for the resources that are able to circulate between nations.[8]

Establishing good eating habits and moderation are inevitably central to this ambitious approach, the goal being to determine the point where "pleasure ends and abuse begins"[9] and "to maintain a balance between one's force and one's needs."[10]

The Question of Creating an "Art of Living Well"

There is no proof, however, that this regimen was generally adopted in the first decades of the nineteenth century.[11] The gastronomy promoted by the "private pleasures of moderns" suggests just the opposite in fact. The bourgeois belly seems to have gone in the direction of profusion. Jean-Paul Aron had long experience depicting the "nineteenth century eater" as unapologetically hungry for a good spread and other pleasures, a figure blithely unconscious of the old image of the transgressive glutton.[12]

"Meals for big stomachs" that might last a whole day were organized in the 1840s.[13] These occasions to "eat and drink without stopping or rest"[14] are evidence that such pleasures were becoming ever more explicit, sought after, and talked about. Léon Gozlan describes Balzac as "superbly full of vegetable Pantagruelism."[15] The Goncourt brothers describe him as "eating like a pig to the point of indigestion, his belly a balloon of chow."[16] The Count of Viel-Castel speaks of making feverish bets such as daring someone to ingest in two hours a five-hundred franc dinner, the annual revenue of an ordinary worker, and still be "fresh and ready to go."[17]

This is undoubtedly a cocksure male attitude, a slightly tipsy swagger propelled by the perceived merit of the individual who ascends along with "the blossoming of industrialists"[18] profiting from an ever higher celebration of abundance and flux. The evocation of the foods of Paris in the early years of the century is characteristic of this confident display of grasping and bustling that views ingestion as a source of pride. "Each year the quantity of provisions swallowed up by this gaping hole increases; instead of becoming full, it becomes wider and deeper as more and more is ingested—a frightful, awesome progression."[19]

What's most important, however, is happening at another level. The deep transformation in the early nineteenth century has less to do with quantities than with qualitative changes. The dominant figure is less the glutton and more the gourmet. The theses of Brillat-Savarin are more important than they seem. Grimod de la Reynière's gastronome inaugurates the theme at the very beginning of the century: "to guide and enlighten big eaters in the labyrinth of pleasures they enjoy most."[20] The first illustration in his book gets the point across. It shows jars of canned goods and other fine products stacked on shelves from floor to ceiling, all arranged in orderly fashion like books in a professor's library. In the middle of the room is the big eater in thoughtful meditation with his head lowered, and seated not at a dining table but instead at a desk.[21] We are witnessing here the emergence of a new "art"[22]—from the kitchen to "cuisine"—the art that will be named in the title of Marc-Antoine Carême's two volume "elementary and practical treatise" published in 1833.[23]

The "bon vivant" praised by the physiology studies at the beginning of the century does not skimp on quantity, but "without being gluttonous, he is first of all a gourmet and grand eater."[24]

The Archaic and the Modern

Every diet recommended in the early nineteenth century does not rely on the new chemistry. Earlier beliefs and habits persist to varying degrees and with more or less public acknowledgment. The conviction about the usefulness of acids is one example. In 1838, William Wadd asserts with pride that regular doses of vinegar cured the Spanish general Chiapin Vitellis of his obesity.[25] In 1846, Antoine Bossu also notes the persistence of popular customs.[26] And in 1857 Michel Lévy continues to miss the use of lemons and other sour foods "by young people secretly hoping to reduce the precocious onset of exuberant forms."[27] This is hardly surprising and demonstrates that in the first half of the century the new chemical knowledge and the "combustion" theory of food had not yet spread beyond a relatively select scientific community. The entry for Diet ["*Régime*"] in the *Encyclopédie moderne* (1830) is evidence of this with its classic recommendation of "sobriety" and not the least mention of the nitrogen or carbon content of foods.[28]

There is however no getting around the striking rupture that the chemistry of Lavoisier and his followers introduced. One can also not overlook the increasingly systematic references to slimming techniques in discussions of obesity. This observation by Brillat-Savarin is typical: "Having the proper amount of plumpness, neither too much nor too little, is for women a lifetime's occupation."[29] Along the same lines, but with a dose of irony, magazine authors of the day could insist on the "fashionable woman's" unceasing watchfulness of what she eats: "What! you say, she's eating! Yes, she sure eats." And what these women are eating are foods and drinks that are "stomachy, chesty, incisive, and softening."[30] This teasing demonstrates the increasing importance of female slenderness that is both sought after and expected—to the point of becoming according to all available evidence a matter of daily concern. There seems little exaggeration in George Sand's declaration during a trip through southwestern France in the 1830s that it was next to impossible for her to eat the "sauces and fat" that she considered to be "a type of poisoning."[31]

Consider, finally, the archaism and modernity of the corset. The old sheath lives on. The flesh remains shapeable even if the conception of its material substance is altered by constant research and demanding commentaries. Patents multiply in the pursuit of flexibility and comfort. Sixty-eight patent applications are filed between 1828 and 1848 alone.[32] The criteria are highly precise: ease of lacing, respect for the various positions, retaining the possibility of movement, and use of noble materials—"watered silk," "satin," "silk taffeta."[33]

Masculine obesity at this time can also incite the wearing of corsets. The wealthy bourgeois described by Eugène Briffault in 1845 at a swimming school is no more than a "deformed" bare-chested figure at the edge of the pool once he has taken off his corset "at the door" of the swim club.[34] The rigid enclosure of the "chest" continues to exert its usefulness in the popular imagination at the beginning of the nineteenth century, including in simplified versions such as the "anti-obesity belt" strongly recommended by Brillat-Savarin.[35]

The "Misfortune" and Me: The New Status of Obesity

Grandville's portrayal of the obese person possesses an undeniable originality, less based on facts however than on the commentaries and sensations it provokes.[36] A new register opens up; a new focus on suffering. Misfortune becomes a central theme. In a story from 1843 narrated in the first person, the obese person gives an account of daily miseries. He shares his feelings, and the sufferings that are recounted are not only physical but moral, even psychological. It contrasts sharply with the personal narrative of Élie de Beaumont from 1760. In that eighteenth century document, the Parisian lawyer tells of his exhaustion and powerlessness. However, the "big, fat, and sad" person in *Small Miseries* from 1843 describes an awkward discomfort that is first of all social.[37] The evil is interior. And humiliation is a big part of it—in particular the feeling of a decidedly unjust ostracism that leads the individual "endowed with a certain fatal corpulence" to view himself "as a veritable social pariah" (300, 302). The word *malheur* (misfortune, sadness, unhappiness) crops up everywhere: "I will not be able to avoid the most poignant misfortunes [*malheurs*] attached to my state," or "Yes, I was rather misfortunate [*malheureux*]" (292, 294). "Misfortune" ["*infortune*"] is spoken of as a fatality, an "*ingratitude*" endured in sadness or in "bitterness" ["*aigrissement*"] (296).

There is hardly any originality as to the circumstances of these "relegated" individuals. There is mockery of the obese person's fatigue, the rebuffs of more "seductive" rivals, and a "feeling of disgrace" that is revived with every social encounter (299). An inventory of schoolyard pranks directed at the obese is minutely eloquent on the subject. There is, for example, the game of "*poste*," whereby the obese child is interminably pushed by joking classmates and obliged to run nonstop to the point of exhaustion. The humiliating experiences start early, occur often, and are deeply wounding. Whether true or invented, however, these testimonies are not the only interesting thing about this text.

Much more important is the evocation of a feeling, an observation that traverses the entire text, namely that the obese person has been "deprived of happiness" (299) and that this privation is to be studied, perhaps for the first time, as a "personal" matter. The originality of the text, therefore, is its emphasis on an "amputation" lived from the inside, a drama between two selves. This gives obesity a new status. No longer a simple infirmity, nor simply the result of deviant behavior, it is now a sufferance, and the distress involved, the psychic abscess, the continuous torment are all to be taken into account. In short, the image of the fat person becomes more complicated. One doesn't necessarily have in mind any longer the erring individual indulging in some culpable passion, the random glutton, nor even the sick person laboring with his physical infirmities as George Cheyne and Élie de Beaumont did at an earlier time. One thinks first of the fat person struggling with social difficulties. The misfortune further intensifies with the pursuit of slimming programs that all come to naught. The diet quickly abandoned, the vinegar, the corset—nothing seems to work and the weight gain continues on as one's fate.

Obesity had to become better understood scientifically for the limits and failures of its treatment to be noticed. The advent of a more modern "me" led to the development of more sophisticated procedures of self-observation with more intimate testimonies, interrogations about sensations, and reports of "moral" suffering.[38] Together these allowed obesity to be increasingly viewed as an overwhelming evil that one underwent, an immoveable suffering, a poorly controlled collapse. Obesity simultaneously becomes a multi-faceted and deeper problem. A more confident, assertive scientific approach combined with a self more successful at introspection make the suffering associated with fatness into a subject of unsuspected interest.

PART 5

TOWARD THE "MARTYR"

The theme of organic combustion developed in the first half of the nineteenth century transformed the way obesity was approached, correcting explanations and modifying treatments. It took the second half of the century, however, for this theme to fully and precisely assert itself. This came, for example, with heightened attention to the caloric specificities of various diets, to exercise and lifestyles, and to distinctions between organisms categorized as more or less "high burning" and therefore more or less susceptible to becoming fat. The idea of the body as a fireplace takes hold definitively. The obese person therefore has a vital weakness that, materially speaking, is a combustion problem.

A new battle begins against weight gain in the second half of the century. The advent of "pastimes," a redefinition of the feminine that allows for more "active" women and different ideas about privacy and nudity all play their roles in making discussions of obesity occur earlier and its rejection more determined.

It is also impossible to ignore the note of disappointment and pain associated with anti-obesity treatments. This is especially true at the start of the twentieth century as accounts of various cures multiply in parallel with the growing number of personal testimonies. Psychological analysis is born and quickly spreads through contemporary society. The obese speak, judge themselves, and detail their "misfortune." Greater knowledge of physiologies and more closely analyzed slimming practices and general body care lead to the acknowledgment of therapeutic obstacles.

The body cannot be transformed on command. Hence the possible "failure" of various therapies—an unavoidable trial against organic laws that are often inflexible. Besides the ordinary stigmatization of the obese person, one now faces the more intimate narrative of the "victim." This allows for a discourse of the "martyr" to emerge—contemporary society's slant on the triumph of the thin and distaste for fat.

16. The Dominance of Aesthetics

An illustration by Crafty in an issue of *Paris on Horseback* from 1884 might seem anecdotal. It shows a heavy female rider being lifted with difficulty into the saddle. The situation is rather delicate and the physical contact not a little bit ambiguous. The helper has his hands full, literally, and the body is "wobbling." Crafty's teasing caption reads, "One of the thousand reasons why women over fifty kilos should give up horseback riding."[1] The derision is clear even without the caption, but the weight reference puts it over the top. Such references are becoming ordinary and resonate in everyone's mind as a certain widely understood indicator. One notes a similar mention of weights in the literature of an arms manufacturer in Saint-Étienne who diversified into bicycles in the 1890s. His sales pitch makes an association between the ideal weight of the bike and the rider: 14–15 kilograms "minimum" for the bike, on condition that the cyclist weigh no more than 70 kilograms "maximum."[2] Bodily weights and measures become progressively more and more commonplace as technology moves into everyday life.

Other practices encourage an unprecedented attention to nuances. For example, people reveal their bodies more at the end of the nineteenth century, a new habit that incites watchfulness of the adipose, as do public and private pastimes as well as fashion and body care. Becoming big is also talked about in years younger than before, and as something generally unpleasant and ugly. Fat's negative publicity definitely gains in intensity throughout the period.

The Spread of Weighing

Widespread weighing is a sign of the standardization of norms that occurs in the last decades of the nineteenth century. In 1887 Albert Millaud speaks of a woman who arrived at a spa town "perched on a scale with a built-in meter." Weighing becomes standard practice, and the appliance used becomes simpler, often with the mechanism enclosed in a wooden case with the needle and numbers raised closer to the eyes. The act is also performed more frequently. The spa goer mentioned by Albert Millaud "weighs herself constantly and tells anyone within earshot that she has lost ten or twelve pounds in a given week."[3] A nearly identical scene takes place in a Maupassant story, "My Twenty-Fifth Birthday," where a spa goer "carefully weighs himself to the closest gram."[4] And a similar scene also occurs in *Parisian Life* (1886) where a coquettish woman weighs herself daily. "She begins her day by weighing herself with almost nothing on."[5] Zola too, in answer to a journalist's question, reports his exact weight loss thanks to a "remarkable" diet he followed. He claims to have lost eight of his original two hundred pounds in ten days, and forty-five pounds in three months.[6] This declaration decisively shows that the act of weighing is now considered worthwhile and especially that it is rendered in both numerical units of mass and in relation to time.

The cumulative effect of various advice givers when it comes to weight, all of whom make increasing use of scales and tables, will result in further stabilization of usage.[7] One can find evidence of a wider use of weighing, also accompanied by a certain popular resistance, in an engraving that appears in an issue of *L'Illustré national* from 1901. It shows a simple man being teased for wanting to weigh himself three times, but only a third of his body each time because the narrow scale was ill-adapted to his size.[8] There is also the provocative engraving in the same periodical of a traveler who wishes to use one of the early scales installed in train stations at the beginning of the twentieth century. He is shocked by the high number that the machine reports as his weight until he notices he has mistakenly placed his packages on the scale's platform along with himself.[9] Here the modern laughs at the unmodern's unfamiliarity and ineptness when it comes to scales and weighing.

Personal scales become more varied. "Apartment scales," for example, are advertised in the *Archives générales de médecine* at the beginning of the twentieth century.[10] Around the same time, the dictionary of Émile Brissaud and Adolphe Pinard proposes placing a scale in the bedroom of the obese person to more easily register the "weight curve."[11]

The practice grows steadily more common, to the point where not weighing is a source of annoyance, such as in the case of Bruno, the servant of Van Mitten, a heavy Dutch merchant in Jules Verne's *Kéraban* (1883). Bruno wants to check his weight loss caused by an exhausting voyage through the Nordic countryside of Georgia. No scale is available—the habits of Georgians not being the same as those of Western countries. He therefore turns to the commercial balances he comes across in the port of Poti.[12] The detailed account of a search for a weighing machine in this novel is further indication of its importance.

The First Conflicts Between Charts

The completely ordinary use of numbers by the end of the nineteenth century leads to another striking development, namely, the diversification of size charts that relate height and weight. The weight expected for a given height is calculated in greater detail, an important stage toward today's "body mass index" graphs.[13] In the years 1860–1880 William Banting and Louis-Alexandre de Saint-Germain offered their own scales beside the scale and weighing apparatus developed by Adolphe Quetelet in 1835.[14] Louis-Alexandre de Saint-Germain set out to simplify the use of such charts. The figure for weight expressed in pounds had to correspond to the figure for height expressed in centimeters. A person 1.68 m tall would be considered "normal" if his weight were 168 lbs or roughly 80 kilos.[15] This number was immediately disputed by Adrien Proust and Albert Mathieu in their study, *Hygiène de l'obèse*, in which they stick closer to Quetelet's tables. For them the weight figure in kilos should correspond to the height expressed in centimeters minus 100.[16] This makes a big difference, since for them the 1.68 m person should weigh 68 kilos. All the recommended figures are now advanced from both a medical as well as an "aesthetic" perspective, but the lingering question of the relative and the contingent remains a problem. The "normal" weight in the 1880s depends on what chart one consults. For the same 1.68-m person, the recommended weight according to Quetelet is 63.5 kilos, whereas for Saint-Germain it is 84 kilos.

These variations also crop up in ordinary circumstances. Lisa, the pork butcher in Zola's *The Belly of Paris* (1878), is a woman with an ample but firm body, a bit overweight but "normal"; she "occupies the width of the door, but she's not too fat at all."[17] She has a "superb freshness,"[18] "white pinkish skin," her complexion recalls "the transparency of fat."[19] Her allure is alert and palpitating despite her bust being intensely "strapped down."[20] This woman, known throughout Les Halles as "beautiful Lisa," is quite different from another entirely "normal," "beautiful," and "alluring" type of woman described in issues of the periodical *Monde élégant* during the same years. This second woman is lankier and more mobile, her thin body compared to that of a "dragonfly."[21] Thus there is the popular sensibility, on one side, and the elitist sensibility, on the other—the threshold in each case of what constitutes "fat" is certainly not the same. The gaze in each case is obviously different, and though the charts, tables, and figures are fully available, they are hardly brought up at all in such circumstances.

Despite these many differences, there is a common accord. In both cases the "fat person" is designated by the same principle, namely, the loss of all "flexibility in the waist," though it might be judged differently in each.[22] The model waist is fundamental. The word *thinness* applies, first of all, to the middle of the body, no matter what the expectations for other body parts. The term is so powerful that it alone can be the focus of nostalgic outpourings about beauty: "She who used to have such a thin waist . . . "[23] It is also the primary attraction of another beauty in Les Halles that Zola describes. Like Lisa, the "beautiful Norman" woman is a popular figure who is close to being overweight (*forte*), but is not really. She has "the big body of a goddess," round arms, a "beautiful," "moving" waist that sways her skirts, and "superb" breasts.[24]

Alongside such figures, there is an intensified will to thinness in the second half of the nineteenth century. The pressure is stronger, more frequent, and exercised first of all on the bodies of women, as may be seen in the fashion magazines whose tone grows markedly more serious, even to the extent of sounding alarms and inciting fears. "Get fat? Why it's the nightmare of every woman!"[25] One also notes the words of fashion designers who associate youth with thinness more than before and link systematically getting thinner with getting younger with the help of close-cut robes, bolero vests, and shift dresses.[26] Lisa is strapped "to the point of suffocation in her corsets," we're told.[27] But the true aim of this remark is a critique by her rivals. If she "tightens herself" in this way, say her "adversaries," it's because "she must be a fright naked."[28] The suspicion of what's underneath is expressed more. Allusions to masked flesh become more frequent, as though clothes ought no longer to betray the anatomy. Allusions to "open" and "closed" corsets become topics in both novels and images. An evocation of the hidden is taken up in memoirs, letters, and stories. In his engravings from the end of the century entitled simply *Around Women*, Henri Boutet multiplies the images of "ordinary" women whose flesh is suggested underneath the clothes—one symptom of a much larger cultural movement tipping in the direction of our contemporary world.[29]

The meanings of words are tipping too. The meaning and connotation of *embonpoint*, for example, shifts in less than a generation. For the *Dictionnaire de l'Académie française* (1884), the term is definitely assigned to "a fat person"; whereas in Emile Littré's *Dictionnaire de la langue française* (1866) it is associated with someone "whose body is in a good state." *Embonpoint* no longer designates an equilibrium, but a "defect" that announces "fat."[30]

The Exposure of Bodies

References to the hidden progressively increase the demand for slimming. The steady increase in "free time" also adds to this demand as bathing and seaside vacations suddenly become one of the abrupt new cultural changes at the turn of the century. Clothes that are more "stripped down" also contribute to the image of a more exposed body. In addition, gazes that are freer linger over more varied bodily deformities. Contours can go awry and provoke surprises and rejection. "Their glowing adiposity is displayed in the sun without their consciousness of other people's disgust."[31]

Starting in the years 1870–1880, the simple "rupture" between the "lightness" of swimwear and the envelopment of women's dresses challenges appearances. "Mademoiselle X, who was the queen of the ball when she circulated through drawing rooms, is no longer at all pretty" on the beach.[32] Jules Michelet makes a "cruel exhibition" out of the wearing of simple swimsuits that make perfectly normal-looking women "ugly."[33] Hugues Rebell recalls the "disdain" that is sometimes leveled against women who, though admired for their "art of dressing well,"[34] are maliciously betrayed by certain body features revealed at the beach.

Sagging bodies are constantly being teased by illustrators of the day. Surprise and wisecracks are visited on bathers taken for "balls," "balloons," "beams," "towers," "buoys," "whales," and "torpedoes."[35] The ridiculousness of "fat ladies" is more liable to be voiced.[36] New pastimes allow "monstrosities" to be glimpsed, and this exerts further pressure to get thin.

Another type of intimate observation that grows common for the first time in the second half of the century is the practice of viewing one's entire body naked in a mirror. Here too it is the underneath that gets revealed, but in a reflection literally never seen before with full-length mirrors, not just the modest oval mirrors that stood atop dressers in old alcoves. Now mirrors can reflect bodies and objects from floor to ceiling. The kind of mirrors that Barbey d'Aurevilly in the 1870s considered indispensable and imagined as "an immense lake at the end of the room."[37]

A number of technical and economic changes made these new mirrors possible in the second half of the century.[38] New and less expensive chemical processes for silvering the glass were developed, thus lowering the cost, while industrial production of glass and better transportation systems also played important roles. Large stores advertise such mirrors through mail-order catalogues as early as the 1870s. This causes the product to become more diversified and widely diffused. Wardrobes with mirrors, large wall mirrors, and double-faced mirrors become standard equipment in the living spaces of the bourgeoisie and petit bourgeoisie, and even enter the homes of small savers by the end of the century. Curiosity increases. The practice of looking at oneself becomes material for literary treatment as well as the visual arts. There is a promotion of the complete vertical silhouette, now revealed with all its anatomical undulations including the lower ones and no longer just the upper ones. Zola makes a major scene of this encounter in *Nana* (1882) after having studied Lucie Lévy, a well-known Paris socialite of the 1870s, for many years. "With a naked belly and throat, she approached her wardrobe mirror and smiled at the reflection of her beauty that had become pink from the flames of the fire behind her."[39] The Goncourt brothers also evoke a certain Manette Salomon standing and observing her naked body's "radiant slenderness."[40] The periodical *Parisian Life* recycles the same scene in systematic ways, playing constantly with desire, the distancing of prudishness, and the wish for emancipation.[41]

The Ascendancy of Women's Hips

Types of attention emerge that did not exist before—a worrisome eye for discreet changes or for clearly localized features. "Standing before the tall mirror of her dressing room, she contemplated with terror what formerly had been only a slight plumpness—her hips had grown, her throat was now swollen, her delicate face as round as the bourgeoisie."[42]

A young woman in *Parisian Life* (1899) has the same experience when she surveys herself each morning before the mirror of her dressing room. She's worried by a "development of the hips."[43] Measuring tape and balance scale are deployed, but the gaze is certainly playing a new role—more subtle, more equipped, more explorative of "folds" not just around the waist but on the hips now that their traits are suddenly apparent and considered to "thicken" before all other body parts.

This development is accentuated by another change that happened during the 1870s, namely, a style revolution when it comes to woman's dress. The traditional amplitude of the lower half disappears, thus eliminating the masking of hips and legs. The customary "flared" female form that spread out in large folds below the waist loses its dominance. The "line" replaces the "bouffant," the continuous curve replaces the broken folds. The hips become more fluid, the curving contours more "natural" as they press almost against the cloth. Hips impose their presence and outline for the first time in the 1870s. *L'Illustration* underlines this point in 1878 in a multitude of texts and drawings. "This bell, which ruled for years and for which no doorway was ever wide enough, has suddenly been overtaken by this sheath that women are wearing now. . . . What was formerly hidden is now shown. . . . Every contour is now on view underneath these skirts without folds."[44]

The clothes in *Nana* that Zola situates at the end of the Second Empire (roughly 1870) mark a stage along the way toward these changes. The front of a dress is described as "straight" and its back curved and lifted slightly by the "bustle" framework—the last vestige of the flaring style. The dress "draws bold attention to the thighs" at a time when skirts were still rather ballooning.[45] The progression is accentuated when the rigid, loin-lifting bustle is abandoned during the 1880s. At that point the hidden becomes more visible than ever before. The silhouette is now more sinuous, more mobile—changes no doubt linked to the changing status of women during the last decades of the century. A more available, supple body—even if the corset continues its encasing hold—corresponds to a more striking female presence in the public sphere and higher expectations as to their initiatives and activities.[46] The greater affirmation of women provokes the affirmation of their profile.

This leads to changes in the way forms are designated. The hips are more visible than ever before, and with that comes the possibility of revealing deformity and excess. The representation of sizes reflects this and now takes into account "the excessive development of the hips" among its forms and degrees.[47] *Le Caprice* explains the phenomenon in 1900, writing of the inevitable "risks" of dresses that are ever straighter focusing attention on the hips, "the first region where female obesity takes hold."[48]

Two types of female obesity are described at the turn of the century. The first is the classic fattening up into a sphere like the protagonist in Maupassant's story *Boule de Suif* (Ball of Fat): "round everywhere, tub of lard . . . with taut, damp skin."[49] The second is lower-body obesity as described, for example, by the Goncourt brothers with "oversized" forms that appear to have "flowed and molded themselves at the lower levels."[50] As a result, closer attention is paid to the hip and pelvis area, vigilance being particularly strong among "delicate" women who worry at the first sign of changes to their features. Thus, for example, there is the "minutely" examined detail inspected "every fifteen minutes in the mirror" by Madame Lanlaire in *Diary of a Chambermaid*.[51] In contrast, there is the overall fattening up of an ordinary character in the same book, Marianne the cook, described as "fat, soft, flabby, and spread out."[52] There is also Gervaise in Zola's *L'Assommoir*, who at the end of her life powerlessly contemplates her round profile—"enormous, squat, grotesque"—which she sees in shadow on the sidewalk at night.[53]

From the Masculine Waist to the Muscular "Discovery"

The advancing belly, however, remains a predominantly masculine image. Bertall "darkens" his illustration in 1874 when he calls the belly "one of the most malicious acts of nature against man."[54] The matter is portrayed for the first time in dramatic, combative terms.

> In youth, the resistance of the soft parts located between the backbone and the hip bones suffices to fight against the enlargement of the abdominal cavity. But with age, this resistance is defeated. Succulent lunches, opulent dinners, and drinks of all kinds accumulate and distend at will the elastic tissues that balloon little by little, becoming a round bump that daily protrudes beyond the straight and narrow. An addition begins to be constructed out front. It is then that with waist belts and cleverly cut trousers, one tries to impede the further expansion of the belly down below.
> Between thirty and thirty-five, the belly carries itself high and mighty, one could say, toward the chest. Then one comes to be a little short of breath while eating. To breath more easily, the belt is loosened. And eventually the battle is lost. One ends up letting things slide. Resignation is unavoidable. Further resistance is impossible when the hour of the belly tolls.[55]

Bertall innovates with this clear depiction of phases of a "battle." It stands in marked contrast to the evocation, also in stages, of the obesity of Tracy Tupman in Dickens's *Pickwick Papers* (1836). Pickwick's friend gradually sags with little opposition; he undergoes a process with hardly any resistance.[56] Bertall orchestrates a reply that is itself a progression. He innovates further with a veritable tapestry of French bellies enumerating for the first time a spectrum of characters and their profiles. "Rouher's belly is a reclamation, Gambetta's a hyperbole, Courbet's an insult." The belly ball of Adolphe Thiers is destined to become "historic."[57] Here the names, bodies, and social milieu of well-known figures are presented and compared. The text points and inspects as though inventorying, insisting on those, like Alexandre Karr or Roqueplan, who "triumph over the enemy" as well as on those, like Jules Sandeau or Jules Janin, who give up "without a fight."[58]

What's more, in the 1870s this theme is no longer separable from references to slimming. Doctors seem to be more frequently invoked. By the end of the century, "My doctor told me . . . " becomes the standard phrase to start a discussion about diet.[59] One also notices pressing, discreet references to veiled resistance to medical advice. "I don't like hunting, but my doctor has prescribed it as part of my thinning program."[60] The names of the prescribing doctors are also mentioned now, especially those of famous people such as Zola and Gambetta.[61] Generally speaking, an obligation takes hold, a new pressure. To evoke a man's large size is to evoke the possibility of erasing it. Already Flaubert seems to consider "the majestic belly" a "useless" marker, an outmoded sign of old-fashioned notoriety when it was "customary for the belly to ennoble."[62] Satirical periodicals from the end of the century insist on this view with parodies of threats and punishments. Consider, for example, the rebuke uttered by Cham's worldly woman from 1869 who falls back in an armchair and scolds her lover, saying, "My dear, we shall interrupt our meetings during Lent. You are fat."[63] Or the wife of a government deputy who makes a crack about budgetary restraint: "You want to reduce the budget when you haven't even been able to reduce yourself!"[64] Or this wife from 1884 pointing out the indignity of it all: "You want to run for election at such a sensitive time with a belly like that?"[65] Close acquaintances also intervene, as in the case of Gambetta, whose friends, worried about his immanent "obesity," exhort him to "act." Partially convinced, the "herald of the Republic" agrees to wear a belly belt and to enroll in exercise sessions under the direction of Eugène Paz; he abandons that project after a long trip in the South;[66] later he thinks he'll substitute mountain walks instead, but these are made impossible by his commitments in Paris, and so at the end of his life his 1.70 m frame weights 112 kilos.[67]

Such cases lend a certain credence to the continued certitude of many that some examples of bigness are "natural"—the idea that there just are some big people who cannot be thought of any other way. This blank conviction is often to be found in popular settings where an inexorable fatalism is more common. Resigned powerlessness and even mild amusement are the rule here, as in the case of Toine, a café owner in Tournevent in a Maupassant story, who becomes a "curiosity"[68] from eating and drinking so much that he no longer reacts to the criticisms of his wife. "There's just so much fat it makes my heart ache."[69] Toine's friends joke, drink with him, and react crudely when apoplexy paralyzes him; and things become even more burlesque when one of them suggests making him "warm eggs" in the damp sheets.[70] The scene illustrates the disparities across different perceptions and sensibilities.

A last novelty during the 1870s when it comes to descriptions of the belly and the "pressure" to slim down are references to the muscular "wall" of the healthy abdomen and invention of the word *bedonnement* (potbelly) to designate the sagging collapse of this wall.[71] Bertall expresses the idea in his characteristic manner in 1874, indicating the progressive softening of the "elastic tissues" situated "between the backbone and the pelvic bones."[72] He proposes no specific belly gymnastics. The image of the body, however, is definitely reconceived as an architectural framework held up by muscles, something the physiologists of the 1880s clearly insist on. "Firm and vigorous abdominal muscles are the best guardrail against obesity."[73] This theme is also taken up in exercise manuals from the turn of the century. They stigmatize "the weakness of abdomen muscles,"[74] to the extent of distinguishing among morphologies a specific "abdominal type," characterized by a "prominent abdomen and slackening of the walls of the bell," and a "respiratory type," with a "prominent chest and slight abdomen."[75]

Nothing seems more ordinary than this muscular vision of the body since anatomists had long drawn muscles, specifying how they were attached.[76] And yet there is nothing newer and more original than this role attributed to the abdomen's movement. It requires a "mechanistic" representation of the body. It presupposes a decomposed vision of movements focusing on the relations of lever to lever that could only be suggested by a technical universe that promotes numerically precise measured gestures, their simplified representation in geometric terms, and an awareness of modern industry's patterns and not simply those of earlier workshops. Physiologists, gymnasts, and engineers of the early nineteenth century were the first to envision these partial movements.[77]

They studied the possible series, montages, decompositions, and recompositions. They were the first to explain in terms of muscular deficiencies certain vertebral deformations, archings, twistings, rigidities, and infirmities of the waist.[78] They transposed the question of muscular mobility into a play of possible supports and levers. However, their universe remained for a long time rather formal and concentrated on dissymmetries and faulty positions more than on the tonic envelope and its overall effects. They had no general musculature theory in mind.

However, the turn-of-the-century importance given to the abdominal wall renews muscle awareness, especially a modular vision with attention to posture and mobility. This is aided by having bigness considered more than before a problem of the silhouette and not merely of specific contours. The image of the body as framework is what counts now—along with its dynamic vectors, forces, tensions—much more than the body as simple volume or container.

From Aesthetics to the Conflict of Images

Everything changes with the surveillance of minute and measured indexes. Aesthetics grows definitively dominant, and people become supremely alert to ugliness. Ugliness is the focus of an interminable array of couples scenes and tableaus of mores featured in satirical magazines at the end of the century, such as the chubby man who questions a potential "conquest." He: "Do you not find me passably attractive?" She: "I find you past attractive."[79] There's the courtesan exasperated by the sunken state of her lover who quips, "Not cheating on him would be an offense against God."[80] And equally put off is the grousing prostitute who laments when faced with an extremely sagging client, "It's all the same, but a girl's got to be pretty hard up to do it with you!"[81] These are portraits of ridicule against a background of seduction. The fat person is above all ugly before being the big eater, the grasper, or the abuser. And this ugliness, as the beach and bedroom scenes attest, is now the earliest concern as well. This is reinforced by the extent to which preferences are announced at the end of the century, affirming a particular desire and its legitimacy and attributing to individual conquest and its inclinations and choices a place it did not formerly have. It also demonstrates how much psychology and taste have won out by then over the older moralizations.

There are inevitably other new scenes featured in the world of satirical magazines. Two of them certainly result from the stigmatization of ugliness. The first extends the old tradition of representing class warfare. A diffuse "radicalism"[82] pervades these scenes; beyond the failure of the Paris Commune in 1871, a particular "intransigence" accentuates tensions and oppositions.[83] The illustrations in the magazine *Le Père Peinard* (The Comfortable Father) get the point across aggressively at the end of the century with sharp oppositions between "redundant" bigwigs and a half-starved looking people that gripe about "the power of fat."[84] Rothschild, for example, has gotten "fat at the expense of our leanness,"[85] just as the most "richly clothed" have the "least burdened shoulders."[86] These are striking images centered on disparities of alimentation that were often recognized but less easily accepted. The investigations of Frédéric Le Play in the last decades of the century offer the clearest evidence—revealing, for example, the small quantities of meat present in the diet of working-class families compared to the sizable quantities eaten by wealthier families.[87] Consequently the clearly different profiles translate the less apparent differences in diet between groups—the real or imagined heaviness of the "rich" functioning as a commentary on the concrete diminution of the "poor." Armand Gautier makes a similar point at the end of the century when he compares the food of the "bourgeois of Paris" with that of the "average" population. He claims the former consumes 90 grams of fat per day as compared to a "standard" consumption of 48 grams.[88] These findings are so stark that the height and weight charts used by the military's medical check-up committees can totally ignore the problem of overweight conscripts from the popular classes. The label *weakness* is only applied to designate the overly thin, such as a recruit who is 1.80 m but less than 70 kilos or someone who is 1.70 m but weighs less than 60 kilos.[89] Was the idea of the obese working-class soldier as yet unthinkable?

In 1878 Zola puts the theme at the center of a major novel, *The Belly of Paris*, that features the unremitting confrontation between "two Frances"[90]—an opposition between "the thin and the fat" engaged in social warfare.[91] The half-starved painter Claude Lantier sums up the confrontation at its climax: "The fat are victorious"[92]—they send off to penal colonies the fantasizing agitators, the men with illusory dreams such as Florent, the very model of the thin camp who had sworn to "crush the reign of pigging out and boozing."[93]

The fat person in *The Belly of Paris* is first of all a figure of allusion. He is an "image." This is all the more clear since the attribution is not limited to "the haves," but is also applied to their admirers, supporters, and in some cases electors; in other words, to the mix-up heterogeneous mass in the Halles markets where in the novel ordinary people, artisans, and shopkeepers dominate. The fat are the "profiteers" who exploit the system and make it prosper. Thus the physical profile is really only part of the argument. The Halles are its physical transposition: potbellied Paris displaying an "egoistic" and contested fortune.[94]

The second type of totally new scene at the end of the century derives from images in conflict and crossed oppositions. Here the "fat" can be ordinary people, grotesque effigies, or crude drunken sacklike people imagined by individuals who are wary of popular public access or who contest the very existence of the Republic. All these oppositions become more emphatic, embittered, and perverted at the end of the century. "The Republic's failure when pitted against Germany . . . a skeptical questioning of modern society . . . in contrast to Republican optimism, confident nationalism, and belief in the progress of science, another France slides into anxiety and pessimism. The feeling of discomfort of this other France is expressed via the notion of 'decadence,' a term that was repeated everywhere."[95]

In 1882 the royalist periodical *Le Triboulet* presents "Today's Kings" as a collection of fallen Sancho Panzas[96]—clog-wearing peasants swollen by drunkenness and other excesses. "The Republic of the defeated" is one of infamy and vulgarity.[97] That same idea is conveyed in an engraving of the author Zola in a 1879 issue of *The Young Guard* where he is presented as a "fattened-up pig"[98]—a fleshy sphere whose paunch and groin dominate over all other features. The same idea is also suggested in the "grotesque" representation of the Jew, which associated the virulent obsession over a foreign "peril" with the pseudo-scientific theories that would have such disastrous effects. In his *Jewish France* Drumont multiplies viperish references to "bleary eyes," "enormous jawbones,"[99] and "the rotundity of the princes of Israel."[100] *Le Grelot* (The Jinglebell) accumulates "charges" in its engravings with references to the "Jewish pig" and to "Jewish dumplings for sale."[101] The image of fatness is further weighted with hate and abjection.

The aesthetic dimension increases its dominance as the caricature of the fat person proceeds along a set of cultural pathways, exhibited differently by different parties in a variety of conflicts.

17. Clinical Obesity and Everyday Obesity

In the second half of the nineteenth century, the way of perceiving and judging bodily forms was influenced by the ascendancy of "free time," the revolutionary changes in customs of dress, and the reorganization of private living spaces. An everyday obesity develops that relies on categorizing profiles, distinguishing hips, chest, belly, and abdominal muscles, differentiating male and female cases, and usually stigmatizing the second more than the first.[1] A threshold of expectations of slenderness is also established even as a certain conviction holds firm, namely, that "there are more obese people in the upper classes than in the working class."[2]

Alongside this lay person's vision of obesity, medical science advances another view. Obesity now enters its "scientific period,"[3] becomes the subject of experiments and calculations, is explored by means of "chemistry and physiology,"[4] and acquires the status of a specific field of study as for other pathologies. New decisive sorts of "verifications" are introduced that no longer simply distinguish sizes but differentiate types of fattening. A new weakness also emerges, one almost measurable by the knowledgeable expert. It concerns the lack of fire, the organic malfunction rooted in the body's organs—a low level of combustion that provokes the accumulation of fat as a result of insufficient burning. The result is the totally new way of distinguishing a fatness from excess that comes from an overaccumulation of food, and a fatness by default, as it were, that comes from a deficiency in the "burner." And there is also the conviction that enlivening the fire will erase fat.

Forms and Numerically Measured Degrees

Are these some of the effects of increased social pressures? Or of better equipment for measuring the organic? In the second half of the nineteenth century, medical science radically changes the categories of sizes and their explanations. Research now focuses on the specification of degrees. Fattening is divided up into "small," "medium," and "large" degrees of obesity. Jean Sicard provides the most precise formulations at the beginning of the twentieth century. "Small" obesity is defined as a weight that exceeds by 3/10 the weight judged normal for a given height; 91 kilos, for example, if the normal weight were 70 kilos. "Medium" obesity is defined as a weight that exceeds the normal weight by 5/10; e.g., 105 kilos versus a norm of 70 kilos. And "large" obesity is defined as all degrees of excess greater than 50 percent over the norm.[5] Measuring instruments establish thresholds such that a thorough diagram with all stages and levels accounted for is definitively available.

More important, the extension of the statistical universe leads to finer differentiation of the categories themselves. In 1882 Charles Bouchard, a professor of pathology at the Paris school of medicine, is one of the first to attempt to evaluate hereditary factors in ninety-four cases. Of these, forty-three had a "strong" presence of obesity among their relatives, in forty-two others there was the presence of illnesses related to food assimilation (gout, diabetes, arthritis, etc.), while only nine had no pathological antecedents whatsoever.[6] In other words, this suggests "predisposing causes," of which one example is family history; and "occasional causes," of which one example is excess food and drink.[7] And this leads to two types of fattening that are more distinct than ever before: one that derives from some superabundant consumption and a second that derives from "ancestral" influence. Other statistics confirm this thesis. Charles Bouchard claims that out of one hundred obese individuals, fifty eat normally, forty eat too much, and ten don't eat enough.[8] Thus the definition of an all new type of bigness that would not be related to excessive eating or an exaggeratedly sedentary lifestyle becomes possible —as well as being far from the former models of slack fibers or overabundance of certain humors. Two ways of being obese now exist that until then had been confusedly grouped together and not distinguished: excess blood (*sanguins pléthoriques*) and anemic lymphatics (*lymphatiques anémiques*).[9] The first tend to get fat from their excesses, the second from their constitution (*complexion*). It's not that the first end up avoiding anemia; they can merely suggest for a time the dynamic appearance of "vulgar" obesity associated with "polysarcia" and "extra large appetites."[10]

These developments mark a definitive break with the former distinction based on temperaments, a distinction that was often imprecise, between a phlegmatic person suffering under excess fluids and an overeater suffering under excess flesh. They also permit a clarification between two contradictory notions—that of the strong obese and the weak obese, the ascendant and the sagging. Two poles marking two distinct paths to obesity become more clearly identifiable: the one is related to "opulence," the other to a "deficit." The latter designates a malady of bigness whose origin is neither overeating nor a sedentary lifestyle.

Retarding Nutrition and Excess Nutrition

Charles Bouchard insists that "a healthy person can consume and even overconsume fat without becoming polysarcous,"[11] while another person can get fat without any exaggerated consumption. The cases of the "anemic" obese, who gain weight from lack of fire, and those becoming ill from their constitution become parts of a new field of research. A particular characteristic identifies them, namely, "their pallor, fatigue or soft flesh."[12] This is confirmed by a final observation: "the exhalation of carbonic acid diminishes" in these obese individuals due to weak breathing, whereas their "fetid quality" increases due to "insufficient combustion of volatile fatty acids."[13] Thus the body susceptible to fattening up is a low "burner."

The caloric principle is generalized to the point of subverting Liebig's division of human alimentation into "respiratory" foods and "plastic" or body-building foods. Now it's believed that all foods can participate in combustion. An experiment conducted by Pettenkofer and Voit in 1873 demonstrates this. A dog nourished exclusively on low-fat meat can "fabricate" fat, thus transforming a "plastic" food into a "respiratory" food.[14] Moreover, albumin can be combusted. "Plastic foods generate heat"—even if less or with less intensity.[15] The three big food groups, "carbohydrates, fats, and albuminous matter,"[16] can all contribute to fattening through the transformation of carbon into a fatty substance. This unifies the theme of the role of energy-production and gives it primary importance. The creation and destruction of fat are now viewed as related systems.

A new argument centered on heat and its effects also emerges now. The application of the caloric principle is not limited to bodily work. It is also present in "plastic" effects; i.e., the organic constructions that renew the life of the tissues themselves. It is active in the very "constitution" of the flesh. In the 1870s, Marcelin Berthelot took an interest in advancing a chemistry of synthesis alongside the usual chemistry of analysis.[17] This explains the presence of fire within the most secret "synthetic reactions"[18] which are increasingly invoked. "We view physiological combustion as the great regulator of functions."[19] This affirmation establishes the primacy of the caloric principle.

Diet can now be expressed almost exclusively in terms of combustive values—those indispensable for life as well as those that signal abuse. The energy-producing reference entirely guides the pronouncement of the diet and its contents: 2,450 calories per day for "an average man, dressed and at rest, in a temperament climate,"[20] but 2,800 to 4,000 calories per day depending on the intensity of "effort undertaken."[21] This caloric reference allows one to express "vital" insufficiency, the lack of fire as well as its excess. It's important to distinguish organisms that have a strong combustive power from those that have a weak combustive power.

Fattening that happens without any excessive eating is now explainable for the first time: "fat burning deficit."[22] Charles Bouchard studied the subject at length and referred to it as "slow nutrition" or "retarding nutrition" (*nutrition retardante*).[23] His systematic study extends to other pathologies such as forms of arthritis and gout, both of which are provoked by the presence of organic acids that are poorly "combusted." "In all these circumstances, the organic acids may not be burned, alkaline levels of fluids diminishes, the uric acid in urine increases, urate crystals form more easily, and oxalic acid appears."[24]

Weak fire is a problem that manifests itself in many forms, a malfunction that varies according to the materials concerned. The proximity long supposed between maladies as different as gout, diabetes, and obesity can now be better understood as being different forms resulting from a unique cause. In each case a different substance causes the problem: "Albuminoids and uric acid for gout, carbohydrates and sugars for diabetes, fat and fatty acids for obesity."[25]

"Retarding nutrition" as a factor in obesity becomes a standard medical explanation at the end of the century with doctors all pointing to "insufficient oxygen supply" as the cause.[26] What causes that remains to be explained, and it is controversy on that point that makes recommending treatment delicate. Some see the problem arising from the composition of the blood; for them a lack of red blood cells explains the presence of unburned material: "as oxidation slows, fat accumulates."[27] Others point to a slowing of the heart, "blood stasis," or of the lungs, "carbonic asphyxiation."[28] Others point to different obscure weaknesses. But all the theories rely on the energy model and view fattening as an imbalance of fire, "a discordance between what's received and the needs."[29] All therefore expect to see a decrease in fat from an increase of combustion.

Two types of obesity that were either poorly or not at all explained by the first "energy" theorists, including Liebig, come into view: a type deriving from excess and a second deriving from lack, the second being linked to an organic insufficiency of the force and use of fire.

The Degenerative Obsession

A more general reference emerges in the context of this very specific weakness, an all-encompassing "insufficiency" that turn-of-the-century culture tends to view as a behavioral trait signaling some unfitness for life. It becomes the "modern" way of invoking some insidious lack lodged in the human heart. The subject is approached in terms of the very requirements for fire. Manuel Levin discusses many cases of patients with "deregulated nervous systems" and "loss of vigor," especially a debilitating "irritation" that is said to provoke spontaneous fattening due to excess amounts of uncombusted carbon.[30] In 1892 the *Review of Medicine and Surgery* links the possible "sudden death" of obese individuals to those that occur in "neuropathological families."[31]

In this way obesity in its anemic version has changed grounds. A sneaky malady, it now becomes part of the larger malady that fin de siècle culture was stigmatizing: an ungraspable vital lack. This is also conveyed by a new term, *degeneration,* that was cautiously put forward by Adrien Proust and Albert Mathieu.[32]

The prestige of the evolutionist vision of the world in the second half of the nineteenth century aggravates the fears of regression.[33] "Inversions" may exist, atavisms may exert an influence over the body. In a medical book destined for the general reader, Jules Rengade claimed to have identified *lymphatiques gras* and *phéthoriques mous* by investigating back up to their related antecedent forms.[34] At the same time, Victor Galippe studied the "stigmata of degeneration" in the Habsburg family and confidently declared that the "hereditary" obesity of the Dukes of Parma in the seventeenth century was a sign of organic recession. It is claimed that the "excessive corpulence" of Ranuce Farnèse, born in 1630, made him "unfit to govern," and so on through to Antoine Farnèse, who died in 1732 without an heir, supposedly because of his "extraordinary corpulence."[35] There is also Cesare Lombroso whose interminable search into the physical anthropology of "born criminals" does not neglect to list weight among the "degenerative" signs of criminals and prostitutes. With quasi-numerical precision, he affirms that their average weight is higher than the norm and, what's more, most of them become with age "enormously overweight" to the point of being "true polysarcous monsters."[36]

The theme of degeneration, which was present in the turn-of-the-century mind to the point of becoming a haunting obsession, inevitably crossed the path of obesity.

The Explosion of Diets

There is a multiplicity of new cases that draw attention at the end of the century and a corresponding number of new treatments are developed in response. There is an insistence on the necessity of different approaches to "flabby" (atonique) obesity and "vigorous" obesity, for example, and between those "predisposed" to obesity and those who are not. There is also greater reliance on chemistry's discriminating capabilities. For example, the advice to conduct "early analysis of urine samples" in order to better detect other factors within the obese individual relating to urea, lymphatism, gout, or anemia.[37] Pathological profiles are more numerous, and so are the propositions for treatment.

The writings in the last decades of the century have the most to say about overcoming excess eating. Reducing calories, reducing sugars and fats, and watching what one drinks. This is evidence of an overall increase in body care. Profiles become more distinct and diet proposals become more diversified. Lewis Worthington describes four in his 1877 treatise on obesity.[38] Paul Le Gendre lists eight in the article "Obesity," in Jean-Marie Charcot's Traité de médecine (1891).[39] Adrien Proust and Adolphe Mathieu offer thirteen in the Hygiène de l'obèse (1897).[40] The variety on offer increases steadily, but the most famous diet of the day remains that of William Banting, a sixty year-old English businessman. In the early 1860s he published a short pamphlet detailing how, by eliminating certain specific foods, he was able to overcome his "distressing" obesity.[41] He says he strictly obeyed the recommendations of chemists—elimination of sugars and carbohydrates—and a strict eye on proteins—lean meat and grilled fish. William Banting reports losing 46 pounds in one year having started at 202 pounds (for a height of five foot five, 1.65 m).

Equally important, the diets are graded in severity according to the severity of the obesity to be treated. The precision of degrees of obesity naturally required corresponding invention of degrees of severity for the cures. Adrien Proust and Adolphe Mathieu suggest thresholds of which the most severe is 1,250 calories—half the daily amount judged "normal."[42] There are now progressions, stages, and levels which all lead to new forms of attention, especially the awareness of the "gnawing sensation of hunger" during the treatment,[43] the fight against obstacles, and the discouragement. Tactics are invented that are supposed to help one cope better with these diets, which are becoming standardized: "small frequent meals," "favoring salads," the occasional drinking of a "tonic" cup of tea or a bowl of light broth.[44]

In addition, there are the happy testimonials of successful treatments of cases "where the polysarcia is caused by nothing other than a vicious exaggerated alimentation."[45] Paul Le Gendre reports weight losses of nearly 25 kilos in a few months;[46] he insists on changes in behavior—becoming active again and regaining vivacity. William Banting lists the improvements in his health beyond the simple recovery of physical lightness. "My sight has come back and I can hear better. My other indispositions are a thing of the past."[47] Zola's friends speak of a changed attitude subtly summarized by Karin Becker. "He is discovering a new joy in living thanks to his rejuvenated body. He cycles, he has taken up photography, and has had amorous relations with the servant Jeanne who is going to bear him two children."[48]

Is this a double emancipation for Zola when it comes to women and physical initiatives? By the end of the century, the cure has become an object of exploration as well as the focus of storytelling. And its success offers quasi-psychological benefits.

Rather more complex, inevitably, are the treatments proposed for those suffering from "atavistic" obesity. The prognosis remains opaque. Certain treatises affirm that the "true obesity" of adults, which "comes on progressively in its most severe form, is not curable."[49] This of course has an effect on the hope of the patient. The evil is central, the deficit all-encompassing, and thus necessitates a "modification of the constitution."[50] This in turn provokes a proliferation of demands to "stimulate the overall vitality and tone up the entire organism."[51] The means proposed refer to the nerves, cells, the blood, and to the liver that some experiments proved had "burning" capabilities.[52] There are also references to "reconstituants, iron, quinine, and bitters,"[53] the use of excitants, the importance of red blood cells, and the multiplication of practices and treatments. The body of the "atavistic obese" is to be solicited and excited so as to steadily improve its burning capacity.[54] The techniques include massage, hydrotherapies, showers, exercises, the application of cold, trips to the mountains and to the sea. The invention of all these practices is part of the nineteenth century's steadily increased investment, for a growing number of people, in various stimulations, changes of air, vacationing, and voyages.

Attention to the body's insides, its balances and chemical compositions, leads to further diversification of diet programs during the 1880s. Investigations into glands, their removal studied in animals, and the presence or absence of their fluids demonstrate a brusque appearance of symptoms that had until then been little noticed. Knowledge about the role of the thyroid, in particular, is completely revised. Its absence in certain animals and humans allows one to observe at once a very particular excess of fat (mucin), accompanied by weakness and debility as well as swelling of the face and skin—a condition known as myxedema or hypothyroidism, a "heavy" illness described for the first time by William Ord in 1878.[55] Confirmation came from the inverse procedure. The mutilating condition could be erased with regular injections of "thyroïdine," an extract of the "normal" gland. This led to a number of adventurous treatments. The *Journal de la beauté* recommends it to readers in 1897, especially thyroid extracts from "sheep or calves" carefully prepared by pharmacists.[56] A few years later, more care was taken, including the recommendation to "avoid thyroïdine."[57] Accidents had happened, unexpected troubles, and failures. But the importance of these attempts and the new vision of the body that emerged is undeniable. The body was now seen as an organism regulated by an interior milieu whose balance needed to be discovered, an organism where the glands and the nervous system combined were part of the "indispensable stimulating principles that contributed to a perfect nutrition."[58] It's a new type of physical "piloting" that becomes evident, now with particular attention to secretions, an awareness about the contribution of the glands, including the "thyroid, ovaries, testicles, and pituitary gland,"[59] a watchfulness about chemical balances, with a new distinction between those provoked by foods and those provoked by the "interior milieu." The certainty of the Paris medical school professors at the beginning of the twentieth century is characteristic: "The more we study nutritional problems, the more we become convinced of the preponderant role played by internal secretions."[60]

Exercise also is completely renovated to fit fin de siècle thinking. Numbers and precision once again are all-important. Joseph Ortel prescribes two hours of morning walking on an empty stomach—and at an intensity level sufficient to "tone up" the heart.[61] The cure of "getting outside," perhaps to do one of several loops of differing lengths and difficulties, became popular in the 1880s, especially in Germany and Switzerland. The walkers would have detailed maps with the distances and uphill sections marked to indicate "flat" or "steep," "long" or "short."[62] This in turn could provoke new difficulties, since exercise "increases appetite,"[63] thus making the diet more difficult to put up with for the patient—not to mention the increased effort and therefore possible threat to the heart.

Oxygen and combustion remain throughout the central tenets of all these "theories" that rely on convictions about fire.

The Socializing and Chemistry of Spa Life

Therapeutic interest in spas or "balneology" becomes important in the second half of the nineteenth century as part of a major transformation of the knowledge and habits of a wide swath of the middle class.[64] Chemistry developed the analysis of waters, spa towns invested extensively in their amenities, and railroad lines made getting to them much easier. These "open air" sites with their greenery and gurgling waters lent themselves to the development of scientific regimens that led to dreams of total physical transformation and restoration of health. Formerly pursued as both a social pastime and casual body care, spa life now becomes a place of study and experimentation as well. Knowledge expands and a multitude of claims are put forward to establish ever more specific benefits of particular spring waters for particular types of maladies. Individuals with different types of obesity, for example, are directed toward the waters most suited for their condition—the "lymphatic" to waters that "tone up" and the heavy eaters to laxative waters.

Thermal spas become specialized. For example, Marienbad and Carlsbad in Germany were said to have purgative waters and were "recommended for those with engorged livers and out-sized abdomens"—a "pathology" judged very common in Germany according to a French guide.[65] In France, Châtelguyon in central France specialized in the "laxative medicalization,"[66] while Brides specialized in "oxidation of the blood." In the 1870s, Émile Philbert, the vice president of the Paris Society for Medical Hydrology, founded a special obesity cure in Brides in the French Alps that "attracted more patients every year."[67] The Paris doctor advertises his regimen extensively, observing and codifying "purgatives, sudation, food lists, and physical exercise" and making daily use of weight charts.[68]

A particular type of care develops at these specialized spa sites, and many testimonies recount its regularity and rigor. The scheduling of particular program elements over several weeks, the prescription of diets, baths, body rubs with friction gloves, massages with soap, cold compresses on the belly, and walks of varying length and difficulty.[69] The fight against obesity is the center of every instant of the day, with most attention accorded to calories and combustion. The increased marketing of these services leads to a multiform specialization of types of care, times, and locations.

The humorous observations in an 1885 issue of *Charivari* make fun of the apparent contradictions that could arise, in this case around the supposed benefits of the waters of Stilba in Corsica. A man says he's leaving "for the waters of Stilba" because he senses the "early stages of obesity," but his mother-in-law is going too "because she suffers from consumption" (*étisie*, extreme thinness).[70] That this can be the punch line of a joke shows the extent to which spa going had grown ordinary as well as how attentive people had become to early and all changes in size. The spa town of Vichy, whose waters were claimed to combat "anomalies of nutrition,"[71] had 2,543 visitors in 1840, 40,000 in 1860, and 100,000 in 1890.[72] Évian, another increasingly popular spa destination, had to entirely redesign itself at the end of the century to accommodate the crowds—building new rail platforms, wider boulevards, a new underground water pipe system, and, of course, more and bigger hotels. The following excerpt, giving an account in rather abstract language of a "medical study trip" undertaken in 1901, insists on the spa's effects on all of the digestive processes. "These osmotic materials aid in completing and activating the organic life, resulting in better respiration, oxidations, assimilations, and cellular discharges, as well as facilitating the breakdown of organic wastes and their elimination, and the solubility of used matter."[73]

Digestive malfunction and the correction of excess eating are the dominant themes in the world of balneology. The "water drinker" represented in the *Physiologies parisiennes* in 1887 is the big eater in search of a new equilibrium. "It is generally a Parisian who has gone on a binge and then retires for three or four weeks to a watering hole situated near some Alpine village or peak in the Pyrenees.[74] The "simplistic" idea of draining the body with some purifying water is the subtle suggestion in many of these enthusiastic initiatives that promote water springs, green meadows, and foreign air. The therapeutic action aims at easing assimilation and digestion, and is expected to work wonders for the skin, rheumatism, excess weight, and the nerves. Multiple positive effects from a single line of action designed, in the language of balneology, to treat "indolent engorgements and obstructions of the viscera of the abdomen."[75]

The Ascendancy of Advertisers

Advertising campaigns in the second half of the nineteenth century further confirm the development of slimming practices and their marketing to the public.[76] Many of these campaigns get started in the 1880s and take a very direct, succinct line.

> Persian Pills: to lose weight while strengthening one's health, a two-month treatment suffices to eliminate all excess weight in both sexes.[77]

A doctor generally associates his name with the product, thereby guaranteeing a certain notability, unlike the "secret formulas" of former times. Thus there are "Doctor Blyn's Persian Pills," "Doctor Smith's Hindu tea," etc.[78] The products vary: pills, potions, baths, belts, corsets. Some traditional ideas continue to exert an influence, as with references to "drying out" or "toning up."

Some allusions to smells and odors may lend an additional persuasiveness. Thus the "Gigartina pills" come from sea algae, Brahms water is perfumed with "Bengal flowers," and the "Ismaël belt" is "composed of aromatic plants."[79] Some references to physical features are added as well in keeping with the "anatomic" gaze of the fin de siècle. Thus "Beautygène tea" is supposed to "reduce the hips, slim the belly, and produce a fine, svelte waist."[80] The "anonymous" product that the Chardon pharmacy in the rue Saint-Lazare in Paris wants to bring to the attention of its customers is supposed to "reduce the belly and hips, slim the waist, and erase double chins."[81] The treatments are as simple as possible: pills, drinks, and belts. The results "certified," "sure and rapid," "a sure success."[82] The rhetoric plays on images and words, such as contrasting pictures showing the big person "before" and the thin person "after," and uses declarations that combine promises with guarantees such as "wonder water," "a truly infallible method," or the maintenance of "eternal youth and firm flesh."[83]

All these exclamations are rushed and intuitive, of course; but their very existence demonstrates the steady emergence of a weight loss market at the end of the nineteenth century as well as the stubborn resistance of traditional notions. The advertising also insists on the abbreviated side of the diets, which are themselves slimmed down to the barest outline: the recourse to magical elixirs. It also reveals the relatively select population pursuing these practices. The products vary in price from between five and twenty francs in the 1880s, a time when the average worker's daily wages were between five and six francs.[84] It also underlines the persistence of traditional ideas that expect slimming to result from the simplest actions.

18. The Thin Revolution

Silhouettes became thinner in the second half of the nineteenth century, and treatments for obesity become more numerous. The multiplication of pastimes, the new attention to the self, and the revolution in medical knowledge were all factors. One important change that is totally decisive takes place in the 1920s and is the outcome not of new knowledge but new habits. The transformation of the status of women brings with it a new thinness—an avoidance of references to breasts and other curves—and a new technically inspired imaginary that insists on fluidity, reactivity, agility, and lankiness. There is also a heightened expectation of control and affirmation of the self. A plain affirmation repeated more than once in Jean Prévost's *Essay on the Human Body* (1925) sums up this new attitude: "Our bodies are mostly muscle."[1] The "athletic" look, with its coordinated lines, is for the first time the norm.[2] It is certainly the case that the body of the 1920s is evoked differently than before. Its dynamic quality takes on an all-new importance. "Only muscle is noble."[3] Muscle tone is hinted at in the static pose, movement is implicit in the curves. Of course this also holds true for the female body, the interminable descriptions of which underline its "straight suppleness," the "serpentine allure," and the "spring in the derriere."[4] The presence of muscle is not a sudden discovery. Its role, however, is entirely rethought, deliberate, and "ennobled." All thinking about fat is concerned: the thresholds being attained earlier, the dangers underlined more. The body of the 1920s is quite simply the herald of today's body.

Another change that emerges are the stronger doubts as to whether certain types of obesity can be successfully treated. A number of cases seem to lead toward the "martyr." The introduction of this new "gravity" also prepares questions that persist today.

The "Defect of Civilization"

The social conscience of bigness changes in the 1920s. Adiposity is suddenly more present in everyday life. Images of the day prove it. Workers and peasants that appear in caricatures of the periodicals *Le Canard enchaîné*, *Rire*, or *L'Illustré national* show a capacity for stoutness that had formerly been "reserved" for the wealthy. The "poor," who had traditionally been represented as half-starved, suddenly acquire a physical volume they didn't have before. The drawings of Albert Dubout from the early 1930s feature many working-class fat people with floating breasts, bellies out of control, and sagging chins. The *Port of Marseille*, which was drawn by the artist at the same time, offers the most vivid example.[5] The stiffness and the neckties of the distinguished silhouettes contrast with the slack appearance and open-necked shirts of the ordinary workers, but the voluminous flesh and fattiness are distributed among the two groups. The ample abdomen is more democratically shared. Consuming and overeating are becoming more widespread as social phenomena.

Certain statistics make this very clear. The CSIR (International Scientific Commission on Nourishment) decrees the ideal consumption of meat and dairy products as "75 grams per day per person of average size" and then gives the actual figures for different countries vis-à-vis this threshold.[6] Germany, England, and France pass above this threshold in the new century, reporting respectively 126 g, 120 g, and 86 g during the period 1909–1913. The higher norms of these three indicate "a radical change in food consumption"[7]—the percentage of proteins and sugars from animals is higher than that coming from vegetables, signaling a more "rich" and "adipose" diet.

Commentaries especially change at this time. In 1913 Georges d'Avenel claims there is a "leveling of pleasures" and an "ease" of nourishment for ever greater numbers of people.[8] In 1930, Francis Heckel claims to see a "defect of civilization" in the alterations of morphologies resulting from the various abuses and disorders provoked by the comforts of technology,[9] the wide diffusion of machines, and surplus nourishment. And the "evil" has spread. "Peasants and working class people are beginning to suffer from maladies that earlier provoked the physical decline of the wealthy and the nobility. Gout, obesity, diabetes, arteriosclerosis, neurasthenia, angina, brain hemorrhages, and paralyses were formerly reserved for the masters. Today they occur among factory workers, servants, and peasants in equally high numbers."[10]

The new situation is that the entire population is now concerned. Another new contributing factor is the "predictable fattening up of automobilists,"[11] given the augmented sedentariness of sitting in cars. All these changes are characterized as "vital perversions."[12] An alert goes out to "civilized man" that denounces bingeing and excess. As a part of this alert, one notices at the beginning of the twentieth century a sudden increase in the number of comparisons that praise "primitives" for the frugality that has preserved them versus the "civilized" whose abuses have deformed them—a total inversion of the earlier hierarchy. A distinct "naturism" emerges in the 1920s that spreads through popular teachings, sports, and pastimes.[13] A certain strident militancy against fat develops as well.

The Dashing Slender Male

Inevitable questions remain. Vague impressions without statistical support of there being more fat people among the driving classes or the working classes don't provoke new expectations for thinness so much as they are its effect.[14] As the denunciation of fat increases, tolerance decreases and the fat person seems all the more present and all the more omnipresent—a sight causing sore eyes.

These changed attitudes derive from alterations in daily perceptions, especially the reorientation of the idea of efficiency and vivacity. The 1909 "Futurist Manifesto" boldly asserts that "a roaring automobile that seems to run on machine-gun fire is more beautiful than the Victory of Samothrace."[15] Paradoxically, it is the world of technology and not nature that transforms the image of the body by enlivening it. The former is a universe of "power and flexible performances" thanks to various machines where functionality and output count.[16] These criteria, in turn, transform practices and make speed and adaptability ever more important. This new tension rewards certain virtuosities that tend to definitively privilege the active and slender.[17] At the same time, there is a corresponding denunciation of the weak and sedentary. The head of employment in Henri Béraud's 1922 novel Le Martyre de l'obèse symbolizes this attitude. He eliminates every job candidate at the slightest hint of stoutness. "Come back after you've lost some weight. We need active men not bloated mice."[18] The American model where one can be fired for any "decrease in output" also gets the point across clearly.[19]

Male fashions in the 1920s adopt these criteria as well, privileging an active look and tightened forms.[20] A multitude of American advertising campaigns affirm these triumphant values by featuring suits with tapered lines.[21] The *Catalogue de la Manufacture de Saint-Étienne* for 1924 features the "double-breasted suit,"[22] a style that is not very wearable by fatter men. Trimmer cut shirts associated with nature and sports also become more popular,[23] and put an end to the ample, flowing style that had been preferred before.[24] There is now a systematic refusal of anything that floats or curves too much, and this explains the obese protagonist in Henri Béraud's novel who declares, "Modern clothes are the enemy."[25]

The Dashing Slender Female

A second cultural shakeup takes place at the beginning of the twentieth century around the image of the female body. The description of Vinca in Colette's 1925 novel *Le Blé en herbe* is a decisive symptom. The allusions to the "thin well-turned spindles" of the young woman are part of a clear insistence on a silhouette of a new type, one that imposes the "line" as the single tenet that dictates all contours.[26] Everything changed in only a few years. The dynamic replaced the static, the straight replaced the curved. The overthrow is total. What's in are long legs, a tapered waist, and a lanky torso. The former *S* profile, with its supple undulation that accentuated the gentle bends of the bust and loins as they cambered and curved, gives way to the *I* profile that insists on a systematic lengthening of physical features and clothing.

The change occurred during the years 1910–1920. The traditional corset that accentuated a cambered look is phased out in favor of resolutely elongated forms, especially a narrow line and "no waist."[27] This gives thinness an entirely new meaning far from the old connotations of delicate and fragile. The narrow has metamorphosed. Stretching and slimming lend a decisive new particularity to the female body, which now rejects contours judged too "mammary" and favors linear physiques that privilege agility and movement. This wiry body mobilizes a culture and especially a manner to single out a woman who occupies public space more than ever—a woman existing "outside" as she both participates more in the work world and enjoys the great outdoors.[28] A major change is this perception of the activity and availability that being thin and narrow make possible. Victor Margueritte's 1922 novel *La Garçonne* symbolizes the movement that triumphs in magazines of the 1920s, playing with masculine codes and entirely transforming the look of hair, hips, and profile. The figure grows ever thinner as the "stunning success" of her will for mobility and emancipation advances.[29]

This provokes a further and even more profound change. The physical form is no longer defined by "flesh" but by "muscle." Fat and thin are now also contrasted via textures and the tactile. The curving contour is now associated with firmness rather than creamy smoothness. It signals the sculpted and marks the tense but real borderline beyond which lies the fat. A shapely dryness is the right thinness.[30] "To be supple, adroit, and harmonious one must have regularly exercised muscles."[31] Colette's Vinca is a good example, with her "long thigh muscles" and "discrete muscles."[32] Another example is Montherlant's character Mademoiselle de Plémeur, in *Les Olympiques* (1924), who languishes between thin and fat from the moment she lacks exercise—"I saw the fat come back and my muscles stiffen up."[33] There is a new profile, which *Vogue* clearly specified around this same time. "The svelte athletic silhouette, the limbs fine and muscular without any lingering fat, an energetic open figure—this is today the ideal of feminine beauty."[34]

This model can be replicated all the more easily and on a large scale thanks to the new information technologies of the day—magazines, cinema, and advertising in the 1920s reach new audiences, multiply their impact, and industrialize their procedures.[35] Communication spreads, standards are made, unified, and become familiar on their way to being turned into a market where a rapidly growing middle class will be invited to circulate.[36]

The "Graduated" Anatomy

These important changes derive from social changes, it should be recalled, more than from any type of "medical pressure."[37] They are so pervasive that anatomists in the 1920s inaugurate a totally new field of research. Weight gain is no longer merely the subject of anecdotes and becomes an object of rigorous study that seeks systematic knowledge of its stages and progressions, much as geologists record findings about sediments and minerals. Forms of heaviness are, little by little, converted into diagrams.

These investigations are so methodical that they review and in some ways reconnect with the earliest established thresholds. For example, the case of "loosening" studied by Louis Chauvois in 1923 where fattening stems from skinniness itself due to the "lamentable muscular thinness" that provokes a sagging "below the navel."[38] There is the idea of a new sort of fat—the "compact" aspect of the "muscled person" is claimed to trigger obesity, starting with the "sacklike" belly of a skinny person caused by the collapse of all body tone.[39]

The systematic study of phases is also new. In 1920 Paul Richer classifies differences in the buttocks, thighs, deltoid area, and pelvis area and works them up into charts so as to fill a void neglected, in his view, by traditional anatomy.[40] The same year George Hébert statistically analyzes their gradations: the three degrees of chubbiness of the neck, the two degrees of swelling of the face, the three stages of sagging breasts, etc.[41] The categories of possible disorders are also extended and detailed: "a belly swollen in all directions," "ball-like round low belly," "a hanging sagging belly," "a belly that becomes progressively a hanging belly."[42] And, inversely, degrees of lankiness are also specified: short lined, medium lined, long lined.[43] Some combinations become nearly incomprehensible due to the multiplication of details, which begin to lose much of their sense. Their mere presence, however, is proof that this new attention to morphologies is keener than ever before.

The Creation of the "Monstrous"

Degrees of obesity are revolutionized.[44] The extension of phases became systematized during the 1920s. This also changes the image of the "ultimate" obesity, which is now more precisely specified, but sometimes takes on the curious cast of a specter without limit, a state of monstrosity that the realism of photography displays as a tragedy with flesh falling to the ground, unbelievable belts, and disproportioned navels.[45] The anatomies of these extreme cases are no longer just strange or unusual; they've become so surprising that a mask is sometimes placed over the face of the subject photographed to protect the person's identify . . . and humanity. All the varying degrees are rethought. The old treatises that limited their attention to "the very fat" are updated.[46] Judgment and its "cursor" have been moved; the focus of worry is now "the fat," and this tips "the very fat" into a tragic extremity.

Over the previous few decades, moreover, the badge of bigness was no longer derived from the world of the fat but associated with that of the monstrous. Extremely misshapen anatomies had become little more than examples of the "grotesque," curiosities presented from behind curtains at fairs, like in the peep shows described by Jules Vallès at the end of the nineteenth century. "The public enters, the attraction rises. . . . You go in, you go out, that's it."[47] Jules Vallès describes the case of "Grassot," glimpsed in a peep show in Paris: "an enormous mass of flesh that looked so unalert one hesitated to think of it as living."[48] Some examples of extreme anatomical heaviness are scrupulously reported at the end of the nineteenth century and presented as symbols of "abnormality." For example, there was Miss Conley, who was exhibited in a traveling circus in America. She weighed almost 300 kilos and had lost the ability to turn over in bed unaided. There was the Parisian café owner who attracted the curious around Notre Dame because he sat on three chairs simultaneously before a bar that had been specially designed to accommodate his corpulence. And there was the 300-kilo young woman who died in Plaisance in 1890. She had agreed to appear in a fair the year before, but, despite the efforts of eight men, was unable to "extract herself" from her room.[49]

Postcards also exploit the monstrosity theme. There is the image of Cannon, for example, which circulated at the end of the nineteenth century: "the heaviest man in the world" is shown crushing a scale before spectators who appear "minuscule" in comparison. And there is Mademoiselle Térésina, another woman in a carnival sideshow, whose monstrous folds of flesh are rendered even more disconcerting by a vaguely erotic pose.[50] Continuity with the merely big is erased. The existence of the "very" big is nothing but a gross error, its appearance nothing more than "monstrosity."

This rupture is, without a doubt, somewhat dated. It asserts itself the moment norms become strongly uniform, the moment when mass society erases old regional differences and the brusque acceleration of all types of communication turns the local "shagginess" that had long been tolerated into "strange oddities." Fairs and carnivals then expose those things that have become "phenomena." They exhibit the "abnormal." A practice that quite simply "has as its goal the propagation of a bodily norm."[51] And this dynamic is reinforced when this same norm is strongly sharpened at the end of the nineteenth century. The game in the sideshow consists in juxtaposing the fattest person with the thinnest or the tallest with the shortest.[52] The spectator thus feels more what "must" be when witnessing what clearly represents necessity's extreme betrayal. The spectator is thus confronted all the more with an "elsewhere."

Starting in the 1920s the rupture widens; a surge of compassion leads to considering anatomical infirmities quite differently. Looking at them only evokes suffering, and they are viewed only as figures of the unbearable. All the norms' strictures created "monstrous obesities" that are totally alien from the universe of the "acceptable."[53] Their reality belongs exclusively to science—no longer to the curious visitor to the amusement park. The "gaze police" shunts them aside,[54] and public amusement turns elsewhere. Obesity cases declare themselves at earlier ages, and bigness is the more worrisome as it becomes more familiar in daily life. But extreme bigness tips toward the unviewable and the unnameable and is abandoned to the exclusive view of the scientist. The "big" are seen to emerge earlier in various discreet forms, while the "extreme" can no longer be seen at all.

19. Declaring "the Martyr"

The specter that rises up in the 1920s behind the increasingly sophisticated weight charts influences the development of a corresponding haunting prospect surrounding pathologies. Obesity's gradations develop, as do its evils. Medical concern changes its tone and embraces the new culture of thinness. Publications of the day show this through their insistence not just on evaluating bigness but on tactics that will guarantee weight loss. *How to Lose Weight, Why Lose Weight? Why We Get Fat—How to Lose Weight, The Art of Losing Weight*, etc.[1] "Weight loss" becomes the priority to the point of imposing a new injunction during the years 1920–1930: "Weight Loss at Any Cost."[2]

This has the effect of displacing the former stigmatizations. No longer the glutton or the oaf, the overweight person is above all now the sneaky one who dodges the order to slim down and refuses to work on himself. His flaw is neglect, his intimate inattention a dereliction of duty. His passions attract less notice than his indifference; he's less culpable for getting carried away than for lack of control, the impossibility of self regulating and transforming oneself.

Failure takes a new shape, one reinforced by the generalization of treatment and the increased significance of psychology. Narratives of suffering multiply, just as self-evaluations, self-descriptions, and intimate memoirs in contemporary culture become increasingly common. The prestigious place accorded to the thin doubles the stigmatization of the fat. The obese are not just fat people but people who cannot change—thus an identity of defeat is stuck to them at a time when working on oneself and adaptability become obligatory criteria of value. Obesity declares a manifest failure to reform oneself.

Revolutionizing the First Degrees

One of the original aspects of 1920s culture was to seek out the fat person in unobservable troubles, in imperceptible conflicts that accumulated within the silence of the body. The very use of the word *obesity* changes at this time in response to the view that it was being used "too late" to designate phases that were "too advanced."[3] This won't do at a time when the fat person is thought to lurk behind an unassuming appearance[4]—when it's considered an invisible presence, a secret mass, hidden within the flesh, there where the form of the body's features comes not from muscle but from fat.

All new "intermediate" phases also take on significance. "Cellulite," for example, with its "padding," offers to the touch the idea of an "orange rind" or the appearance of "marquetry" that signals an early stage of fatness.[5] Invention is important during the 1920s as part of the intense renewal of the demand for form. It becomes important to uncover formerly ignored anatomies and to turn into objects of contemplation those nuances that the eye for a long time had already distinguished. Debates arise about the causes of these discreet deformities. Does inflammation of the skin develop simply from the infiltration of fat? Is stiffening due to some resistance opposed to fatty textures? Are superficial deposits the sign of incompletely eliminated wastes? Such questions linger as cellulite and the associated veining are increasingly discussed. The imaginary develops, combining classic fat disorders to those judged more specifically feminine. "Sedentariness, extended time spent in tiring positions, neuro-arthritus, marriage trauma [*traumatisme conjugal*], and among virgins trouble with the rhythm of utero-ovarian circulation and hormonal secretions."[6] Cellulite is long the focal point of aesthetic anxieties about skin imperfections, the early signs of weight gain, and all other symptoms of precocious obesity.

It's impossible not to notice the extent to which traditional views were upended at the beginning of the twentieth century. The doctor no longer has to evoke some caricatured infirmity to incite worried concern;[7] he only has to mention the early phases, the first signs of weight gain that aren't "normal." It's not that thinness is being valorized for the first time.

The change is not a sudden turnaround from a rejected slenderness to a praised slenderness, but a long evolution of the gaze that leads to the new manner of triggering unease on the basis of signs that didn't exist before and of redefining thinness in relation to fluidity and tone.

The Multiplication of Pathologies

The more pronounced suspicions around fat lead to a reinterpretation of the related pathologies, starting with the nearly unutterable problems associated with "small obesity" that quietly trouble the sensibilities: "bloating, acid stomach, heart burn, diarrhea."[8]

Worries and studies grow apace. The pathology becomes more general and unites the classic maladies of "shortness of breath, poor circulation, and digestive troubles" with numerous other disorders of various sorts.[9] There is intoxication, for example, which recalls the internal infection associated with visions of badly processed waste. Also cancer, which, according to the explanatory models of the time,[10] was thought to come from "parasitical" accumulations.[11] The sole presence of adiposity is considered noxious: "Chronic poisoning," "brain poisoning," "excess toxins and organic poisons."[12] A new vision comes gradually into focus at the beginning of the century—the idea that the threat comes no longer just from heaviness, the mass weighing down the organism, but from an internal pollution, the spread of this deleterious substance—fat.

One result is the endless and wide discussion of chemical processes, unassimilable fats, and their dangers. It is also an occasion to renew old cultural oppositions as well. For example, the criticism of "big" Germans by some French experts in 1917 as part of research into what they called "ethno-chemistry."[13] They claimed their neighbors east of the Rhine exhibited an "abnormally overactive intestinal function," with consequences for their internal acidity and exhalation; i.e., the alleged "stinky breath of the German race" is stigmatized by the French savants' hatred.[14]

The psychological dimension is invoked more than ever before with other possible exaggerations. A number of markers are posited that differentiate the "excited plethorics" from the "depressed anemics."[15] These juxtapositions of "anxious faces" and "dull faces,"[16] for example, are all psychological versions of older moral categorizing. One example would be the caricatured view of Édouard Herriot after his term as *Conseil* president in 1924 as being a victim of "the fat person's mentality." It is an extreme interpretation that illustrates how bigness had been turned into a general evil. "An erudite grammarian, honest but weakened by ill health and lack of judgment, he shared some of the responsibility for the collapse of the franc, the secret inflation, Alsatian autonomy, the exploitation of small savers, religious intolerance, the dishonorable recognition of the Soviets."[17]

More serious are the statistics about obesity-related mortality that make a sudden appearance at the beginning of the century, first in North America then in Europe. Insurance companies in particular are behind this initiative. Starting in the 1910s, American issuers of life insurance categorize policyholders according to eight levels ranging from 12 kilos underweight to 23 kilos overweight. Their chart is not directly applied in France, but it is adapted by popular magazines that make the ideas behind the progressions, degrees, and numbers more widely known.[18] The Metropolitan Life Insurance company refines their numbers and degrees in 1922, claiming, for example, that mortality is 30 percent higher than average among men 20 percent overweight who measure 1.70 m and are between forty and forty-four years old. It is said to be 80 percent higher for individuals in the same height and age group who are 40 percent overweight. In general, longer life expectancy is promised to people with lower than average weight, so long as it's a moderate deficit that doesn't fall into "skinniness."[19]

The Multiplication of Therapies

With the extension of scales, pathologies, and the sophisticated calculation of risks, the vision of obesity by the 1920s approximates our contemporary views. The fat person is both an aesthetic threat and a health risk. And he or she is both these things from the earliest stages of barely perceptible signs. As a result, therapeutic proposals become more numerous, diverse, and widely available.

First of all, the scale becomes standard equipment. "A constant guide, an imperturbable judge."[20] The tool again changed shape—now lowered and fitted with a horizontal magnifying glass that enlarged the needle and number dial. American advertisers in the 1920s are the first to propose it "for those wishing to lose weight scientifically."[21] The scale is "artistic," practical, and gives everyone the chance to use it in one step.[22] It quickly gains its place in France as well. At the end of the 1920s the magazine *Fémina* insists that "the compact scale is to be found in every well-ordered bathroom."[23] It's recommended for daily use—"an inseparable part of one's morning bathroom routine."[24] There are also a growing number of public personal scales such that, by the mid-1920s, 500 million weighings per year are recorded on them in the United States alone.[25]

Therapeutic practices intensify the use of scales as well as recourse to daily tracing of "barygraphic" curves. The major goal is to follow the results obtained step-by-step and fine-tune one's diet according to changes in the curve—thus, in effect, transforming eating into a scientific experiment. Over the course of hypotheses, tests, and reorientations, the diet becomes a guiding narrative, a long-term adventure with its expectations, surprises, and twists of fate.

> Weighing patients during the treatment at different moments, at rest and during physical activity, when food intake is restrained in variety and quantity; weighing them again to measure the effects of all attempted practices; following day to day, even sometimes hour to hour, the variations in their weight during these experiments— these procedures are not beyond the abilities of a good observer, if he is patient, tenacious, and has at his disposal a large amount of information.[26]

Beyond dieting, a large cohort of practices get started, with their specialists and their clearly defined techniques, thus confirming the definitively pathological status of obesity and the definitive existence of an obesity treatment market. Anti-obesity services become more professional. There are specific massages, "superficial" and "deep"; "light touch," "vibrations," and "tappings";[27] even "massage under water,"[28] a specialty at Vichy, and "self-massage" recommended as a regular activity.[29] Then there are gymnastics—from "global" exercises to "abdominal" exercises all designed to "prevent obesity forever."[30] There is also an ever wider array of specialized physical agents: electricity (electrotherapy), the sun (heliotherapy), heat (thermotherapy), showers and baths (hydrotherapy), and machines and passive movement (mechanotherapy).[31] Obesity receives enormous attention from technical and body care experts. There are even adventurous "grafts" attempted in the 1920s by Serge Voronoff who implanted extracts of monkey and billy goat testicles with the idea of reversing symptoms of swelling and anemia. There is the notable case of the retired English government official suffering from "obesity and general sagging" who in 1924 allegedly became thin and statuesque after being grafted with "baboon testicles." "The fat melted, the muscles became firm, the body straightened."[32] The procedure did not catch on, but it shows the extent to which body care had become wide-ranging and experimental.

The true originality of the new treatments lies elsewhere, however, and has to do with the new vision of the progressive stages one undergoes over an extended period and their association with a whole gamut of new sorts of projects at the beginning of the twentieth century that all aim at personal development, work on oneself, and personal training. The goal: "to accomplish every day and without great fatigue an amount of work greater than the day before."[33] The treatments are also accompanied by a new literature promoting "self-reliance" and "self-confidence,"[34] detailing how to "become stronger" and "make one's way in life."[35] Their priority is clear: to develop a person in a society facing greater equality and competition. A large part of the population applies these precepts in various ways, finding in them a way to "brace themselves" and work on themselves so as to progress better in life. This is the reality of a world overtaken by services, scales, grades, positions, and promotions in a hierarchy the conscientious employee sets out to conquer step-by-step.

Indoor exercise becomes so popular at this time that a Danish book on the subject published in 1904, *My System: 15 Minutes Exercise a Day for Health's Sake*, sells 21,000 copies in its first French edition in 1905, then another 40,000 copies of a fourth edition in 1908, and 376,000 copies the same year in a dozen European countries The author, J. P. Muller, instantly became one of the world's first fitness gurus.[36]

The Evidence of Therapeutic Failures

There is a paradox however. It is precisely when obesity becomes the object of detailed investigations, when numbers relating to it abound, and different programs and routines to treat it sprout up everywhere, that obesity therapy begins to reveal its limitations. What had been evident is suddenly less so. Treatments as they're studied further become more opaque, not less. Obesity, as it's followed more closely, becomes more "complex." News of failure, formerly neglected, spreads. The suffering of the obese person is heard for the first time.

A turning point is the discovery of an innovative theoretical instrument, basal metabolism, in a New England laboratory at the end of the nineteenth century. Wilber Olin Atwater, Francis Gano Benedict, and Edward Bennett Rosa, researchers at Wesleyan University in Connecticut, set out to perfect Lavoisier's original measuring chamber[37] and build a sophisticated four-by-eight foot steel respiration calorimeter to rigorously measure oxygen intake, carbon dioxide output, and all other fluctuations.[38] Their conclusions are precise: a person placed at rest on an empty stomach in a sealed room that can measure all changes "produces" a measurable quantity of heat, namely, forty calories per square meter per hour—a figure that is roughly constant among "normal" individuals.[39] These experiments provided a unified, measurable calculation of the amount of energy indispensable to maintain the body at rest, known as the basal metabolic rate (BMR) or resting metabolic rate (RMR).[40]

The consequence for the obese seems obvious—it's impossible for many of them to attain this normal condition, victims as they are of the insufficient combustion capability that has resulted in their fatness.[41] This had been alleged for decades according to the theory of the "retarding foods" and sagging energy that characterized anemic obese people hereditarily.

Very quickly, however, metabolic experiments on obese people reveal a surprising fact. The figures obtained "ruin" the theory of combustive weakness.[42] At the end of the 1910s, Marcel Labbé and Henri Stévenin discover a normal metabolic rate among most of the obese subjects studied. Only a small minority have a lower metabolic rate, which they explain as the result of lower endocrine levels (from thyroid problems among other causes) that have slowed combustion.[43] In other words, certain types of fattening must continue to be understood as the effect of excess intake, exactly as with the "forced feeding of geese."[44] Others become more obscure, the results of weaknesses that escape analysis. But lack of fire is no longer a sufficient explanation. How high weight gain could be possible among people leading normally active lives once again becomes mysterious. Obese subjects at rest and on an empty stomach conserved normal combustive force as indicated by their basal metabolic rate; however, for some unknown reason, it was deficient when they ate food. Emotions, rate of eating, general rushing, lack of taste, lack of interest were some of the guesses. Francis Heckel, alerted by some cases of accidents and nervous shocks followed by uncontrollable weight gain, advances the hypothesis of a possible "imbalance of glands and nerves."[45] Marcel Labbé, targeting not combustive force but the obstacles it may encounter, suspects poor diffusion and evaporation through the skin. "Obesity is caused by the inability in certain individuals of getting rid of the excess heat produced by eating due to a malfunction of the skin."[46]

So the idea is that the obese person's "burner" is normal except when faced with food. What exactly the explanations are is less important than their diversity, which all link up to a single irremediable avowal: in some individuals dieting is difficult and gives limited results.

The consequences are major. On the one hand, the existence of a regulating principle that modulates energy—higher or lower—becomes more certain. On the other hand, although the combustive principle and the regulating principle are considered in balanced association as being that which permits increasing or decreasing the energy level based on food availability and needs, what the mechanism is that maintains that balance remains unknown. In 1929 Marcel Labbé sums up the situation with professorial authority: "A regulating mechanism exists, but we don't know what it is."[47] Regulation and deregulation remain rather obscure. It seems as though the fire can be available without being put to use.

Thus obstacles to treatment arise—identifiable but unexplainable—especially unalterable weight gain despite numerous efforts. Certain types of obesity prove resistant to diets, physical therapies, and chemicals. A very particular image of the obese person arises, which is that of a patient whose frustrated expectations symbolize failure. This is not true for all, of course; a number of plethoric people and heavy eaters respond to treatment. However, it is inevitably the case for a growing number of patients as treatments become more widely available. A double vexation arises for these individuals that extends down to today—first, the suffering caused by the difficult acceptance of fat people and, second, the suffering caused by the difficulty of obtaining weight loss.

A new type of health practitioner also emerges—a person whose discourse is far removed from the old certitudes and "simple" gestures and who agrees to accompany the patient through long-term treatment filled with obstacles and even impossibilities.

Between Trial and Martyr

Treatment narratives therefore take on real poignancy. Their increase alone is striking, as is the standard plot line: first fat becoming a dominant preoccupation, then therapy, which becomes either a heroic or tragic adventure, to the point where the treatment becomes the defining focus of a life.

On first glance these narratives display no doubts. Magazines in the 1920s concentrate mostly on the success stories of weight loss by men and women who routinely report how much and how long. "Galton pills allowed me to lose 3 kilos between September 15 and October 20. Since then, I have continued to have remarkable results without having to stop work or any trouble whatsoever."[48]This is typical of the sort of upbeat stories that were more or less solicited by these magazines.

However beyond the feel-good formulas, three totally new story genres emerge in the 1920s that will contribute to define our "modernity."

The first is the story of relentless fixation on subtly discrete signs. For example, the "mutation" of a Berlin Marlene Dietrich into a Hollywood Marlene Dietrich at the end of the 1920s. The comparison is constant, though her body, already lanky, shows off tapered legs and an angular face. There is this frequently repeated affirmation: "I am too fat. . . . I must take more laxatives, drink more coffee and smoke without eating anything else." The remark "I am too fat" becomes more frequent and insistent over time,[49] followed by food "restrictions" and coffee laced with "magnesium sulfate" to stimulate fat burning. There is the added tension of it going on for a long time and always having to begin again. It!—a slimming program organized around the invisible. So begins one of the contemporary forms of dieting: a preoccupation with something that can hardly be seen—slimming as a constant combat, and one given such importance that it can hardly fail to fail.

The second story genre is more complex. It is the narrative of a health practitioner facing a particularly stubborn case of obesity and relating his hesitations and choices. There are discussions of progressively revised calculations, procedures, and experiments and fine-tuning various trial efforts such that the whole treatment turns into a saga of successive episodes. One hears about the effect of different diets, various baths and massages, and combinations of exercise and medications. The doctor's own experience becomes the subject of commentary. He shares his detailed reactions to changes in relation to the weight curve and to any adaptations and adjustments. "I tried various experiments with nearly all my patients during the treatment. . . . Nerve trouble and violent emotions have a particular influence on weight.[50]

The doctor recounts a case history as an adventure overlaid with the unexpected where things are always changing and numerous determining figures and variables enter and exit.

The third story genre consists of the testimony of obese people trying with difficulty to lose weight. Magazines relate these painful experiences, evoking cases of obesity that persist despite much determination and planning. "My chest is fat and falling, I'm 1.70 m tall, and I would never dare wear a bathing suit; I'm desperate."[51] The Goncourt Prize–winner for 1922, *The Martyrdom of the Obese Man* by Henri Béraud, is a prime example of this type of story. Here obesity is as "invincible" as it is plainly visible.

At first, the "evil" does not seem tragic. The "fat person" does not suffer physically. He is neither "incapacitated" nor "tired." He is "enormous" in the eyes of others, perhaps, but not to himself. He is moderately over-weight, in other words, the originality being that this assessment is made by the subject himself.

The plot turns on examples of failed seduction. A long love quest described by the obese man turns tortuous when the woman he yearns for refuses his advances and regularly calls him "my fatty," "my nice fatty," and "my poor fatty."[52] His suffering becomes suddenly more acute when his appearance seems to engender a loss of identity. The otherwise endear-ing attributes of "bonhomie," "ingenious," and "without malice" are reg-istered as harmful misunderstandings of his true self, errors of judgment about how he really is.[53] Physical appearance is lived as a misleading mes-sage. So the narrator seeks to lose weight, tries various diets, undergoes massage, does gymnastics, takes drugs, and visits Turkish baths—all to no effect. Worse, the scale suddenly announces he's reached 100 kilos, thus confirming the undeniable. The novel dramatizes a most painful par-adox: an apparently treatable evil, mentally resolved with ease, persists and resists all treatment.

The pain deepens for another reason as well, namely, the fact that one exhibits a body visibly unchanged, which is prima facie evidence that one is incapable of changing oneself. This is all the more damaging since the practice of slimming had definitively imposed itself as a social priority since the beginning of the twentieth century. The employment director said it all in his imperative to the obese person: "Lose weight!"[54] What's different about the stigmatization now is this pointing out of a lack of work on oneself, a negligence of one's intimate self, and not the old moral-izing. "The obese man is the life of the party, especially when he sets out to lose weight."[55] With the new incapacity comes a new kind of teasing. The flaw turns around an obscure inadequacy—alleged lack of mastery, a crack in one's power over oneself—that becomes significant against a backdrop where losing weight has come to be regarded as "well-adjusted" behavior.

A "progression" in personal testimonies during the modern period is clearly perceptible now when one considers the evidence over a long time span. Jean-Baptiste Élie de Beaumont, one of the first individuals in the eighteenth century to express his personal suffering at being fat, concen-trates on physical difficulties, his sexual impotence, and general insen-sibility.[56] His unhappiness came especially from physical suffering, from feeling weak, and from the wounded pride of not being able to father children. The obese figure in Granville in the middle of the nineteenth century talks more about a relational suffering—about social humiliations, solitude, and a "feeling of disgrace."[57] His unhappiness stems from a rejection he has suffered and from repeated vexations undergone. Henri Béraud's twentieth-century obese man, on the other hand, underlines a more intimate desperation—the impossible satisfaction of a desire judged socially legitimate plus the added difficulty of getting one's true identity properly recognized. It's no longer a question of simple rejection; here feelings are trampled upon, interiority is denied. The unhappiness of this obese person stems from being able to neither seduce nor take pleasure nor be taken for what he truly is. In some ways he is already the archetype of the contemporary individual affirming his singularity. His misfortune, let's repeat, stems from revealing to everybody that he cannot change; he's stuck in a body that everyone considers moldable but that everyone can plainly see is not budging. Between the personal account of Élie de Beaumont and that of Béraud, it is without a doubt the interrogation of the self that has deepened.

With Béraud's generation, the malaise of the obese person undergoes another turn of the screw, this time more stabbing and interior. Condemned to appear different from what he is, the potential for a new failure emerges—that of not being able to reduce the gap between what he is and what he would like to be. His "martyr" feelings grow—all the more since the "uselessness" of dieting strengthens the revolt by reducing his guilty feelings. Instead, the feeling of an unheard of injustice emerges—that of living in a humiliated body that everyone and everything demonstrates to the obese person is not really his body at all but some foreign thing.

This is a central theme that underscores not only the appearance of a new sort of suffering but also how the discourse of obesity has come to be increasingly shaped by self-testimony, interior analysis, and personal narrative. Beyond the old stigmatizations, beyond insults and humiliations, the culture of obesity turns into a narrated commentary of failure and suffering. The growing importance given the subject in Western society inevitably favors the corresponding importance accorded to the victim and humility.

PART 6

CHANGES IN THE CONTEMPORARY DEBATE

An Identity Problem and an Insidious Evil

An entirely new phenomenon shaping all discussions of obesity today is its epidemic status. Obesity has become a common "malady" that is generally identifiable and identified. It is considered to be a steady invasion, ill-controlled, and attributed as much to overconsumption as to certain lifestyles. These attitudes sharpen the public's view of the obese person and of his or her problem, which is judged a public disturbance—a social malady and costly problem resulting from this individual's lack of will. In addition, there are the ambiguities of treatment that ordinary thinking considers simple and straightforward but empirical evidence and testimonies reveal to be complex and obscure.

Self-testimony has also changed. The increasing identification in today's society between the individual and his or her body accentuates in the obese person an insurmountable interior tearing: living a "broken" identity while at the same time noting the impossibility of overcoming that breakage. More profoundly, the person is living with a body that the subject feels betrayed by and that yet constitutes a basic expression of one's self. It is a body that is foreign and oneself at the same time (*autre et soi en même temps*). There arises then the new difficulty of abandoning what is, after all, one's own identity. In the end, this is a way to intensify as never before the contemporary investment in one's bodily condition as a manifestation of absolute identity, which from now on is susceptible to maladies and misunderstandings. Today's obesity culture confirms how much things have swung from accusation to self-testimony, from stigmatization to victimization.

The Affirmation of an "Epidemic"

Statistics eventually became an undisputed mental tool.[1] Measuring obesity, which had long been subjective and approximate, has today become standardized. Contours and weight are definitively quantified according to universal norms. Quetelet's figures are still used, but now translated by a single simple index of "body mass" calculated according to the relationship between weight in kilos to the square of the height (in square meters). The spectrum of degrees is normalized: first "overweight," which is situated between the numbers 25 and 29.9; then "obesity," which is defined as any figure over 30 with three subcategories: "moderate," "severe" (above 35), and "very severe" (above 40).[2]

This scale takes the older statistical measurement to its logical conclusion. It details thresholds, describes levels, and creates its own vocabulary, notably the term *overweight*, which today has become as ordinary as it is unthinkable without its quantified definition. There is thus no surprise when Christiane Collange and Claire Gallois begin their 1994 exchange of views about "fat" and "skinny" by sharing with the reader their own measurements on the very first page.[3]

The originality of today's calculations lies elsewhere. It has to do with a new statistic that evaluates the presence of this "evil" (*mal*). Studies confirm its increase. In 2005 1.2 billion people in the world were categorized as overweight, 400 million as obese,[4] and 700 million are expected to be obese by 2015.[5] The prevalence is also increasing. In France, 5.5 percent of the population was obese in 1992, 12.4 percent in 2006, and 14.5 percent in 2009,[6] whereas the percentage was stable in the years 1980–1990. The increase is more striking in the United States where the obese population doubled in the twenty years between 1980 and 2000, and a decade later in 2010 two-thirds of adult Americans are either overweight or obese.[7]

This explains the dramatic remarks one hears, such as the following from one of the latest studies conducted in France: "For roughly two decades now, a new epidemic has spread throughout the world; it's called 'obesity,' and France has not been spared. If we include those who are 'overweight,' there are now 20 million people concerned with the problem of excess weight."[8]

Another observation that has become common knowledge today is that the prevalence of obesity is inversely proportional to household income.[9] This overturns the "bourgeois" schema of an obesity that is specific to the dominant class, modifies the more recent idea of a socially shared obesity, and gives rise to interminable questions about the new "faults" and "insufficiencies" of the eating habits of the poor, especially speculation about easy calories and inexpensive foods that are particularly fattening. One thus has the totally new paradox of an exponential increase of excess weight that "strikes" and penalizes the poor—an excess shared by all, but very differently distributed.[10] This suggests indispensable future reflection about reducing growth, controlling markets, and conveying clear product information.

This dimension of social inequality is increasingly underlined. Among the countless factors that are receiving more thorough study are a lack of nutrition information among lower-class populations, lack of care when it comes to cooking and combining various foods, access to foods that are less "noble" or "supervised," and diverse forms of compensation via the display of quantity and surplus. The differences are backed up by numbers: on average, the middle and upper classes ingest two hundred calories less per day than the lower classes.[11]

The "invasion" theme is highly present in any case. Obesity is now a "health threat," a growing epidemic, an insidious global plague. And there are related risks such as hypertension, which is three or four times more frequent among obese or overweight individuals, diabetes mellitus, which is four to nine times more frequent,[12] and a nearly linear relation between mortality rates and body mass index.[13] There are also cost factors. The health costs are double for an "obese" person as compared to a "normal" person, 2,500 euros versus 1,263 euros.[14] Overall, obesity represents between 5.7–7 percent of health care costs in the U.S. and 2–3.5 percent in Europe,[15] with the prediction that 14 billion euros will be spent on this pathology alone in France by 2020,[16] which has led some to speak of a "new French evil."[17]

"Counterattacks"?

These same statistics establish the danger of obesity as a public health problem. Two expressions establish that image: "social plague" and "social challenge."[18] A high-intensity mobilization has gotten underway with calls for "emergency"[19] measures and a politicized debate.[20]

It is important to underline apprehensions that take on for the first time an institutional dimension, namely, the construction of collective defenses against obesity. They reveal the extent to which excess weight has come to be perceived differently with unprecedented inquiries into types and concurrent factors, such as advertising, industrial distribution, the deritualization of meals, forms of sedentariness, etc.[21] At the same time, food brands are perceived differently and also alter their strategies.

There is the denunciation of excess, of higher doses of sugar and fat, for example; criticisms of portions and drinks, of vending machines and their strategic placement that seek to capture and keep a hold on the consumer.[22] Statistics confirm this, such as the 90 percent increase in calories from snacks consumed by American men between 1977 and 1996, and the 112 percent increase for women.[23] The consumption of sugary drinks by adolescents in France stands at 200 ml per day, while adult consumption is less than half that.[24] The statistics about health effects focus more than ever on fat; for example, the daily consumption of a high-sugar drink by teenagers can increase their risk of obesity by 60 percent,[25] whereas limiting fatty foods can, on the other hand, lead to a "modest but significant loss of weight."[26] The hygienic theme has tilted toward the danger of the adipose.

The counterattack invents a legislative strategy. For the first time, obesity appears before the law. On January 25, 2005, the Second Circuit U.S. Court of Appeals in New York State overturned a lower court decision and reinstated the charges of two adolescents who accused McDonald's of being responsible for their obesity.[27] On February 27, 2007, a French government decree required all food advertising to include a "health message aimed at avoiding the progression of obesity."[28] On September 18, 2008, the consumer protection group *UFC-Que choisir* asked the French parliament to pass "a law forbidding advertisements for high-fat and high-sugar products during children's programming."[29] As a more general measure, a proposal for "a law related to preventing and fighting obesity" was introduced in the French Senate during the 2007–2008 session.[30]

There are also prevention campaigns such as the National Healthy Nutrition Program (PNNS), started in 2001 and followed by PNNS 2 and PNNS 3, which became more focused on the multiplication of messages and advice. Naturally criticisms and disputes also multiply, such as complaints that "the problem is not the message, but its application."[31] And imperfections are noted, such as the view that "it's the absence or lack of physical activity that has received the least attention and improvement."[32]

The adipose theme now occupies a certain terrain in the area of public health, with all its norms and rules. The battle against obesity is waged in the name of all. The evil of "fat" is no longer a private evil.

The Dynamics of Thinness, The Dynamics of Obesity

Two social problems, long viewed together, can today be disjoined: the growing presence of an imperative of thinness and the growing presence of a denunciation of fatness. The first remains a norm of social public appearance, the second becomes an indicator of a health threat. Their origins especially are different. For the first, they are cultural, with the codified silhouette and pose; whereas for the second they are economic, as the threat is viewed as a measurable collective risk. Nor are the worries that they provoke focused on the same objects. And in each case the consequences of possible failure do not involve the same stakes. There is no question that the "thin" imperative makes the presence of the "fat" all the more striking today. It tends to underline its greater frequency and "evidence." The rigor exerted to obtain or maintain a slender profile makes all wayward forms more noticeable and makes us hyperaware of contour failure. A major, indisputable disparity remains, however: the striking presence of obesity in our societies comes more from lifestyles and their "fattening" effects than from the contrast suggested by the thin and its impact. Obesity has imposed itself especially through changes in behavior and less through changes in the public's gaze. And again there is this important distinction: the crusade against excess lipids and sugars and the heightened worry about the risks and costs have not been provoked by a search for thinness but by the fear of a new specifically organic attack, a danger that engulfs the physical and the social. In other words, the driving vision is not the ideal of the svelte, but the ordeals of dysfunctions and disorders.

The sharpening attention that for centuries led to more precise observation of sizes, to graduated measurements of their degrees and nuances of language to capture their diversity, is not of central importance here. What dominates is the affirmation of an unprecedented adipose invasion, its geographic extension, and its public harm. This distinction is decisive and explains the novelty of this "epidemic." More generally, it is what accompanies the questioning of risk factors in our societies and the increase in collective vigilance they provoke.

The Effects of Thinness

Once the important distinction between these two imperatives—the one for thinness, the other against obesity—has been made, it is easy to see that crossing or blending them in various ways can make the problem more complex and confusing. The collective imagination also fabricates its criteria, and subjectivity can win out. The increased tenseness around thinness is a deeper problem than it appears, favoring a particular type of "haunting" with its psychological and organic consequences. A number of testimonies demonstrate this, with their tendency to disregard all degrees or nuances and judge the slightest amount of excess as "fat." These are testimonies of a general public, used to being sensitive and scrutinizing of physical details, keenly attentive to the body mass index, and in the habit of viewing the slightest increase as a sure sign of heaviness. "For me, one is either fat or skinny. There is no intermediate weight. If I gain one kilo, I'm done for, I feel heavy and bloated."[33]

The imperative of a new type of thinness, tonic and tense, begins in Western countries in the 1920s, spreads, and today has become almost a unanimously shared norm. Evidence of it abounds in contemporary studies. For example, the man mentioned by Christine Durif-Bruckert for whom one or two kilos too much is enough to signal a decisive excess: "The criterion is I'm either OK or I'm not OK."[34] Or the testimony of a young woman in the same study who considers the slightest sign of "too much" weight "unbearable." "It doesn't take much for me to slump and feel unloved. When that happens, it's over."[35] The borderline becomes razor sharp. "The body is either thin or it isn't."[36] No modulation is considered possible. "Transgression" becomes ordinary and going over the borderline practically becomes the common lot or risk of everyone in their own judgment of what is "too much." "Dieting is part of a woman's normal everyday life."[37] "Too much" thickness or weight becomes the horizon of daily contemplation.

However there is nothing clearly "alarming" at this stage. Feeling fat can remain an inner personal feeling. What emerges is only a possible uneasiness: contours that are hard to bear yet "normal," a reality that's difficult to accept and yet barely stigmatized, if at all. There is, however, the sharpened "listening" to one's body, a deepening of self-perception, a focus that becomes fundamental in the culture of our individualistic societies. There is no objective obesity here, no grave public declaration, even if the worry that is triggered cannot be ignored.

A "Multifactor" Universe

Everything changes, however, with certain possible modifications of eating habits, notably those provoking bulimic compensations and anxiety-related disorders. Everything changes as well with certain organic vulnerabilities. The rigorous attention to thinness can paradoxically provoke an onset of weight gain with eating disorders, crises, or uncontrolled excesses. "The overlap of the psychological and the alimentary" proves unavoidable in every approach to contemporary obesity.[38]

A totally new phenomenon can be seen today more than ever: weight gain deriving from the imperative itself to lose weight. This is the resulting image of the failed dieters who end up with just the opposite of the desired outcome—with an anomic lawless fatness that has been denounced ever since dieting became an everyday practice. This explains the alarmed declarations such as, "I do diet after diet, but they don't work";[39] "I stayed the same for only two weeks and then very quickly I became bulimic, something that I had never experienced before."[40] Longer and more frequent periods of dieting become necessary, the anxiety about thinness intensifies as well as the ever deeper pursuit of psychological analyses that reveal some insight or further raise some consciousness. These are the usual observations of contemporary studies that are described hundreds of times by dieticians. "When I was about eleven or twelve, just before getting my period, I started getting plump. Today, I know this was normal, but for my mother it was a big deal. . . . So then there were diets, one after another, I was starving, so much so that I snacked in secret. . . . That's how I became bulimic. Very quickly I ballooned up to over sixty kilos, it was monstrous."[41]

A "vicious circle"[42] gets established whereby the subject tends "to eat significantly more when the point was to eat significantly less."[43] The obstacles change. A "fasting syndrome" can get going with chaotic consequences,[44] notably the "deleterious" effect of self-imposed controls, random snacking, and phases of accentuated weight gain. The difficulty increases even more when specific genetic factors also enter in. For example, the classic case of the child "with a genetic disposition like his parents to carry more weight than others," but whose first episodes of weight gain trigger worried responses.[45] Preventive measures are attempted. Diets and interdictions follow. Then come crises and difficulties. Then come failure and disappointment. It's true that on the organic side there is resistance, its "logic" continues and holds up with its usual functioning. It may not "obey," thus aggravating the psychological effects more than ever. "The subject is walled behind his/her weight and his/her revolt is hopeless."[46] This explains the high stakes of all drifting off and the irremediable distance between what is wished for and what is obtained.

Beyond the psychological dimension, therefore, it is necessary to consider genes. Their discovery significantly altered science's knowledge about fat. It also confirmed its limits and multiplied its complexity. They became an indispensable reference in all discussions of obstacles to treatment. The first genetic studies in the 1960s set the example. The mouse "ob," for example, that lacked the "leptin" gene ate more than normal since it lacked any sense of a threshold of "too much."[47] That mouse had lost a sense of satiety and was thus insensitive to the quantities of food it was eating, which explains why it stuffed itself. An inverse phenomenon is triggered by "neuropeptide Y," whose presence stimulates eating while its absence triggers abstinence.[48] Besides that, a number of different genes are found to effect leptin levels to various degrees.[49]

Other genes, just as numerous, modulate energy levels. Instead of food intake rates, it is physiological functioning that alters, not just fueling up but burning up or oxidation. Certain genes can affect the feeling of "too much" in the organism itself. Disparities exist here between subjects capable of a "significant caloric supplement" without weight gain and those who are not.[50] The first are strong "burners" when their caloric intake is increased, the others aren't. This distinction had been observed for a long time,[51] but the reason for it was not well understood and is explained now thanks to an ensemble of inside information, as it were, related to genes.

The new genetically informed model of the body accentuates the image of an "intra-organic" piloting that associates energy principles more closely with regulatory principles. This does not mean that the idea of internal control is a new invention.[52] References to it are present from the end of the nineteenth century onward, notably with the discovery of endocrine glands. But it has now become firmly established and occupies a central place of both knowledge and half-knowledge. Moreover, there seems to be an infinite variety of gene messages sending "sensory signals about satiety," "inhibiting signals to the stomach," "hormonal metabolic signals," "signals emitted by reserve organs," "leptin signals," etc.[53] What ensues is the increasingly new representation of a body submitting an energy plan to an informational plan, one of messages issuing from organs designed to better regulate the burner.[54] "Fat accumulation" here is confirmation of the failure of the "regulatory system."[55]

With so many genes and their crossings, the consciousness of greater causal complexity inevitably grows. The possibilities of combinations also multiply. "The majority of obesity cases are the result of interactions between environmental and genetic factors."[56] The inventory of possible determinants becomes the new challenge alongside the truism that "obesity is a multifactor phenomenon."[57] This inevitably extends the aura of mystery. A decisive point is that the obstacles and difficulties of treatment become directly affected. Many genes remain poorly understood despite the clear links established between about seventy different ones and obesity.[58] "Uncertainties" and obstacles persist, especially since the "diversity of factors to be taken into account" has risen,[59] and because of the number of mechanisms that "must still be elucidated."[60] Such language sometimes allows a rhetoric of hope about knowledge to come to substitute for science's customary language of affirmation. "One of the future tasks will be to determine the combinations of genes and the mutations favoring the development of obesity and in which sort of environment."[61]

Knowledge is obviously not "impossible." It is simply difficult to acquire, opaque, heterogeneous, and sometimes "inaccessible," and therefore doctors come to speak with a great deal of tact.

The clinical problem is to attempt to determine for each patient which factors and mechanisms seem to predominate and, of those, which ones are subject to treatment.[62]

The bottom line is that successful treatment is not guaranteed and an aggravation of suffering can occur.

The Self, the Trial, and Identity

This resistance is at the heart of all approaches to the adipose situation. It constitutes the specificity of the obese martyr in 1922—the person who complains about his image and yet cannot change it. The situation is probably more oppressive still today when this resistance is met with new expectations, especially an altered vision of the obese person with the insistence on his or her neglect of changing, and the anathema directed at their supposed abandonment, their indifference toward others and themselves. Earlier criticisms were based on supposed faults and weaknesses that provoked obesity. Contemporary criticism is increasingly based on the idea of insufficiencies and a certain audacious casualness that are preventing weight loss. The obese person is somehow "incapable."

The difference could not be more clear. The old criticism says if he eats too much it's because he overdoes things. The current criticism says if he does not know how to lose weight it's because he has no self-control and cannot change himself. The first does too much, the second does too little. This difference occurs against the backdrop of the domination of the long and lanky silhouette, a figure that is ever more required and expected. Another factor is that the body comes to be judged as somehow more malleable and flexible in analogy with the universe of contemporary technological innovation, which has itself come to be inundated by machines that are surgically designed and appended with computerized supplements.[63]

The feeling of a broad organic efficiency has developed. Working on one-self is displayed, training becomes common practice, and self-transfor-mation is celebrated and on view. And it's precisely the public's common postulate that this work is absent in the case of the obese person that accentuates the stigmatization. "He has no will."[64] This notion is rein-forced by contemporary "heroes" in satirical publications such as Dupuy or Berbérian, for example—slumped characters with no self-regard who put up with dirt and disorder and prefer screens and video games to all other activities.[65] The themes converge: isolation and letting oneself go.

The chasm widens especially with another recent change that has overtaken our societies, namely, the changed outlook on the body. Not its importance, of course, nor its treatment, but the displacement of its status to the central spot that organizes one's identity. This major dis-placement, which has been studied at length, is an important feature of individualistic societies where the "subject" is presumed to be entirely self-reliant and independent,[66] identifying point for point with what one's physical body, with its traits and limits, expresses. The foundation of self erected on a foundation of expression and sensibility.

This change depends in large part on the dismantling of institutions that traditionally guided norms and mores. A grand overarching society with its pedagogical traditions operating through schools, churches, and the military is no longer telling each person what he or she must become.[67] Looks, silhouettes, and clothes are less and less markers of one's social origins or caste as they increasingly convey one's personality and particu-larity instead. Individuals no longer feel constrained to represent a group or milieu. One's singularity reveals itself by itself. These manifest changes suggest a decisive consequence: the subject "is" his or her appearance.[68] What's more, the subject erects in the dense core of his or her organic being, with its singular history, traumas, and trials, the heart of one's iden-tity. This explains the new quests that transform the organic into a place of explanation with answers to questions about the physical past of each per-son, and of reflection also on one's fleshy self that is supposed to be the key to another interiority now totally intimate and psychologized. *The Body Remembers*,[69] *The Talkative Body*,[70] *The Body Has Its Reasons*,[71] *The Body That Speaks*.[72] This is a totally unprecedented exploration where subjects claim to discover themselves based on what they physically undergo and feel. "We are witnessing the emergence of what could be called a 'body cogito' that would replace the 'I think therefore I am' with 'I am my body.'"[73]

It is a redoubled affirmation of the subject with the body as the prime anchor of one's identity. Pierre Pallardy summarizes the theme in a book whose title flirts with caricature as it affirms the new odd logic that the society supposedly leads one to adopt: *And What If It Came from the Belly? Fatigue, Weight Gain, Cellulite, Sex Problems, Beauty Problems, Depression, Insomnia, and Back Ache Explained.*[74] In this way the subject, along with his or her history, troubles, and difficulties, are "identified" with management of the body.

The consequences are decisive for the obese person who is encouraged to abandon the betraying profile even though this profile, according to the deeper logic evoked earlier, is the one the obese subject identifies with. The "martyr" can become highly complex, with various identifiable levels, even if they are not all at work—far from it—in every case of obesity.

The first feeling of betrayal comes with the declaration of the diagnosis. "The simple fact of being told one is overweight increases depression and lowers self-esteem."[75] The obese person, as Béraud already demonstrated, is confronted with the impossibility of "inhabiting" one's image. The person is led toward a lower sense of self-worth and even disappropriation. The person is "displaced." Whereas slimming down, on the contrary, would be proof of adaptability, of overcoming the social trial, and "realizing" oneself. Advertising gets this point across clearly: "So that those pounds no longer weigh down on you and your social relations."[76] Being fat amounts to being "disregarded."

The second feeling of betrayal comes from the organic resistance. The change doesn't happen despite all efforts to lose weight. This is a familiar situation that has been related in much greater detail today. "After two dieting attempts during which I lost 20 kilos, I quickly went back up to 120 kilos and have stayed there."[77] The situation is all the more painful when confronted with the new law of identity according to which "everyone is responsible for how one is."[78] The stigmatization focuses on "lack of will" and "weak self-control."[79] The fault of the obese person is inability to change, with the suffering constantly increasing as this inability is rendered more visible.

The third feeling of betrayal is more complex and perhaps deeper. This body is the one the person has identified with despite the desire to change it. The painful mixed feelings increase with the quasi-contradictory resistance to "leaving" a body that has become one's identity. Moreover, today refusals and revolts exist, all claiming to be opposed to this "injustice." François Coupry was able in his day to write *In Praise of Fatness in a World Without Substance.*[80] He underscores the necessity of taking distance from "the gaze of others" and the importance of cultivating a will not to submit to "their criteria."[81] Institutions have been founded "to fight against discrimination."[82] The association Allegro fortissimo has organized many initiatives since 1989.[83] Their goal is to aid "very corpulent people" "to recover their self-esteem," to build a reassuring environment, and to create forums and shared activities favoring "the highest levels of tolerance and diversity."[84]

These could perhaps be considered minor activities occurring on the margins of the inexorable social tumult surrounding obesity, the necessity to overcome it and to respect "required" norms. The new relation between the body and identity provokes especially a more central and complex question that reveals the insidious identification of the obese person with his or her size and underscores the difficulties of changing for this very reason. A number of testimonies expand on this paradox: the authentic will to change, on one hand, and the obscure resistance to getting change to occur, on the other. "I know deep down that this plump body also gives me pleasure."[85] Such confidences come up repeatedly in various studies, all underlining a similar ambiguity. "I've learned to love my body" and/ versus "I suffer from my obesity."[86] Joëlle Boucher has insisted most eloquently on the "anxiety" of "becoming different" through the process of dieting even though she wants to go through with it.[87] Her long testimony repeats many of the lines of argument one finds in the 1922 novel *The Martyrdom of the Obese Man*, but with an even finer psychological acuity. "This obesity ended up becoming my signature."[88] The obesity corresponds to times and ways of living during which the author claims to have "succeeded" or to have lived most intensely. The result is this particular difficulty of reconciling a desire to change the body and an equally tenacious desire not to change it. Joëlle Boucher comments on this obscure resistance, this ill-discerned refusal to efface an obesity that has become a way of life, a slow adjustment and adaptation, a precarious balancing act, and sometimes even a deliberate affirmation. "When losing weight, obese people are apprehensive about themselves changing."[89] The testimony is extremely valuable for revealing this simultaneous acceptance and denial, both welcoming and refusing change. There is both the "misfortune" of recognizing oneself in an unappreciated body and the recognition of being oneself in that body—and so be it.

The obese person pushes to the extreme a central paradox of contemporary identity: to be led to identify entirely with one's own body while this body is at once both foreign and oneself. At the same time, obese people exhibit a new way of being as they speak of their suffering and misfortune.

Conclusion

There is no doubt that the stigmatization of the fat person is strongly dominant in a history of obesity. This stigmatization changes over time, which justifies the historical approach. The medieval glutton does not receive the same denigration as the modern oaf or the obese person of today who is often considered "incapable" of losing weight. The values of a culture are at the center of the denunciations. Those centered around "the sinner," for example, in a predominantly religious context are not the same as those directed at round-bellied graspers who make others starve in a world of class warfare, which in turn are different from the denunciations of the fat person with no allure or will in today's individualistic societies.

An important difference that traverses all these stigmatizations concerns the double standard between the male case where relatively big sizes are tolerated versus the female case where thinness is obligatory, a rule confirmed by the systematic and long-standing presence of the corset. It is thus impossible to conceive of any ancient general attachment to an ideal of big women. It is more the transformation of criteria of thinness that must be inventoried. In former times, for example, bodies tightly belted at the waist bound "unctuous" or "rounded" flesh; whereas today's model body is just as thin in the waist but composed of muscle and sculpted curves. On one hand, there is a delicate soft thinness, on the other, a tense thinness of dynamism and firmness. The changed status of women is at the center of the evolution of the female silhouette and its contours. Thinness, however, no matter how it is inflected, is an uncontested rule across the centuries.

It is also indispensable to take into account the role played by differing conceptions of the body's functioning that condition the vision of the fat person at different times. Exaggerated contours caused by imbalanced humors and improper liquid flows, as was recounted centuries ago, are not the same as those caused by unburned calories and improper energy levels, as nineteenth-century theories explained. Over time there are different explanations of where fat comes from, what it is, and how it stays. And there are particularly differences in treatments and body care. Excess humors were supposed to be treated by privileging "drying" foods and a lifestyle that favored evacuation with purges and bloodletting as necessary. Fat that came from noncombusted matter is best treated by privileging low-calorie foods and a life that favors combustion: exercise, the great outdoors, and other physical stimulations. The history of the fat person inevitably runs parallel to the history of the body and the organic in general, with its changing models of structures and functions.

Besides the models of what's going on inside, the transformations of related external phenomena are also central to any history of obesity. Inventions of indexes and markers developed gradually over time different categories of bigness, and the advent of numerical evaluation of size and weight have all played crucial roles in this history. There is also the history of the gaze and social regard and disregard that have been conditioned by a structured and inventive play with images, expressions, and words. There is also the emergence of the individual with his or her precise, singular, codified characteristics. And, finally, the mastery of measurements with the development of precise techniques and operations that plot and graph the masses and volumes of the body. One must also recall the slow and relatively recent arrival of weighing machines in everyday life, with the bathroom scale becoming commonplace only at the very end of the nineteenth century. Only then does one's personal weight become ordinary information in Western culture and begin to influence daily habits and self-observation.

These personal observations open up another inside history of obesity. We see this intimate history of attention to one's own image and personal body care and assessment beginning in the sixteenth century with Cardan's interest in preventing weight gain and his close monitoring of mass via the pressure that his rings would exert on his fingers. A century later we see Madame de Sévigné evaluating her slimming efforts by evaluating the fit of her clothes. Another century later and we see the elegant woman in the fashion magazines of the end of the nineteenth century scrutinizing the verdict of one of the early personal scales. This history of obesity conveys important information about changing personal reactions over time to the stigmatization undergone by the fat person.

A history of obesity is thus a history of intimate feelings. Social suffering, as we've seen, comes in different types and degrees. In the eighteenth century Jean-Baptiste Élie de Beaumont complains about the pain of his obesity, especially his infirmity and impotence, but without citing the social ostracism that he might have suffered, a "useless" theme perhaps in his eyes, a secondary wound compared to the physical obstacles he encountered. The social wound becomes more important in nineteenth-century testimonies when increased importance is given to the psychological and to self-exploration. This tendency increases in the following century to the point of becoming a central obsession. In addition, the twentieth century sees the advent of feelings of loss of identity and of intimate relations with a rejected body. This provokes the implacable tearing or breaking in the mind of the obese person faced with a body rejected by the obese person himself, but which is yet that with which he or she identifies and is in many ways attached to. For now our history ends here, at this extreme contemporary stage of our condition with respect to our bodies. More than ever before, identity comes from the body, and more than ever before we have the anxious feeling that this body can double-cross us.

NOTES

Introduction

1. C. É. d'Orléans, princesse Palatine, *Correspondance complète* (Paris, 1855), 2:33.

2. Ibid.

3. *The Diary of Samuel Pepys M.A.F.R.S.* (London: George Bell, 1893 [1825]), June 3, 1667.

4. Ibid., April 30, 1669.

5. L. de Rouvroy, duc de Saint-Simon, *Mémoires* (17th–18th century) (Paris, 1828 [1819]), 3:397.

6. Pepys, *Diary*, June 16, 1665.

7. *Grosse crevée:* letter of July 8, 1676, M. de Rabutin-Chantal, marquise de Sévigné, *Correspondance* (Paris: Gallimard, 1972), 2:339.

8. In French the shift is all the more abrupt since it comes with the change of a single vowel: *gros* (big) to *gras* (fat). —TRANS.

9. A. Carrache, *Portrati carici*, drawings (seventeenth century), Paris, École de Beaux-Arts.

10. G. Andral, L. J. Bégin, and Ph. Fr. Blandin, "Obésité," in *Dictionnaire de médecine et de chirurgie pratiques* (Paris, 1834).

11. É. Daurant-Forgues and J. J. Granville, *Les Petites Misères de la vie humaine* (Paris, 1843), p. 294.

12. Ibid.

13. M. Leven, *La Névrose: Étude clinique et thérapeutique* (Paris, 1887).

14. Since here the author is referring specifically to a linguistic evolution within the French cultural context, it makes no sense to include English translations of the four French terms he lists that express degrees of chubbiness: *grasset, rondelet* (sixteenth century), *grassouillet, ventru* (seventeenth century). —TRANS.

15. N. P. Adelon et al., "Polysarcie," in *Dictionnaire de médecine* (Paris, 1827).

16. See H. Béraud, *Le Martyre de l'obèse* (The martyrdom of the obese man) (Paris, 1922).

Part 1. The Medieval Glutton

1. Because *gros* can mean "big" or "fat," and because the possibility exists in French to turn some adjectives into nouns or even people simply by putting a definite article in front—*riche, le riche, pauvre, le pauvre, gros, le gros*—the author here deploys several ideas at once: bigness, fatness, the big thing or person, the fat thing or person. Here, *gros* will be translated as "big" when the associations are mostly positive, and as "fat" when they are mostly negative. —TRANS.

2. See É. Barbazan, *Fabliaux et Contes des poètes François des XIe, XIIe, XIIIe, XIVe et Xve siècles* (Paris: B. Warée, 1808 [1756]).

3. *Le Roman de Renart* (13th century) (Paris: Gallimard, 2006).

1. The Prestige of the Big Person

1. "C'est li fabliaus de Coquaigne" (13th century), in É. Barbazan, *Fabliaux et Contes des poètes François des XIe, XIIe, XIIIe, XIVe et Xve siècles* (Paris: B. Warée, 1808 [1756]), 4:175.

2. R. Fossier, "Le Temps de la faim," in J. Delumeau and Y. Lequin, eds., *Les Malheurs du temps* (Paris: Larousse, 1987), p. 135.

3. See, R. I. Rothberg and T. K. Rabb, *Hunger and History: The Impact of Changing Food Production and Consumption Patterns on Society* (Cambridge: Cambridge University Press, 1985), p. 13.

4. Barbazan, *Fabliaux et Contes des poètes François*, 3:37, ibid., 4:147.

5. G. de Lorris, *Roman de la rose* (13th century), in A. Pauphilet, R. Pernoud, and A.-M. Schmidt, eds., *Poètes et Romanciers du Moyen Âge* (Paris: Gallimard, 1952), p. 561.

6. "Des grands géants," in D. Régner-Bohler, ed., *Le Coeur mangé: Récits érotiques et courtois, XIIe et XIIIe siècles* (Paris: Stock, 1983), p. 289.

7. *Le Ménagier de Paris* (Paris: Crédit Lyonnais, 1961 [1391]), p. 62.

8. *La Bourgeoise d'Orléans* (13th century), in R. Guiette, ed., *Fabliaux et Contes* (Paris: Stock, 1960), p. 105.

9. Thibaud, roi de Navarre, *Poésie lyrique* (13th century), in Pauphilet, Pernoud, and Schmidt, *Poètes et Romanciers du Moyen Âge*, p. 899.

10. Barbazan, *Fabliaux et Contes des poètes François*, 1:376.

11. See J. Le Goff, *La Civilisation Médiévale* (Paris: Arthaud, 1964), pp. 414–15. Here Le Goff is quoting from a Dominican book of legends.

12. Ibid.

13. See A. Lombard-Jourdan, *Aux origines de carnaval* (Paris: Odile Jacob, 2005), p. 120.

14. Ibid.

15. Marco Polo, *Le Divisement du monde: Le Livre des merveilles* (13th century), in É. Charton, *Voyages anciens et modernes* (Paris, 1861), 2:413.

16. Ibid.

17. Cited in L. Gauthier, *La Chevalerie* (Paris, 1890 [1888]), p. 632.

18. Ibid.

19. Ibid, p. 633.

20. Ibid., p. 634, note 5.

21. Ibid, note 6.

22. A. Riera-Melis, "Société féodale et alimentation (XIIe–XIIIe sècle)," in J.-L. Flandrin and M. Montanari, eds., *Histoire de l'alimentation* (Paris: Fayard, 1996), p. 407.

23. See M. Montanari, *La Faim et l'Abondance: Histoire de l'alimentation en Europe* (Paris: Seuil, 1995), p. 83.

24. Cited by Montanari, "Les paysans, les guerriers et les prêtres: image de la société et styles alimentaires," in Flandrin and Montanari, *Histoire de l'alimentation*, p. 407.

25. Riera-Melis, "Société féodale et alimentation," 407.

26. See R. Fossier, *Ces gens du Moyen Âge* (Paris: Fayard, 2007), p. 75.

27. M. Pastoureau, *L'Ours* (Paris: Seuil, 2007), p. 90.

28. See J. D. Lajoux, *L'Homme et l'Ours* (Paris: Glénat, 1997), p. 35.

29. J. Froissart, *Chroniques* (14th century), in *Historiens et Chroniqueurs du Moyen Âge* (Paris: Gallimard, 1952), p. 833.

30. Ibid., p. 531.

31. Ibid.

32. See N. Gonthier, *"Sanglant Coupaul!" "Orde Ribaude!": Les injures au Moyen Âge* (Paris: Presses Universitaires de Rennes, 2007), p. 104.

33. English, *crass*; Latin, *crassus* = solid, thick, fat, dense. —TRANS.

34. Gonthier, *"Sanglant Coupaul!" "Orde Ribaude!"* p. 66.

35. See A. Brachet, *Pathologie mentale des rois de France, Louis XI et ses ascendants* (Paris, 1903), p. 214.

36. See P. Zumthor, *Guillaume le Conquérant* (Paris: Hachette, 1964), p. 377.

37. Suger, *Vie de Louis le Gros* (12th century) (Paris: Honoré Champion, 1929), p. 271.

38. Brachet, *Pathologie*, p. 217.

39. See G. Henry, *Guillaume le Conquérant* (Paris: France Empire, 1996), p. 273.

40. J. Michelet, *Histoire de France* (Paris: Flammarion, 1879 [1876]), 2:306.

41. Suger, *Vie de Louis le Gros*, p. 237.

42. Ibid., p. 273.

2. Liquids, Fat, and Wind

1. Hippocrates, *Aphorisms* (400 B.C.E.), trans. Francis Adams, see section 5, *On Athletes*. http://classics.mit.edu/Hippocrates/aphorisms.html.

2. C. Aurelianus, *De morbis actutis et chronicis* (5th century) (Amsterdam, 1709), p. 596.

3. H. de Mondeville, *La Chirurgie* (Paris, 1893 [1306–1320]), p. 22.

4. Barthélemy l'Anglais, *Le Grand Propriétaire de toutes choses* (13th century) (Paris, XVe siècle), book 5. Bartholomaeus Anglicus, *De proprietatibus rerum: Texte latin et réception vernaculaire* (Turnhout: Brepols, 2006).

5. Ibid.

6. Ibid. On the humors in medieval medicine, see also "Essences: The Classical Trail," in N. Agrika, *Passions and Tempers: A History of the Humours* (New York: Ecco, 2007), p. 43. I thank D. Sicard for bringing this study to my attention.

7. Bartholomaeus Anglicus, *De proprietatibus rerum*, book 5.

8. H. de Bingen, *Les Causes et les Remèdes* (12th century) (Grenoble: Jérôme Million, 1997), p. 53.

9. Aldebrandin de Sienne, *Le Régime du corps* (13th century) (Paris, 1911), p. 47.

10. M. Scot, *De secretis natura* (13th century) (Amsterdam, 1655), p. 302.

11. Aldebrandin de Sienne, *Le Régime du corps*, p. 47.

12. Scot, "Signa repletionis malorum humorum," in *De secretis natura*, p. 300.

13. Ibid.

14. Arétée de Cappadoce, *Causes et Signes des maladies aiguës* (2d century) (Paris, ,2000).

15. J. Yperman, *Traité de médecine pratique* (13th century) (Anvers, 1867), p. 22.

16. B. de Gordon, *Ci commence la pratique de Bernard Gordon qui s'appelle fleur de lys en médecine* (13th century) (Paris, 1990), p. 400.

17. See Wikipedia entry for "Syndrome oedémateux généralisé" or, in English, the entries for "Edema" and "Anasarca."

18. Yperman, *Traité de médecine pratique.* Yperman distinguishes four types of hydropsy.

19. Ibid., p. 22.

20. Gordon, *Ci commence*, p. 402.

21. Yperman, *Traité de médecine pratique*, p. 22.

22. *Vie de sainte Douceline* (13th century), in D. Régnier-Bohler, ed., *Voix de femmes au Moyen Âge: Savoir, mystique, amour, sorcellerie, XII-XVe siècle* (Paris: Robert Laffont, 2006), p. 348.

23. Gordon, *Ci Commence*, p. 401. The words used are *tympanite* and *ventosité*.

24. G. de Salicet, *Chirurgie*, trans. P. Pifteau (Toulouse, 1898 [1275]), p. 197.

25. A. de Villeneuve, *De conservanda bona valetudine* (13th century) (Paris, 1575), p. 14.

26. Mondeville, *La Chirurgie*, p. 709.

27. G. de la Tour Landry, *Le Livre du chevalier de la Tour Landry pour l'enseignement des ses filles* (Paris, 1854 [1374]).

28. C. de Pisan, *La Vision de Christine* [1405], in Régnier-Bohler, *Voix de femmes au Moyen Âge*, p. 438.

29. See the "disgrégation des jointures" in G. de Chauliac, *La Grande Chirurgie* (Paris, 1890 [1363]), p. 387.

30. See "Goutte," in É. Littré, *Dictionnaire de la langue française* (Paris, 1866). The French king Louis XVIII (1755–1824) would be called *le roi podagre*.

31. See, J.-N. Monmerqué and F. Michel, *Le Théâtre français au Moyen Âge* (Paris, 1839), p. 251.

32. Bartholomaeus Anglicus, *De proprietatibus rerum*, book 7, chapter 57.

33. Ibid.

34. Ibid.

35. Ibid.

36. Rutebeuf, cited in G.-J.-A. Witkowski, *Les Médecins au théâtre: De l'antiquité au XVIIe siècle* (Paris, 1905), p. 65.

37. Chauliac, *La Grande Chirurgie*, p. 389.

38. Witkowski, *Les Médecins au théâtre*, p. 65.

39. Suger, *Vie de Louis le Gros*, p. 275.

40. Yperman, *Traité de médecine pratique*, pp. 22–23.

41. Chauliac, *La Grande Chirurgie*, p. 119.

42. Ibid., p. 120.

43. Ibid., p. 121.

44. Ibid.

45. On the theme of bloodletting, evacuations, and incisions, see J.-Cl. Schmitt, *Le Corps, les Rites, les Rêves, le Temps: Essais d'anthropologie médiévale* (Paris: Gallimard, 2001), p. 329.

46. Salicet, *Chirurgie*, p. 198: "Saisir cette fumée entre deux ligatures."

3. The Horizon of Fault

1. É. Barbazan, *Fabliaux et Contes des poètes François des XIe, XIIe, XIIIe, XIVe et Xve siècles* (Paris: B. Warée, 1808 [1756]), 4:48.

2. At age twenty-four, William the Conqueror is described as being "taller than average, but not by much, and having a wide and robust corpulence," in G. Henry, *Guillaume le Conquérant* (Paris: France Empire, 1996), p. 113.

3. Suger, *Vie de Louis le Gros* (12th century) (Paris: Honoré Champion, 1929), p. 83.

4. N. Bulst, "L'Essor (Xe–XIXe siècle)," in J.-P. Bardet and J. Dupâquier, eds., *Histoire des populations de l'Europe*, vol. 1: *Des origines aux prémices de la revolution démographique* (Paris: Fayard, 1997), p. 176.

5. See "Ars praedicandi," in H. Martin, *Le Métier de prédicateur en France septentrionale à la fin du Moyen Âge (1350–1520)* (Paris: Cerf, 1988), p. 28.

6. Jean de Salisbury, *La Guerre et le Débat entre la langue les membres et le ventre. C'est assavoir la langue, les yeulx, les oreilles, le nez, les mains, les piedz, qu'ils ne veulent plus rien bailler ne aministrer au ventre* (12th century) (Paris, n.d. [c. 16th c.]).

7. See André Vauchez, ed., *Faire croire: Modalités de la diffusion et de la reception des messages religieux du XIIe au XVe siècle*, Rome, École française de Rome (Paris: de Boccard, 1981).

8. See M. Vincent-Cassey, "Les animaux et les péchés capitaux: de la symbolique à l'emblématique," in *Le Monde animal et ses représentations au Moyen Âge (XIe-XVe siècle)*, Proceedings of the Fifteenth Congress of the Society of Medieval Historians of

Public Higher Education, Toulouse 1984 (Toulouse: Université de Toulouse-le Mirail, 1985), p. 125.

9. A. Lecoy de la Marche, *La Chaire française au Moyen Âge, spécialement au XIIIe siècle, d'après les manuscrits contemporains* (Paris, 1868), p. 76.

10. See C. Casagrande and S. Vecchio, *Histoire des péchés capitaux au Moyen Âge* (Paris: Aubier, 2003 [2000]), pp. 223–24.

11. J. Le Goff, *La Civilisation Médiévale* (Paris: Arthaud, 1964), p. 624.

12. C. de Pisan, *Le Livre des trois vertus* (14th century), in D. Régnier-Bohler, ed., *Voix de femmes au Moyen Âge: Savoir, mystique, amour, sorcellerie, XII-XVe siècle* (Paris: Robert Laffont, 2006), p. 567.

13. Ibid.

14. H. de Mondeville, *La Chirurgie* (Paris, 1893 [1306–1320]), p. 622.

15. See D. Jacquart and M. Nicoud, "Les régimes de santé au XIIIe siècle," in P. Guichard and D. Alexandre Bidon, eds., *Comprendre le XIIIe siècle: Études offertes à M. T. Lorcin* (Lyon: PUL, 1995).

16. Aldebrandin de Sienne, *Le Régime du corps* (13th century) (Geneva: Slatkine, 1978), p. 15.

17. B. de Gordon, *Ci commence la pratique de Bernard Gordon qui s'appelle fleur de lys en médecine* (13th century) (Paris, 1990), p. 337.

18. G. de Chauliac, *La Grande Chirurgie* (Paris, 1890 [1363]), p. 422.

19. See "Le temps des chavaux," in Ph. Contamine, *La Guerre au Moyen Âge* (Paris: PUF, 1980), p. 241. See also J. Barnie, *War in Medieval English Society: Social Value and the Hundred Years War, 1337–1399* (Ithaca: Cornell University Press, 1974).

20. *Belle Erembourc* (12th century), in *Poètes et Romanciers du Moyen Âge* (Paris: Gallimard, 1952), p. 828.

21. *La Quête du Graal* (12th century) (Paris: Seuil, 1965), p. 94.

22. Chrétien de Troyes, *Yvain ou le Chevalier au lion* (12th century), in *Poètes et Romanciers*, p. 243.

23. Ibid., p. 174.

24. A. Franklin, *La Vie privée au temps des premiers Capétiens* (Paris, 1911), 1:267.

25. *Le Lai d'Ignauré* (13th century), in D. Régner-Bohler, ed., *Le Coeur mangé: Récits érotiques et courtois, XIIe et XIIIe siècles* (Paris: Stock, 1983), p. 237.

26. Franklin, *La Vie privée*, 1:237.

27. Aucassin et Nicolette (13th century), in *Poètes et Romanciers*, p. 464.

4. The Fifteenth Century and the Contrasts of Slimming

1. See Andrew Bridgeford, *1066: The Hidden History in the Bayeux Tapestry* (New York: Walker, 2005).

2. Mâitre de Wavrin, *Le Roi de Babylone distribuant ses terres à ses deux fils* (Paris, BNF), ms. Fr. 12566, f. 3v. See also P. Charrun, *La Mâitre de champion des dames* (Paris, CTHS/INHA, 2004), in particular, "Le Mâitre de Wavrin," p. 143ff.

3. N. Froment, *Le Buisson ardent*, in the cathedral in Aix-en-Provence, France, 1476.

4. J. Fouquet, *Le Livre d'Heures d'Étienne Chevalier* (15th century) (Paris, Draeger, 1971), miniature 25

5. V. de Beauvais, *Miroir historial* (Paris: BNF, 1463), ms. Fr 50, f. 25.

6. P. de Commynes, *Mémoires* (1464–1498), in A. Pauphilet and E. Pognon, eds., *Histoiriens et Chroniqueurs du Moyen Âge* (Paris: Gallimard, 2005 [1952]), p. 1289.

7. G. Phoebus, *Le Livre de la chasse* (text 13th century, illustrations 15th century) (Paris, BNF), ms. Fr., 616.

8. See E. Pognon, *Boccace, Le Décaméron, Manuscrit enluminé du XVe siècle* (Paris: Seghers, 1978), p. 54.

9. Ibid., p. 70.

10. É. Barbazan, *Fabliaux et Contes des poètes François des XIe, XIIe, XIIIe, XIVe et Xve siècles* (Paris: B. Warée, 1808 [1756]), 4:168.

11. Ibid., p. 288.

12. I. Origo, *Le Marchand de Prato: La vie d'un banquier toscan au XIVe siècle* (Paris: Albin Michel, 1989 [1957]), p. 281.

13. Ibid., p. 288.

14. See D. Jacquart and M. Nicoud, "Les régimes de santé au XIIIe siècle," in P. Guichard and D. Alexandre Bidon, eds., *Comprendre le XIIIe siècle: Études offertes à M. T. Lorcin* (Lyon: PUL, 1995), p. 217.

15. J. Le Fèvre de Saint-Rémy, *Chroniques* (15th century) (Paris, 1876–1881), 2:158–72.

16. See "Festins et banquets médiévaux," in É Birlouez, *À la table des seigneurs, des moines et des paysans au Moyen Âge* (Rennes: Ouest France, 2009), p. 71ff.

17. H. Heingarter, (Paris: BNF), ms. 7446, 15th century.

18. J. Van Eyck, *Madonna of Chancellor Rolin* (1425), London, National Gallery.

19. B. Gozzoli, *The Procession of the Magi* (1459), Florence, Cappella Medici.

20. P. di Cristoforo Vannucci, called Perugino, *Self-Portrait* (late 15th century), Perugia, Collegio del Cambio.

21. *Calendrier des bergers* (Paris: PUF, 2008 [1491]).

22. É. de Fougères, *Le Livre des manières* (Geneva: Droz, 1979 [c. 1175]).

23. See M.-P. Phan, "Pratiques cosmétiques et idéal féminin dans l'Italie des XVe et XVIe siècles," *Actes du Colloque International*, Grasse 1985 (Nice: Centre d'Études médiévales de Nice, 1987).

24. See A. Cabanès, *Remèdes d'autrefois* (Paris, 1901), p. 181.

25. Anne de France, *Les Enseignements d'Anne de France à sa fille Suzanne de Bourbon* (Marseille: Lafitte, 1978 [1490]), pp. 40–41.

26. *Traité de la forme et devis d'un Tournois* (15th century) (Paris: BNF), ms. fr. 292.

27. Théséide, Vienna, Staatsbibliothek, ms. 2617. See also F. Piponnier, *Costume et Vie sociale: La cour d'Anjou, XIVe-XVe siècle* (Paris: Mouton, 1970).

28. See, in particular, *Mare historiarum* de Giovanni Colonna, written and painted by Guillaume Jouvenel in 1448–1449 (Paris: BNF), ms. lat., 4915.

29. *Histoire de Bretagne* (late 15th century) (Paris: BNF), ms. fr. 8266, pl. 24b.

Part 2. The "Modern" Oaf

1. J. de La Fontaine, "La Belette entrée dans un grenier," *Fables* (17th century) (Paris: GF-Flammarion, 2007). See "The Weasel in the Granary" (book 3, fable 17), in *The Complete Fables of Jean de La Fontaine*, trans. N. R. Shapiro (Urbana: University of Illinois Press, 2007).

5. The Shores of Laziness

1. M. de Navarre, *L'Heptaméron* (16th century), in *Conteurs français du XVIe siècle* (Paris: Gallimard, 1956), p. 943.

2. *Les Cent Nouvelles Nouvelles* (late 15th century), ibid., p. 43.

3. S. Le Prestre, chevaliler marquis de Vauban, *Moyens d'améliorer nos troupes*, *Les Oisivetés de Monsieur Vauban* (Seyssel: Champ Vallon, 2007 [1730]), p. 1020.

4. T. Garzoni, *Le Théâtre des divers cerveaux du monde* (Paris, 1586 [1583]), p. 130.

5. Cited by P. Erlanger, *Les Idées et les Moeurs au temps des rois* (Paris: Flammarion, 1969), p. 63.

6. C. de Seyssel, *La Grant Monarchie de France* (Paris, 1557 [1519]), p. 42.

7. A. Paré, *Les Oeuvres divisées en 28 livres* (Paris, 1585), p. 1055.

8. Ibid., p. 1051.

9. N. Guérard, "Le paresseux," in *Les Moralités* (17th century) (Paris: BNF): "ne jamais se fatiguer ni se 'crever le coeur au ventre.'"

10. See, for example, J. Delumeau, "Mobilité sociale: Riches et pauvres à l'époque de la Renaissance," in *Ordres et Classes, colloque d'histoire sociale, Saint-Cloud, 24–25 mai 1967* (Paris: Mouton, 1973).

11. J. A. de Thou, *Mémoires* (16th century), in J.-F. Michaud and J.-J.-F. Poujoulat, eds., *Nouvelle Collection des Mémoires pour servir à l'histoire de France depuis le XIIIe siècle jusqu'à nos jours*, 1st series (Paris, 1836–1839), 11:331.

12. N. Faret, *L'Art de plaire à la cour* (Paris, 1665 [1630]), p. 19.

13. E. Garin, *L'Éducation de l'homme moderne: 1400–1600* (Paris: Fayard, 1995 [1957]), p. 139.

14. T. Artus, *Les Hermaphrodites* (16th century) (Paris, 1709), p. 22.

15. See, for example, J. Revel, "Les usages de la civilité," in Ph. Ariès and G. Duby, eds., *Histoire de la vie privée*, vol. 3: *De la Renaissance aux Lumières* (Paris: Seuil, 1986); *History of Private Life*, vol. 3: *Passions of the Renaissance*, trans. Arthur Goldhammer (Cambridge: Belknap, 1993).

16. F. Queller, *La Table des Français: Une histoire culturelle (XVe–début XIXe siècle)* (Rennes: Presses universitaires de Rennes, 2007), p. 95.

17. Ibid., p. 95.

18. B. Castiglione, *Le Livre du courtisan* (Paris: Flammarion, 1991 [1528]), pp. 49, 47, 53; *The Book of the Courtier: Baldesar Castiglione*, ed. Daniel Javitch, trans. Charles Singleton (New York: Norton, 2002).

19. Faret, *L'Art de plaire à la cour*, p. 16.

20. Castiglioni, *Le Livre du courtisan*, p. 88.

21. P. de Bourdeille, dit Brantôme, *Les Grands Capitaines étrangers, Oeuvres complètes* (Paris, 1854), 1:23.

22. *Les Cents Nouvelles Nouvelles*, p. 86.

23. Ibid., p. 178.

24. Ibid., p. 179.

25. Ibid., p. 85.

26. B. Des Périers, *Les Nouvelles Récréations et Joyeux Devis* (16th century), in *Conteurs français du XVIe siècle*, p. 549.

27. É. Pasquier, *Des recherches de la France* (Paris, 1633 [1560]), p. 787.

28. http://www.shakespeare-online.com/plays/1kh4_2_4.html.

29. *Alizon a l'oeil charmant* (1633), in J. B. Werckelin, *L'Ancienne Chanson populaire en France: XVIe et XVIIe siècle* (Paris, 1887), p. 15.

30. F. de Sagon, *Plusieurs Traictez par aucuns nouveaulx poètes du différent de Marot* (Paris, 1539).

31. *Épitaphe anagrammatique de Daniel Chamier, gros et gras Ministre de Montauban* (Montauban, 1621).

32. *Luther et sa femme Bora* (16th century), anonymous print, in J. Grand-Carteret, *L'Histoire, la Vie, les Moeurs et la Curiosité* (Paris, 1927), 2:32. On Luther see also O. Christin, "La foi comme chope de bière: Luther, les moines, les jeûnes," in J. Csergo, ed., *Trop gros? L'obésité et ses représentations* (Paris: Autrement, 2009), p. 45.

33. *La Genèse et la Naissance de l'Antéchrist* (1525–1530), anonymous print, in Grand-Carteret, *L'Histoire, la Vie, les Moeurs et la Curiosité*, p. 28.

34. F. Rabelais, *Gargantua* (1534), *Oeuvres Complètes* (Paris: Gallimard, 1955), pp. 47, 50, 57; F. Rabelais, *Gargantua and Pantagruel*, trans. M. A. Screech (London: Penguin, 2006).

35. Ibid., p. 718.

36. Ibid., p. 86.

37. F. Béroalde de Verville, *Le Moyen de parvenir* (Paris, 1841 [1610]), p. 166.

38. M. de Cervantes, *Don Quichotte de la Manche* (Geneva: Rencontre, 1962 [1605]), 1:97, 2:418, 1:15, 2:401; Cervantes, *Don Quixote*, trans. John Rutherford (London: Penguin, 2003).

39. See C. Fischler, *L'homnivore* (Paris: Odile Jacob, 1993 [1990]), p. 337. Fischler analyzes the theme very accurately here—recalling "the sympathy that seems often to be evoked by the fat person" and "the quasi-phobic rejection" that he can provoke, especially today.

40. Cervantes, *Don Quichotte de la Manche*, 1:269.

41. Ibid., 2:75.

42. Ibid.

43. Ibid., 2:42.

44. Brantôme, *Les Dames galantes* (16th century) (Paris: Gallimard, 1981), p. 250.

45. *Les Cent Nouvelles Nouvelles*, p. 47.

46. P. Brueghel the Elder, *The Harvesters* (oil on wood, 1565), New York, Metropolitain Museum.

47. Albrecht Dürer, *Les Quatre Livres de la proportion des parties et pourtraict des corps humains* (Paris, 1613 [1515]); *Albrecht Dürer (1471–1528): On Human Proportion*, introduction by Peter Moser (Bamberg: Babenberg, 2005).

48. Brantôme, *Les Dames galantes*, p. 243.

49. G. Cinzio, *Nigella et le docteur* (16th century), in *Conteurs italiens de la Renaissance* (Paris: Gallimard, 1993), p. 1036.

50. G. Straparola, *Les Facétieuses Nuits* (1550), ibid., p. 407.

51. Ibid., p. 410.

52. P. l'Arétin, letter of June 15, 1538, in *Lettres* (Paris: Scola, 1988), p. 95.

53. P. de L'Étoile, *Mémoires, journaux* (16th–17th century) (Paris, 1875–1896), 2:340.

54. J. Liébault, *Trois Livres de l'embellissement et ornement du corps humain, pris du latin de M. Jean Liébaut, . . . et faict français* (Paris, 1582), p. 556.

55. Ibid., p. 564.

56. See the letter from Erasmus to Thomas More, July 10, 1517, Érasme, *Correspondance*, ed. A. Nauwelaerts (Brussels: Presses académiques européennes, 1974), 3:9.

57. Brantôme, *Recueil des dames* (16th century) (Paris: Gallimard, 1991), p. 409.

58. P. l'Arétin, *Les Six Journées* (16th century), in *Conteurs français du XVIe siècle*, p. 801.

59. Navarre, *L'Heptaméron*, p. 749.

60. F. Bacon, *Histoire de la vie et de la mort* (Paris, 1647), p. 30. F. Bacon, *The History of Life and Death* (Whitefish, MT: Kessinger, 2010 [1638]). *Historia Vitae et Mortis* (London: Haviland and Lownes, 1623).

61. *Relations des ambassadeurs italiens sur les affaires de France au XVIe siècle, recueillies par M. N. Tommaseo* (Paris, 1838), 2:631.

62. J. de Indagine, *La Chiromancie et Phisionomie par le regard des membres de l'homme* (Paris, 1585 [1543]), p. 78.

63. A. Dürer, *Melancholy* (engraving, 1514), Paris, Petit Palais Museum; see also "Inquiétudes renaissantes," in Y. Hersant, ed., *Mélancolie: De l'Antiquité au XXe siècle* (Paris: Robert Laffont, 2005), p. 64ff.

64. See "Un monde qui se dérègle," in J. Delumeau and Y. Lequin, *Les Malheurs du temps: Histoire des fléaux et des calamités en France* (Paris: Hachette, 1991 [1960]), p. 253.

65. Marsile Ficin, quoted by G. Minois, *Histoire du mal vivre: De la mélancolie à la dépression* (Paris: Fayard, 2003), p. 117.

66. Ibid., p. 127.

67. T. Bright, *Traité de la mélancolie* (Grenoble: Jérôme Millon, 1996 [1596]), p. 252.

68. J. de la Bruyère, *Les Caractères ou les Moeurs de ce siècle* (Paris: Garnier, n.d. [1688]), p. 179. *The Characters of Jean de la Bruyère*, trans. Henri Van Laun (Whitefish, MT: Kessinger, 2007).

69. Ibid.

70. L. de Rouvroy, duc de Saint-Simon, *Mémoires* (17th–18th century) (Paris, 1828 [1819]), 3:72.

71. Ibid., 10:177.

6. The Plural of Fat

1. A. Paré, *Les Oeuvres divisées en 28 livres* (Paris, 1585), p. xvi.

2. J. Du Chesne, *Le Pourtraict de la santé, où est au vif représentée la reigle universelle et particulière de bien sainement et longuement vivre* (Paris, 1620 [1606]). See, in particular, the examples of "some gluttons, gourmets, and drunkards who looked more like monsters than men," p. 253.

3. L. Guyon, *Le Cours de médecine en français contenant miroir de beauté et santé corporelle* (Lyon, 1664 [1612]), 1:252.

4. *Relations des ambassadeurs italiens sur les affaires de France au XVIe siècle, recueillies par M. N. Tommaseo* (Paris, 1838), 1:429.

5. L. Joubert, *Des erreurs populaires touchant la médecine et le régime de santé: Seconde partie* (Paris, 1587), "Épistre apologitique."

6. See "The Problem of Knowledge," in E. E. Harris, *Nature, Mind and Modern Knowledge* (London: Allen and Unwin, 1968), p. 43.

7. L. Fusch, *Méthode ou Brième Introduction pour parvenir à la cognoissance de la vraye et solide medecine* (Lyon, 1552 [1542]), p. 174.

8. J. Fernel, *Les Sept Livres de la thérapeutique universelle* (16th century) (Paris, 1655); J. Fernel, *La Pathologie ou discours des maladies* (16th century) (Paris, 1655); see also J. Roger, *Jean Fernel et les problèmes de la médecine de la Renaissance* (Paris: Palais de la Découverte, 1960).

9. Fernel, *Les Sept Livres*, p. 71.

10. See "la pléthore comme 'cause antécédante' de l'apoplexie," in B. de Gordon, *Ci commence la pratique de Bernard Gordon qui s'appelle fleur de lys en médecine* (13th century) (Paris, 1990), p. 175.

11. J. Froissart, *Chroniques* (14th century), in *Historiens et Chroniqueurs du Moyen Âge* (Paris: Gallimard, 1952), p. 832.

12. L. de Rouvroy, du de Saint-Simon, *Mémoires* (17th–18th century) (Paris, 1828 [1819]), 3:153.

13. Ibid., p. 157.

14. G. Flamant, *L'Art de se conserver en santé ou le Médecin de soi-même* (Paris, 1692), p. 48–49.

15. Rouvroy, *Mémoires*, 3:153.

16. J. Lommius, *Tableau des maladies ou Description exacte de toutes les maladies qui attaquent le corps humain* (16th century) (Paris, 1760), p. 108.

17. N. A. de la Framboisière, *Oeuvres* (Lyon, 1669 [1616]), p. 261.

18. J. Riolan, *Artis bene medeni methodus generalis* (Paris, 1638), pp. 75–76.

19. P. de L'Étoile, *Registre-Journal d'un curieux* (16th–17th century), in J.-F. Michaud and J.-J.-F. Poujoulat, eds., *Nouvelle Collection de Mémoires pour servir à l'histoire de France depuis le XIIIe siècle jusqu'à nos jours*, 1st series (Paris, 1836–1839), 1:529.

20. G. Patin, *Lettres* (17th century) (Paris, 1846), 2:208.

21. H. de Monteux, *Conversations de santé et Prolongation de vie: Livre fort utile et nécessaire* (Paris, 1572 [1556]), p. 108.

22. M. Ettmüller, "La corpulence," in *Pratique spéciale de médecine sur les maladies propres des hommes, des femmes et des petits enfants* (Lyon, 1693 [1691]), p. 331.

23. J. Devaux, *Le Médecin de soi-même, ou l'art de se conserver la santé par l'instinct* (Leiden: Claude Jordan, , 1687), p. 56.

24. J. Riolan, *Manuel anatomique et pathologique au Abrégé de toute l'anatomie et des usages que l'on en peut tirer pour . . . la guérison des maladies* (Paris, 1661 [1648]), p. 114.

25. I. De Diemerbroeck, *L'Anatomie du corps humain* (Paris, 1723 [1688]).

26. Fabrice de Haldan, *Opera observationum et curationum medico-chirurgicarum, quae exstant omnia* (Frankfurt, 1682), p. 321.

27. Ettmüller, *Pratique spéciale*, p. 648.

28. S. Sanctorio, *Methodi vitandorum errorum omnium qui in arte medica contingunt* (Venice, 1630 [1603]), p. 593.

29. W. Charleton, *Exercitationes de oeconomia animali novis in medicina hypothesibus superstructa, Editio novissima* (London, 1685).

30. Cl. Perrault, *Essais de physique ou Recueil de plusieurs traités touchant les choses naturelles* (Paris, 1680–1688), 3:295.

31. See M. Malpighi, *Discours anatomique sur la structure des viscères, sçavoir du foye, du cerveau, des reins, de la ratte, du polpe du coeur et des poulmons* (Paris 1683 [1669]).

32. Perrault, *Essais de physique*, 3:294.

33. Paré, *Les Oeuvres divisées en 28 livres*, p. 307.

34. Lommius, *Tableau des maladies*, p. 250.

35. See "Hydropsie extraordinarie," in *Journal de médecine* (1679): 247–48.

36. Ibid., p. 241.

37. Devaux, *Le Médecin de soi-même*, p. 83.

38. Ettmüller, *Pratique spéciale*, 1:669.

39. J. Lhermite, *Le Passetemps* (16th century) (Geneva: Slatkine, 1971), p. 141.

40. Paré, *Les Oeuvres divisées en 28 livres*, p. 310.

41. Framboisière, *Oeuvres*, p. 407.

42. L. Rivière, *Observations de médecine* (Lyon, 1724 [1659]), p. 490.

43. T. Sydenham, *De podagra et hydrope* (London, 1683).

44. Rivière, *Observations*, p. 623.

45. F. S. W. de Bayreuth, *Mémoires (1706–1742)* (Paris: Mercure de France, 1967), p. 64.

46. M. A. Severini, *De abscessuum recondita natura* (Lyon, 1724 [1632]), p. 207.

47. T . Campanella, *La Cité du soleil ou Idée d'une République philosophique* (1613), in *Voyages aux pays de nulle part* (Paris: Robert Laffont, 1990), p. 261. The inhabitants of the City of the Sun "never have gout, rheumatism, inflammation, sciatica, colic, hydropy, or gas."

48. A. Furetière, "Goutte," in *Dictionnaire universel contenant généralement tous les mots français* (Paris, 1701).

49. J. Fernel, *Chirurgie* (Toulouse, 1667 [1550]), p. 39.

50. A. du Laurens, *Oeuvres* (Lyon, 1593; Rouen, 1621), p. 352.

51. Framboisière, *Oeuvres*, p. 677.

52. Ibid., p. 352.

53. Ibid., p. 354.

54. T. Sydenham, *Traité de la goutte* (1683), in *Oeuvres de médecine pratique* (Paris, 1816), 2:139.

55. Framboisière, *Oeuvres*, p. 679.

56. Sydenham, *Traité de la goutte*, p. 141.

57. P. Dubé, *Maladies des pauvres* (Paris, 1680 [1640]), p. 209.

58. *Journal de santé de Louis XIV, écrit par Vallot, Daquin et Fagon (XVIIe et XVIIIe siècle)*, ed. S. Perez (Grenoble: Jérôme Millon, 2004), p. 297.

59. Framboisière, *Oeuvres*, p. 675.

60. P. Pigray, *Épitome des préceptes de médecine et de chirurgie* (Rouen, 1653 [1608]), p. 457.

61. Sydenham, *Traité de la goutte*, p. 133.

7. Exploring Images, Defining Terms

1. L. Guyon, *Les Diverses Leçons* (Lyon, 1604), p. 133.

2. See N. Laynerie Dagen, *L'Invention du corps* (Paris: Flammarion, 1997)—an essential text for understanding the emergence of a "new" body with Renaissance painting.

3. J. Hale, *La Civilisation de l'Europe à la Renaissance* (Paris: Perrin, 1998), p. 549. John R. Hale, *The Civilization of Europe in the Renaissance* (New York: Scribner, 1993, 1995).

4. See "Les voies de la mutation," in P. Francastel, *La Figure et le Lieu: L'ordre visuel du Quattro-cento* (Paris: Gallimard, 1967), p. 178ff.

5. See J. Cérard, *La Nature est les Prodiges* (Geneva: Droz, 1996), p. 437.

6. See "Dieu permet que les enfants imparfaits et monstrueux de cette sorte soient engendrés ou pour châtier les crimes ou en signe d'une punition prochaine," ibid., p. 440. See also J.-J. Courtine, "Le Corps inhumain," in J.-J. Courtine, A. Corbin, and G. Virgarello, eds., *Histoire du corps*, vol. 1: *De la Renaissance aux Lumières* (Paris: Seuil, 2005).

7. H. Bosch, *The Hay Wagon* (oil on panel, 15101550), Madrid, Prado Museum.

8. L. Cranach, *Herzog Jahanns des Beständigen* (oil, 1532, Coburg); *Johann Friedrichs des Grosmütigen* (oil, 1533), Tokyo.

9. U. Graf, *The Witches' Sabbath* (1514), Vienna, Albertina Gallery.

10. G. della Porta, *La Physionomie humaine* (Rouen, 1655 [1586]), pp. 329–30.

11. L. Cranach, *Dem Kalvarienberg* (engraving, 1510), Nürnberg, Germanisches Nationalmuseum; see J. Jahn, *1472–1553: Lucas Cranach D. Ä. Das gesamte graphishe Werk* (Munich: Rogner and Bernhard, 1972), p. 317.

12. A. Dürer, *A Big Man Before a Mirror*, ink drawing (n.d.), Gdansk Municipal Museum. See also in *Das gesamte graphische Werk Handzeichnungen* (Munich: Rogner and Bernard, 1971), 1:721.

13. A. Dürer, *Women Bathing*, ink drawing (1496), Kunsthalle Museum, Bremen.

14. C. Mellin, *Alessandro del Borro* (1630), Gemäldegalerie, Berlin. I thank Geneviève and Serge Koster for telling me about this particularly striking painting.

15. See the commentary insisting on the staging of the pictorial space, in M. C. Beardsley, *Aesthetics: Problems in the Philosophy of Criticism* (New York: Harcourt Brace, 1958), p. 300.

16. Peter Paul Rubens, *The Fall of the Damned* (1618–1620), Munich, Alte Pinakothek; *Studies for The Fall of the Damned* (1617), London, British Museum.

17. R. de Piles, *Dissertation sur les ouvrages des plus fameux peintres* (Paris, 1681), p. 82.

18. Ibid., p. 101.

19. Rubens, *The Drunken Silenus* (1615–1619), Munich, Alte Pinakothek.

20. Ibid. Rubens, *Bacchus* (1635), St. Petersburg, Hermitage.

21. See N. Laynerie Dagen, *Rubens* (Paris: Hazan, 2003), p. 120.

22. See S. Alpers, *La Création de Rubens* (Paris: Gallimard, 1996), p. 84. Svetlana Alpers, *The Making of Rubens* (New Haven: Yale University Press, 1995).

23. See F. Baudoin, *Rubens's House: A Summary Guide* (Anvers, 1967).

24. G. Neret, *Peter Paul Rubens: Homère de la peinture* (Paris: Le Monde, 2008), p. 14.

25. P. Muray, *La Gloire de Rubens* (Paris: Grasset, 1991), p. 35.

26. See J. Foucart and J. Thuillier, *Rubens: La galerie de Médicis* (Paris: Robert Laffont, 1969).

27. A. Félibien, *Entretiens sur les vies et sur les ouvrages des plus excellents peintres anciens et modernes* (Paris, 1725 [1705]), 3:429.

28. Rubens, *The Garden of Love* (1630), Madrid, Prado Museum.

29. Ibid., *Study of a Woman* (1630), Rotterdam, Boymans van Beuningen Museum.

30. Ibid., *The Honeysuckle Bower* (1609), Munich, Alte Pinakothek.

31. See Dagen, *Rubens*, p. 120, "le symbole de l'énergie de la vie."

32. See *Abraham Bosse: Savant graveur*, catalogue d'exposition (Paris, BNF, 2004).

33. See the effigy of fat William in the engraving *Hôtel de Bourgogne* (1633–1634), ibid., p. 135.

34. *Felix et Thomas Platter à Montpellier* (Montpellier, 1892 [1552–1559, 1595–1599]), p. 87.

35. P. Ronsard, *Gayetés* (1584), *Oeuvres complètes* (Paris: Gallimard, 1993), 1:539.

36. F. Rabelais, *Quart Livre* (1552), in *Oeuvres Complètes* (Paris: Gallimard, 1955), p. 721.

37. J. Liébault, *Trois Livres de l'embellissement et ornement du corps humain, pris du latin de M. Jean Liébaut, . . . et faict français* (Paris, 1582), p. 556.

38. G. Tallemant des Réaux, *Historiettes* (17th century) (Paris: Gallimard, 1960), 2:274.

39. Letter of August 12, 1714, in *Lettres inédites de Madame de Maintenon et de Madame des Ursins* (Paris, 1826), 3:98.

40. M. Lister, *Voyage de Lister à Paris en 1698* (Paris, 1873), p. 151.

41. G. Patin, *Lettres* (17th century) (Paris, 1846), p. 253.

42. R. de Piles, *Cours de peinture par principes* (Paris, 1708), p. 146.

43. See P. Rambourg, "Manger gras, lard, saindoux, beurre et huile dans les traités de cuisine, du Moyen Âge au XXe siècle," in J. Csergo, ed., *Trop gros? L'obésité et ses représentations* (Paris: Autrement, 2009).

44. M. Charas, *Pharmacopée royale* (Paris, 1670), p. 115.

45. J. Delumeau, "Mobilité sociale: Riches et pauvres à l'époque de la Renaissance," in *Ordres et Classes, colloque d'histoire sociale, Saint-Cloud, 24–25 mai 1967* (Paris: Mouton, 1973), p. 132.

46. J.-L. Flandrin and M.-Cl. Phan, "Les métamorphoses de la beauté féminine," *Histoire*, June 1984.

47. *Les Cent Nouvelles Nouvelles*, in *Conteurs français du XVIe siècle* (Paris: Gallimard, 1956), p. 90.

48. Ibid., p. 174.

49. B. Des Périers, *Les Nouvelles Récréations et Joyeux Devis* (1558), in *Conteurs français du XVIe siècle*, p. 389.

50. J. Regnault de Segrais, *Honorine* (1656), in *Nouvelles du XVIIe siècle* (Paris: Gallimard, 1997), p. 279–81.

51. Letter of January 6, 1672, in M. de Rabutin-Chantal, marquise de Sévigné, *Correspondance* (Paris: Gallimard, 1972), 1:411.

52. Letter of June 11, 1677, ibid., 2:411.

53. Letter of August 6, 1677, ibid., 2:517.

54. Letter of October 18, 1688, ibid., 2:370.

55. Letter of August 3, 1677, ibid., 2:512.

56. Letter of July 3, 1677, ibid., 2:482.

57. Letter of July 22, 1676, ibid., 2:345.

58. Letter of July 8, 1676, ibid., 2:339.

59. Letter of June 12, 1676, ibid., 2:317.

60. Letter of March 22, 1676, ibid., 2:256.

61. Letter of June 11, 1677, ibid., 2:462.

62. Liébault, *Trois livres*, p. 415.

63. S. de Cyrano de Bergerac, "Contre un gros homme" (c. 1665), *Oeuvres comiques, galantes et littéraires* (Paris, 1858), p. 143.

64. A. Furetière, *Le Roman bourgeois, ouvrage comique* (1666), in *Romanciers du XVIIe siècle* (Paris: Gallimard, 1958), p. 1022.

65. J.-B. Poquelin, dit Molière, *L'Impromptu de Versailles* (1663), *Théâtre complet* (Paris: Garnier, 1955), p. 522.

8. Constraining the Flesh

1. J. Cardan. *Ma vie* (16th century) (Paris: Belin, 1991), pp. 41–42.

2. Ibid., p. 45.

3. B. Castiglione, *Le Livre du courtisan* (Paris: Flammarion, 1991 [1528]), p. 240.

4. G. Tallemant des Réaux, *Historiettes* (17th century) (Paris: Gallimard, 1960), 1:447.

5. L. Paris, *Négociations, Lettres et pièces diverses relatives au règne de François II* (Paris, 1841), p. 718. See also S. Édouard, *Le Corps dúne reine: Histoire singulière d'Élisabeth de Valois, 1546–1568* (Rennes: Presses universitaires de Rennes, 2009), p. 179.

6. Letter of November 17, 1675, in M. de Rabutin-Chantal, marquise de Sévigné, *Correspondance* (Paris: Gallimard, 1972), p. 164.

7. C. É. d'Orléans, princesse Palatine, *Correspondance complète* (Paris, 1855), 2:341.

8. Ibid., 2:217.

9. P. du Moulin, *La Philosophie divisée en trois parties, sçavoir, éléments de la logique, la physique ou science naturelle, l'éthique ou science de morale* (Rouen, 1661 [1638]), p. 170.

10. *The Diary of Samuel Pepys M.A.F.R.S.* (1825) (London: George Bell, 1893), April 5, 1661.

11. In the entry for September 2, 1667, Pepys is surprised by the king's curiosity about his weight loss from playing tennis and by his desire to be weighed: "But this puts me in mind of what I observed in the morning, that the King playing at tennis had a steele-yard carried to him; and I was told it was to weigh him after he had done playing; and at noon Mr. Ashburnham told me that it is only the King's curiosity, which he usually hath of weighing himself before and after his play, to see how much he loses in weight by playing; and this day he lost 4 1/2 lbs." —Trans.

12. P. Braunstein, ed., *Un banquier mis à nu: Autobiographie de Matthaus Schwarz, banquier d'Augsbourg* (16th century) (Paris: Gallimard, 1992), p. 114.

13. See P. Mantellier, "Mémoire sur la valeur des principales denrées et marchandises qui se vendent ou se consomment en la ville d'Orléans, au cours des XIVe, XVe, XVIe, XVIIe, et XVIIIe siècles," *Mémoire de la Société d'archéologie de l'Orléanais* 5 (1862): 206–7.

14. D. Sennert, *Medicina practica, Tomus primus* (Lyon, 1629), p. 21.

15. D. Panarolo, *Polycarpoponia, seu Variorum fructuum labores . . . opus philosophis, iatris, aliisque philoponis admodum utile* (Rome, 1647).

16. M. Ettmüller, *Pratique spéciale de médecine sur les maladies propres des hommes, des femmes et des petits enfants* (Lyon, 1693 [1691]), p. 634.

17. A. Le Fournier, *La Décoration d'humaine nature et ornement des dames* (Paris, 1542).

18. J. Liébault, *Trois livres de l'embellissement et ornement du corps humain, pris du latin de M. Jean Liébaut, . . . et faict français* (Paris, 1582), p. 445.

19. L. Guyon, *Le Cours de médecine en français contenant miroir de beauté et santé corporelle* (Lyon, 1664 [1612]), 1:243.

20. Liébauilt, *Trois livres*, p. 444.

21. M. de Romieu, *Instructions pour les jeunes filles par la mère et fille d'alliance* (Paris: Nizet, 1992 [1597] . . .), p. 71.

22. G. della Porta, *De humania physionomia* (Naples, 1686), p. 19.

23. G. della Porta, *Della fisionomia dell'huomo* (Venice, 1644), pp. 38–39.

24. For an earlier extensive development of this theme, see G. Vigarello, *Histoire de la beauté* (Paris: Seuil, 2004).

25. O. de Serre, *Le Théâtre d'agriculture et mesnage des champs* (Paris, 1600); see especially "Garder la face du hasle" and "Blanchir les mains" in chapter 8.

26. See, for example, C. Gesner, *Trésor de Evonime Philatre des remèdes secrets* (Lyon, 1555 [1552]).

27. M. de Montaigne, *Essais* (Paris: Gallimard, 1958 [1595]), p. 417.

28. Letter of June 24, 1537, in P. l'Arétin, in *Lettres* (Paris: Scola, 1988), p. 153.

29. Ibid.

30. Ibid.

31. L. Cornaro, *De la sobriété: Conseils pour vivre longtemps* (Grenoble: Jérôme Millon, 1991 [1558]), p. 43.

32. L. Lessius, *Conseils pour vivre longtemps* (Grenoble: Jérôme Millon, 1991 [1613]), p. 119.

33. B. Des Périers, *Les Nouvelles Récréations et Joyeux Devis* (1558), in *Conteurs français du XVIe siècle* (Paris: Gallimard, 1956), p. 450.

34. Ibid., p. 483.

35. See R. and M. Wittkower, *Les Enfants de Saturne: Psychologie et comportement des artistes, de l'Antiquité à la Révolution française* (Paris: Macula, 1985), p. 93; Margot and Rudolf Wittkower, *Born Under Saturn: The Character and Conduct of Artists* (New York: NYRB Classics, 2006 [1963]).

36. Cornaro, *De la sobriété*, p. 52.

37. J. Héroard, *Journal* (17th century) (Paris: Fayard, 1989), p. 632ff.

38. Guyon, *Le Cours de médecine*, 2:253.

39. N. A. de la Framboisière, *Oeuvres* (Lyon, 1669 [1616]), p. 69.

40. N. de la Mare, *Traité de la police où l'on trouvera l'histoire de son établissement les fonctions et les prérogatives de ses magistrats, toutes les lois et tous les règlements qui la concernent* (Paris, 1722 [1705]), 2:721.

41. Ibid., 2:704.

42. Ibid., 3:17.

43. See H. de Monteux, *Conversations de santé et Prolongation de vie: Livre fort utile et nécessaire* (Paris, 1572 [1556]), p. 41.

44. An opinion shared by all European doctors. See "Diet," in P. Earle, *The Making of the English Middle Class: Business, Society and Family Life in London (1660–1730)*, (Berkeley: University of California Press, 1989), p. 272.

45. Guyon, *Le Cours de médecine*, 1:208.

46. P. Pigray, *Épitome des préceptes de médecine et de chirurgie* (Rouen, 1653 [1608]), p. 147.

47. N. Lemery, *Pharmacopée universelle contenant toutes les compositions de pharmacie qui sont en usage dans la médecine* (Amsterdam, 1748 [1697]), pp. 115, 127, 140, 141.

48. Framboisière, *Oeuvres*, p. 93.

49. *Relations des ambassadeurs italiens sur les affaires de France au XVIe siècle, recueillies par M. N. Tommaseo* (Paris, 1838), 1:429.

50. F. Rabelais, *Gargantua* (1534), *Oeuvres Complètes* (Paris: Gallimard, 1955), p. 186.

51. D'Orléans, *Correspondance complète*, p. 154.

52. A. de Bandole, *Les Parallèles de César et de Henri IV* (Paris, 1609), p. 32.

53. Ettmüller, *Pratique spéciale de médecine*, p. 672.

54. Framboisière, *Oeuvres*, p. 90.

55. M.-M. de Caylus, *Souvenirs de Madame de Caylus* (18th century) (Paris: Mercure de France, 1986), p. 120.

56. P. Alpino, *Histoire naturelle de l'Egypte: 1581–1584* (Cairo: Institut français d'archéologie orientale, 1979), 1:60.

57. Letter of October 21, 1673, in Rabutin-Chantal, *Correspondance*, 1:603.

58. E. Rodocanachi, *La Femme italienne à l'époque de la Renaissance: Sa vie privée et mondaine, son influence sociale* (Paris: Hachette, 1907), p. 110.

59. Émery, *Nouveau Recueil de curiosités rares et nouvelles des plus admirables effets de la nature et de l'art* (Paris, 1685), p. 83.

60. Liébault, *Trois livres*, p. 37.

61. Ibid.

62. On lemons, see P. Laszlo, *Citrus: A History* (Chicago: University of Chicago Press, 2008).

63. R. de Bussy-Rabutin, *Histoire amoureuse des Gaules* (Paris: Garnier, 1967 [1663]), p. 153.

64. G. de Tallemant des Réaux, *Historiettes*(17th century) (Paris: Gallimard, 1960), 2:427.

65. Ibid., 2:435.

66. Ibid., 2:633.

67. M. Charas, *Pharmacopée royale* (Paris, 1670), p. 98.

68. B. Castiglione, *Le Livre du courtisan* (Paris: Flammarion, 1991 [1528]), p. 233.

69. Cited by J. Delumeau, *La Civilisation de la Renaissance* (Paris: Arthaud, 1967), p. 437.

70. Brantôme, *Recueil des dames* (16th century) (Paris: Gallimard, 1991), p. 58.

71. Liébault, *Trois livres*, p. 15.

72. See also A. Croix, "De la différence à l'intolérance," in J.-P. Rioux and J.-F. Sirinelli, eds., *Histoire culturelle de la France*, vol. 2, *De la Renaissance à l'aube des Lumières* (Paris: Seuil, 1997), p. 139.

73. G. de Minut, *De la beauté. Discours divers. Avec la Paulegraphie ou Description des beautez d'une Dame Tholosaine, nommée la belle Paule* (Toulouse: B. Honorat, 1587), p. 259.

74. C. Vercellio, *Costumes anciens et modernes* (Paris, 1840 [1590]), 1:213, 2:246.

75. Fournier, *La Décoration*, p. 31.

76. J. Liébault, *Thrésor des remèdes secrets pour les maladies des femmes* (Paris, 1685), p. 729.

77. See entries for 1592 in P. de l'Étoile, *Registre-Journal de Henri IV et de Louis XIII* (17th century), in Michaud and Poujalet, eds., Nouvelle Collection, op. cit., 2e série, t, I, deuxième partie, p. 92.

78. See J.-B. Poquelin, dit Molière, *Théâtre complet* (Paris: Garnier, 1955), p. 1397.

79. See A. Blanc, ed., *Théâtre du XVIIe siècle* (Paris: Gallimard, 1986), 3:1268.

80. J. Liébault, *Quatre livres des maladies et infirmitez des femmes* (Rouen, 16th century), (Paris, 1649), p. 726.

81. Liébault, *Thrésor*, p. 726.

82. Tallemant des Réaux, *Historiettes*, 1:60.

83. Ibid.

84. *Felix et Thomas Platter à Montpellier* (Montpellier, 1892 [1552–1559, 1595–1599]), p. 408. See also F. Libron and H. Clouzot, *Le Corset dans l'art et les moeurs du XIIIe au XXe siècle* (Paris, 1933). In this book, still the most informed on the subject, the authors underline correctly that before the sixteenth century most all strapping procedures made use of only a simple belt.

85. *Relations des ambassadeurs*, 2:559.

86. Montaigne, *Essais*, p. 81.

87. Vercillio, *Costumes*, 2:266.

88. See *Le Livre commode contenant les adresses* (Paris, 1692), 2:61.

89. Jaubert, *Dictionnaire raisonné et universel des arts et métiers* (Paris, 1773), 4:176.

90. Madame de Maintenon, quoted in Libron and Clouzot, *Le Corset*, p. 32.

91. Letter of March 14, 1696, to P. H. Coulanges, in Rabutin-Chantal, *Correspondance*, 3:1148.

9. Inventing Nuance

1. Joseph Addison, *Spectator*, no. 25, Thursday, March 29, 1711.

2. See L. Dacome, "Living with the Chair: Provate Excreta, Collective Health, and Medical Authority in the Eighteenth Century," *Science History Publications* 39 (4), no. 126 (December 2001): 467–500. I thank Rafael Mandressi for bringing this text to my attention.

3. B. Robinson, *A Dissertation on the Food and Discharges of Human Bodies* (Dublin, 1747). J. Lining, "Extract of the Letters from Dr. John Lining," *Philosophical Transactions of the Royal Society of London* (1744–1745): 318.

4. J. Floyer, *A Treatise of the Asthma* (London, 1698), p. 238.

5. T. Secker, *Disputatio medica inauguralis de medicina statica* (Leyden, 1721). G. Rye, *Medicina statica Hibernica, Or Statical Experiments to Examine and Discover the Insensible Transpiration of The Human Body* (Dublin, 1734).

6. J. Leupold, *Theatrum machinicorum* (Leipzig, 1726).

7. P. Burguburu, "Balances publiques," *Revue de métrologie pratique et légale* (July 1941): 224.

8. F. M. Arouet de Voltaire, *Micromégas* (1752), in *Romans et contes* (Paris, 1931), p. 165. J. Swift, *Gulliver's Travels* (New York: Norton, 2001 [1726]).

9. *Journal de médecine*, 1757, 1760, 1762.

10. See especially his interventions in the famous Jean Calas case, J.-B. Élie de Beaumont, *Choix de plaidoyers et mémoires* (Paris, 1824).

11. D. Teysseire, ed., *Obèse et impuissant: Le dossier médical d'Élie de Beaumont, 1765–1776* (Grenoble: Jérôme Millon, 1995).

12. This figure alone, without a corresponding measurement of height, has become a sign of pathology today; but eigteenth-century culture was still relatively indifferent to the relationship between height and girth.

13. Teysseire, *Obèse et impuissant*, p. 58.

14. See A. Guerrini, *Obesity and Depression in the Enlightenment: The Life and Times of George Cheyne* (Oklahoma City: University of Oklahoma Press, 2000), p. 8.

15. See B. Kisch, *Scales and Weights: A Historical Outline* (New Haven: Yale University Press, 1965), p. 76.

16. M. Flemyng, *A Discourse on the Nature, Causes and Cure of Corpulency, illustrated by a Remarkable Case, Read before the Royal Society, November 1757, and now first Published* (London, 1760).

17. G. L. Buffon, *De l'homme*, in *Oeuvres complètes* (Paris, 1836 [1749–1767, 1777]), 4:102.

One pound equals 453.60 grams; and "pound" is the translation of the French *livre;* however the French *livre* is actually 500 grams (i.e., half a kilo).—TRANS.

18. F. Boissier de Sauvages, *Nosologie méthodique dans laquelle les maladies sont rangées par classes* (Paris, 1770–1771), 3:277.

19. Louis René Villermé possessed the unpublished manuscript of Tenon. Adolphe Quételet, who was given the manuscript by this Parisian savant, published the results in 1869 in *Physique sociale ou Essai sur le développement des facultés de l'homme* (Brussels, 1869), 2:90.

20. G. L. Buffon, "Probabilité," in D. Diderot and J. Le Rond d'Alembert, eds., *Encyclopédie ou dictionnaire raisonné des sciences, des arts et des métiers* (Paris: 1751–1772), 27:463. For an online version of the *Encyclopédie*, see http://encyclopedie.uchicago.edu/. See also G. Leclerc, *L'Observation de l'homme: Une histoire des enquêtes sociales* (Paris: Seuil, 1979).

21. P. de Marivaux, *Le Paysan parvenu* (1735), in *Romans* (Paris: Gallimard, 1949), p. 715.

22. P. de Marivaux, *Le Voyageur dans le nouveau monde* (1734), ibid., pp. 942–43.

23. See, "De la jeunesse et de la vieillesse," in G. Lavater, *Essais sur la physiognomie destiné à faire connoître l'homme et à le faire aimer* (Paris, 1781–1803 [1772]), plates, 3:155.

24. Ibid., 2:180.

25. See D. Chodowiecki, "Soldats" and "Suite d'ecclésiastiques berlinois," ibid., 3:192–95.

26. See Francis Grose, *Principes de caricature, suivis d'un Essai sur la peinture comique* (Leipzig, n.d.), *Rules for drawing caricaturas, with an essay on comic painting* (London: Samuel Hooper, 1788).

27. E. H. Gombrich, *L'Art et l'Illusion* (Paris: Gallimard, 1971), p. 434. *Art and Illusion: A Study in the Psychology of Pictural Representation* (Princeton: Princeton Univesity Press, 2000 [1960]).

28. J. F. von Goez, *Exercices d'imagination de différents caractères et formes humaines* (Paris, 1784).

29. On the theme of singular types, see J. Sébastien, *Le Corps des Lumières: Émancipation de l'individu ou nouvelles servitudes?* (Paris: Belin, 2006). It is at this same time that "individual" criteria of beauty begin to be asserted. See "La beauté de l'individu," in G. Vigarello, *Histoire de la beauté* (Paris: Seuil, 2004), p. 111.

30. See, in particular, *Monument du costume: Les vint-quatre estampes dessinées par Moreau le Jeune en 1776–1783 pour servir à l'histoire des modes et du costume dans le XVIIIe siècle* (Paris: L. Conquet, 1883 [1789]).

31. *Galerie des modes* (Paris, 1878–1888), pl. 112.

32. A. J. Duclos, *Le Bal paré* (c. 1770) (Paris, BNF, département des Estampes).

33. On the history of the word *silhouette*, see the entry in A. Rey, ed., *Dictionnaire historique de la langue française* (Paris: Le Robert, 1992). The word does not appear in the mid-eighteenth-century encyclopedia of Diderot and D'Alembert.

34. *Les Costumes français représentant les différents états du royaume avec les habillements propre à chaque état* (Paris, 1776), pl. 5.

35. B. Castiglioni, *Le Livre du courtisan* (Paris: Flammarion, 1991 [1528]), p. 52.

36. P. La Touche, *Les Vrais Principes de l'épée seule* (Paris, 1670), p. 6.

37. D. Chodowiecki, "Attitudes," in G. Lavater, *Essais sur la physiognomie destiné à faire connoître l'homme et à le faire aimer* (Paris, 1781–1803 [1772]), 3:192ff.

38. See "Angleterre, scènes d'intérior," in A. Racinet, *Le Costume historique* (Paris, 1888), vol. 5.

39. *Galerie de l'ancienne cour ou Mémoires et anecdotes pour servir à l'histoire des règnes de Louis XIV et de Louis XV* (Paris, 1789 [1786]), 8:238.

40. Berny de Nogent, *Atlas de portraits et figures de traits et entrelas à la plume. Ouvrage unique en ce genre dédié aux amateurs* (Frankfurt, 1761).

41. Ibid. See in the same series the portrait of Rubens's wife.

10. Stigmatizing Powerlessness

1. See R. Rey, *Naissance et Développement du vitalisme en France, de la deuxième moitié du XVIIIe siècle à la fin du Premier Empire* (Oxford: Voltaire Foundation, 2000), p. 126.

2. See "Des animaux machines aux animaux sensibles," in the appendix prepared by S. Luste Boulbina that accompanies D. Diderot, *Le Rêve d'Alembert* (Paris: Gallimard, 2008), p. 110.

3. S. A. Tissot, *Traité des nerfs et de leurs maladies* (Paris, 1770–1779), p. 59.

4. See "Quelles vibrations peut-on attendre des fibres laches?" in A. Le Camus, *Médecine de l'esprit*, 2 vols. (Paris, 1769 [1753]), 1:434.

5. Ibid., 1:23.

6. See D. Macbride, *Introduction méthodique à la pratique et à la théorie de la médecine* (Paris, 1787 [1774]), 1:53: "Le relâchement et l'insensibilité se combinent."

7. A. de Nobleville, *Cours de médecine pratique* (Paris, 1781 [1769]), 1:75.

8. C. de Peyssonnel, *Les Numéros* (Paris, 1783), 1:83–84.

9. See D. Teysseire, "Un médecin dans la phase de constitution de l'hygiénisme, Louis Lépecq de la Clôture (1736–1804)," in P. Bourdelais, ed., *Les Hygiénistes: Enjeux, modèles et pratiques* (Paris: Belin, 2001).

10. L. Le Pecq de la Clôture, *Collections d'observations sur les malades et constitutions épidémiques* (Rouen, 1778), 1:272.

11. Ibid., p. 387.

12. J. Raulin, *Traité des affections vaporeuses du sexe* (Paris, 1758), p. 325. Raulin includes "nervous tension," "convulsions," and "spasms" as causes of obstruction and eventual weight gain—a claim that reinterprets the nervous tension and agitation attributed to certain excesses of civilization into a poorly controlled tension susceptible, paradoxically, of provoking fatness (*grosseurs*).

13. See the entry for "Obésité" in A. Furetière, *Dictionnaire universel contenant généralement tous les mots français* (Paris, 1701).

14. J. Liébault uses the term in the sixteenth century. Other authors such as T. Venner (*Via recta ad vitam longam* [London, 1638]) use it in the seventeenth century. For more on this point, see S. L. Gilman, *Fat: A Cultural History of Obesity* (Cambrige: Polity, 2008), p. 19.

15. See the entry for "Obésité" in D. Diderot and J. Le Rond d'Alembert, eds., *Encyclopédie ou dictionnaire raisonné des sciences, des arts et des métiers* (Paris: 1751–1772).

16. "Observation sur une enfant d'une grosseur extraordinaire," *Journal de médecine, chirurgie et pharmacie* 1 (1755):92.

17. W. Cullen, *Éléments de médecine pratique* (Paris, 1785), 2:126. W. Cullen, *First Lines of the Practice of Physic*, 4 vols. (Edinburgh: Bell and Bradfute and William Creech, 1777, 1778, 1781, 1784).

18. L. Le Pecq de la Clôture, *Observations sur les maladies épidémiques, Année 1770* (Paris, 1776), p. 347.

19. L. de Préville, *Méthode aisée pour conserver sa santé jusqu'à l'extrême vieillesse* (Paris, 1752), p. 188.

20. C. von Linné (Linnaeus), *Systema naturae* (Leyden, 1735). See also the entry for "Nosologie" by F. Dagognet in D. Lecrout, ed., *Dictionnaire de la pensée médicale* (Paris: PUF, 2004).

21. F. Boissier de Sauvages de la Croix, *Nosologie méthodique, ou Distribution des maladies en classes, en genres et en espèces, suivant l'esprit de Sydenham et la méthode des botanistes*, 10 vols. (Lyon: J. M. Bruyset, 1772), a French translation by Gouvion of the Latin original, *Nosologia methodica sistens morborum classes genera et species juxta sydenhami mentem et botanicorum ordinem*, 4 vols. (Amsterdam, 1763), 3:274.

22. J.-B. Morgagni, *Recherches anatomiques sur les lieux et les causes des maladies* (Paris, 1837–1838 [1761]), 2:365.

23. A. Monroe, "Hydropsie extraordinaire causée par un épiploon devenu stéatomateux," in *Essais et Observations de médecine de la société d'Édimbourg* (Paris, 1747 [1745]), 4:553.

24. G. Cheyne, *The English Malady, or a Treatise of Nervous Diseases of all Kinds* (London, 1733), p. 326.

25. See "A soul in crisis," in A. Guerrini, *Obesity and Depression in the Enlightenment: The Life and Times of George Cheyne* (Oklahoma City: University of Oklahoma Press, 2000), pp. 3ff.

26. Cheyne, *The English Malady*, p. 328.

27. D. Teysseire, ed., *Obèse et impuissant: Le dossier médical d'Élie de Beaumont, 1765–1776* (Grenoble: Jérôme Millon, 1995), p. 56.

28. J.-B. Moheau, *Recherches et Considérations sur la population de la France* (Paris, 1912 [1778]), p. 258. A. Burguière, "Le prêtre, le prince et la famille," in A. Burguière, C. Klapisch-Zuber, M. Segalen, and F. Zonabend, eds., *Histoire de la famille* (Paris: Le Livre de Poche, 1994 [1986]), 3:184.

29. J.-J. Expilly, "Avertissement," *Dictionnaire historique, géographique et politique de la Gaule et de la France* (Paris, 1767), 1:n.p.

30. Teysseire, *Obèse et impuissant*, p. 62.

31. D. Diderot, *Les Bijoux indiscrets* (Paris: Gallimard, 1951 [1748]), p. 147. *The Indiscreet Jewels*, trans. Sophie Hawkes (Venice: Marsilio, 1993).

32. É. Raunié, *Chansonnier historique du XVIIIe siècle* (Paris, 1879), 6:237.

33. See "La subordination impatiente," in P. Goubert and D. Roche, *Les Français et l'Ancien Régime*, vol. 2, *Culture et Société* (Paris: Armand Colin, 1984), p. 336.

34. R. Chartier, *Les Origines culturelles de la Révolution française* (Paris: Seuil, 1991), p. 62. J. Nicolas, *La Rébellion française, 1661–1789* (Paris: Gallimard, 2008), p. 383. T. Wright, *Caricature History of the Georges* (London, 1867 [1848]), p. vi.

35. W. Hogarth, *Le Banc des magistrats* (1758), etching, BNF, département des Estampes. W. Hogarth, *The Complete Engravings* (Edison, NJ: Wellfleet, 1988).

36. Raunié, *Chansonnier historique*, 6:249, 211, 239.

37. *Le Pressoir*, etching (1790), Paris: BNF, département des Estampes.

38. Massard, *Convoi d'un fermier général* (1791), Paris, BNF, département des Estampes.

39. C. Thomas, *La Reine scélérate: Marie-Antoinette dans les pamphlets* (Paris: Seuil, 1989), p. 116.

40. J. de la Viguerie, *Louis XVI: Le roi bienfaisant* (Monaco: Rocher, 2003), p. 93.

41. See the secret correspondence between Marie-Thérèse and the Count of Mercy-Argenteau, cited in J.-C. Petitfils, *Louis XVI* (Paris: France Loisirs, 2005), p. 239: "Louis XVI began to be stuffed. Without attaining the thickness of his precociously fat brother the Count of Provence"—the future Louis XVIII, the gouty king, *le roi podagre.*

42. Ibid., p. 238.

43. See the words of Louis XV about *gaucherie* in Viguerie, *Louis XVI*, p. 24.

44. F. de Hézecques, *Souvenir d'un page* (18th century), in A. de Maurepas and F. Brayard, *Les Français vus par eux-mêmes: Le XVIIIe siècle* (Paris: Robert Laffont, 1998), p. 899.

45. On the personalilty of Louis XVI, see É. Lever, *Louis XVI* (Paris: Fayard, 1985). See also J.-D. Bourzat, *Les Après-Midis de Louis XVI* (Paris: La Compagnie littéraire, 2008).

46. "Nouvelles de la cour" (1776), in Raunié, *Chansonnier historique*, 9:79.

47. "Sur Monsieur de Maurepas," ibid., 9:32.

48. "Noël pour l'année 1777," ibid., 9:139.

49. See A. Duprat, *Histoire de France par la caricature* (Paris: Larousse, 1999), p. 196.

50. Cited by A. de Baecque, *Le Corps de l'histoire: Métaphores et politique (1770–1800)*, (Paris: Calmann-Lévy, 1993), p. 94.

11. Toning Up

1. D. Teysseire, ed., *Obèse et impuissant: Le dossier médical d'Élie de Beaumont, 1765–1776* (Grenoble: Jérôme Millon, 1995), pp. 53–54.

2. Ibid, p. 115.

3. See W. Cullen, *Éléments de médecine pratique* (Paris, 1785), 2:531–532.

4. A. Baumé, *Éléments de pharmacie théorique et pratique* (Paris, 1770 [1762]), p. 505.

5. Teysseire, *Obèse et impuissant*, p. 42.

6. *L'Avant-Coureur*, February 18, 1760.

7. G. F. Bacher, *Recherches sur les maladies chroniques, particulièrement sur les hydropsies* (Paris, 1776), p. 480 sq.

8. See A. Monroe (the son), *Essai sur l'hydropsie et ses différentes espèces* (Paris, 1789 [1761]), p. 54–55.

9. See "Balsamiques," in D. Diderot and J. Le Rond d'Alembert, eds., *Encyclopédie ou dictionnaire raisonné des sciences, des arts et des métiers* (Paris: 1751–1772), 2:49. For an online version of the *Encyclopédie*, see http://encyclopedie.uchicago.edu/.

10. Ibid., see the entry for "Menthe" (Beaumont index).

11. Teysseire, *Obèse et impuissant*, p. 29.

12. A. P. Jacquin, *De la santé: Ouvrage utile à tout le monde* (Paris, 1771 [1762]), p. 270.

13. A.-L. Jourdain, *Préceptes de santé ou Introduction au Dictionnaire de santé* (Paris, 1772), p. 123.

14. C. de Montesquieu, *Mes pensées* (18th century), in *Oeuvres complètes* (Paris: Gallimard, 1956), p. 1195.

15. See "Tabouret d'équitation," in *Affiches, Annonces et Avis divers* (1761), p. 185.

16. See "Équitation," in Diderot and D'Alembert, *Encyclopédie*.

17. Teysseire, *Obèse et impuissant*, p. 28.

18. Cullen, *Éléments*, 2:531.

19. Teysseire, *Obèse et impuissant*, p. 58.

20. Ibid., p. 63.

21. Cullen, *Éléments*, 2:531.

22. See "Les bains Turquin," in G. Vigarello, *Le Propre et le Sale* (Paris: Seuil, 1985), p. 138.

23. P. J. Marie de Saint-Ursins, *L'Ami des femmes, ou Lettres d'un médecin concernant l'influence de l'habit des femmes sur leurs moeurs et leur santé* (Paris, 1804), p. 234.

24. L. de Préville, *Méthode aisée pour conserver sa santé jusqu'à l'extrême vieillesse* (Paris, 1752), p. 371.

25. J. N. Dufort de Cheverny, *Mémoires* (18th century) (Paris: Les Amis de l'histoire, 1970), 2:22.

26. P. Pomme, *Traité des affections vaporeuses des deux sexes* (Paris, 1765 [1763]), p. 21.

27. C. J. A. Schwilgué, *Traité de matière médicale* (Paris, 1805), 2:27.

28. P. Bertholon, *De l'éléctricité du corps humain* (Paris, 1786 [1780]), 2:157.

29. Ibid.

30. Ibid., 2:81–82.

31. Ibid.

32. N. Retz, *Fragments sur l'éléctricité humaine* (Amsterdam, 1785), p. 22.

33. W. Buchan, *Domestic Medicine* (London, 1770), 5 vols. The first French edition was published in 1775. Important commentaries supplement the translation by J. D. Duplanil.

34. Ibid., 3:132.

35. Préville, *Méthode*, p. 98.

36. Ibid., p. 39.

37. Ibid., p. 96.

38. Buchan, *Domestic Medicine*, 1:161.

39. Jacquin, *De la santé*, p. 149.

40. Buchan, *Domestic Medicine*, 1:153.

41. Préville, *Méthode*, p. 33.

42. C. de Ligne, *Mémoires, Lettres et Pensées* (18th century) (Paris: François Bourin, 1989), p. 690.

43. J. Boswell, *Journal intime d'un mélancolique, 1762–1768* (Paris: Hachette, 1986), pp. 42, 49, 98, 135. J. Boswell, *London Journal, 1762–1763* (London: Penguin, 2010).

44. See letter for October 10, 1772, in H. Walpole, *Lettres* (Paris, 1872 [1818]), p. 58.

45. J.-F. Marmontel, *Mémoires* (18th century) (Paris, 1891), 2:264.

46. G. Cheyne, *The English Malady, or a Treatise of Nervous Diseases of all Kinds* (London, 1733), p. 362, *The English Malady* (Ann Arbor: Scholars; Facsimiles and Reprints), 1976. A searchable online version is available through Internet Archive (book contributor, York University Libraries): http://www.archive.org/details/englishmalady-ortoocheyuoft (accessed February 13, 2012). The spelling and punctuation have been modified to reflect modern usage.

47. F. Queller, *La Table des Français: Une histoire culturelle (XVe–début XIXe siècle)* (Rennes: Presses universitaires de Rennes, 2007), p. 96.

48. Ibid., pp. 88–89. See S. Mennell, *All Manners of Food: Eating and Taste in England and France from the Middle Ages to the Present* (Urbana: University of Illinois Press, 1995).

49. P. Verri, *Opere varie*, cited in P. Camporesi, *Le Goût du chocolat, L'art de vivre au XVIIIe siècle* (Paris: Tallandier, 2008), p. 83.

50. A. Le Camus, *Abdeker, ou L'art de conserver la beauté* (Grenoble: Jérôme Millon, 2008 [1754]).

51. Verri, *Opere varie*. A. Le Camus, *Médecine de l'esprit*, 2 vols. (Paris, 1769 [1753]), 1:73.

52. See, in particular, J. E. Chamberlin and S. L. Gilman, eds., *Degeneration: The Dark Side of Progress* (New York: Columbia University Press, 1985). This volume contains the following essays: "History and Degeneration"/M. Eksteins; "Anthropology and Degeneration"/J. A. Boon; "Sociology and Degeneration/R. A. Nye; "Sexology, Psychoanalysis, and Degeneration/S. L. Gilman; "Biology and Degeneration"/N. Stepan; "Medicine and Degeneration"/E. T. Carlson; "Technology and Degeneration/W. Leiss; "Political Theory and Degeneration/S. C. Gilman; "Literature and Degeneration"/

S. Siegel; "Art and Degeneration/P. Bade; "Theater and Degeneration"/S. Williams; "Images and Degeneration"/J. E. Chamberlin.

53. J. J. Rousseau, *Émile, ou De l'Éducation* (Paris: Garnier, n.d. [1762]), p. 37. J.-J. Rousseau, *Emile, or On Education*, trans. C. Kelly and A. Bloom (Lebanon, NH: Dartmouth College Press), 2009.

54. J. N. Demeunier, *L'Esprit et l'Usage des coutumes des différents peuples* (London, 1776), 1:7. See also C. Spencer, *The Heretic's Feast: A History of Vegetarianism* (Lebanon, NH: University Press of New England, 1995 [1993]), in particular "To Eat Meat or Not?" p. 211.

55. Cited by K. Thomas, *Dans le jardin de la nature: La Mutation des sensibilités en Angleterre à l'époque moderne* (Paris: Gallimard, [1983] 1985), p. 215. K. Thomas, *Man and the Natural World: Changing Attitudes in England, 1500–1800* (Oxford: Oxford University Press, 1996).

56. See the entry for "Viande" in Voltaire, *Dictionnaire philosophique* (1764), *Oeuvres complètes* (Paris, 1827), 2:1906.

57. Jacquin, *De la santé*, p. 146.

58. G. L. Buffon, *De l'homme*, in *Oeuvres complètes* (Paris, 1836 [1749–1767, 1777]), 4:104.

59. See A. L. Lavoisier and A. Seguin, "Premier mémoire sur la respiration des animaux," *Mémoires de l'Académie des Sciences* (1789): 570.

60. See F. Hoefer, *La Chimie enseignée par la biographie* (Paris, 1865), p. 117.

12. The Weight of Figures

1. See, for example, *Les Recherches statistiques sur la ville de Paris et les départements de la Seine* (Paris, 1821).

2. A. Maccary, *Traité sur la polysarcie* (Paris, 181), pp. 41–42.

3. G. Dupuytren, "Observations sur un cas de polysarcie," *Journal de médecine et de chirurgie* 12 (1805): 262.

4. Maccary, *Traité sur la polysarcie*, pp. 39–41.

5. J. A. Brillat-Savarin, *Physiologie du goût ou Méditations de gastronomie transcendante* (Paris, 1826), vol. 1.

6. A. Quetelet, "Recherche sur le poids de l'homme," *Bulletin de l'Académie royale de Bruxelles* (1832): 20.

7. A. Quetelet, "Le poids de l'homme aux différents âges," *Annales d'hygiène publique et de médecine légale* (1833): 24.

8. See M. Halbwachs, *La Théorie de l'homme moyen: Essai sur Quetelet et la statistique morale* (Paris: Alcan, 1913).

9. See M.-N. Bourguet, *Déchiffrer la France: La statistique départementale à l'époque napoléonienne* (Paris: Éditions des Archives contemporaines, 1989); see also P. Abrams and M. Janowitz, eds., *The Origins of British Sociology, 1834–1914* (Chicago: University of Chicago Press, 1968).

10. Quetelet, "Le poids de l'homme," p. 10.

11. See J.-P. Aron, P. Dumont, and E. Le Roy Ladurie, *Anthropologie du conscrit français* (Paris: Mouton, 1972), p. 61.

12. Ibid.

13. V. Cazenave, *Recrutement de l'armée, Contingent de la classe de 1840, Département du Nord, Année 1841, Rapport adressé à M. le préfet du Nord sur les opérations du Conseil de révision pendant l'année 1841, rapport dans lequel sont examinées les causes de détériorations des hommes dans les villes de fabriques; suivi de quelques considérations sur les maladies qui entraînent la réforme* (Lille, 1842), p. 21.

14. *Physiologie du conscrit* (Lille, 1846), p. 13.

15. H. de Balzac, *Eugénie Grandet* (1833), in *La Comédie humaine* (Paris: Gallimard, 1947), 3:488.

16. H. de Balzac, *Le Curé de Tours* (1832), ibid., 3:783.

17. É.-A. d'Osmond, comtesse de Boigne, *Mémoires* (Paris: Mercure de France, 1971 [1901]), 2:89.

18. F. A. Barde, *Traité encyclopédique de l'art du tailleur* (Paris, 1834), p. 110.

19. A. Dumas, *Mes Mémoires (1802–1830)* (Paris: Robert Laffont, 1989), p. 494.

20. J. A. Brillat-Savarin, *Physiologie du goût* (Paris, 1848), méditation 22, p. 221.

21. See the letter of June 30, 1807, in G. G. Byron, *Correspondance à un ami* (Paris: Calmann-Lévy, 1911), p. 9; see also G. Matzneff, *La Diététique de Byron* (Paris: Table ronde, 1984), p. 22.

22. C. d'Ennery, *Gras et Maigres, Bouffonerie en acte* (Paris, 1838).

23. H. Daumier, "Tiens! poupoule . . . ," *Le Charivari*, July 20, 1844.

13. Typology Fever

1. Ch. Philipon, "Physionomies, poses, gestes, grimaces," in *Musée ou Magasin comique de Philipon* (Paris, 1842–1843), p. 14.

2. Anonymous, *Les Anglais peints par eux-mêmes*, trans. Émile de Labédollierre (Paris: Louis Curmer, 1840 [1839]); H. de Balzac, *Les Français peints par eux-mêmes: Encyclopédie morale du dix-neuvième siècle* (Paris: Louis Curmer, 1841–1842); L. Huart, *Le Muséum parisien, Histoire physiologique, pittoresque, philosophique, grotesque de toutes les bêtes curieuses de Paris et de la banlieue* (Paris: Beauger, 1841).

3. Honoré de Balzac is guided throughout by the zoological metaphor that the work of Buffon revived in the eighteenth century. "Does not society fashion man, according to the context in which he lives, into as many different men as there are varieties in zoology?" ("Avant propos," in *La Comédie humaine* [Paris: Gallimard, 1947]). Metaphors aside, the project clearly undertakes a complete inventory of all classifications and categories. The "type" is a constant theme: "When you meet someone [*un type*] in Paris, it's not a man, it's a spectacle"—*Splendeurs et misères des courtisans* (1847), ibid., 5:745.

4. See, in particular, S. Le Men, "Les images sociales du corps," in A. Courbin, J.-J. Courtine, and G. Virgarello, eds., *Histoire du corps*, vol. 2: *De la Révolution à la Grande Guerre* (Paris: Seuil, 2005).

5. See P. Kaenel, "Daumier, 'au point de vue de l'artiste et au point de vue moral,'" in *Daumier, L'écriture du lithographe* (Paris: BNF, 2008). Here, as with the *Comédie humaine*, one has a case of *comédie graphique*, p. 46.

6. C. Dickens, *The Pickwick Papers* (Oxford: Oxford University Press, 2008 [1836]), p. 3.

7. See "Le bourgeois," in *Bibliothèque pour rire: Les physiologies parisiennes* (Paris, 1850), p. 7.

8. "La femme la plus malheureuse au monde," ibid., p. 16.

9. *Musée ou Magasin comique*, p. 15.

10. Ibid.

11. Ibid, p. 62.

12. See J.-P. Bardet, "Le lent recul de la mort," in J.-P. Bardet and J. Dupâquier, eds., *Histoire des populations de l'Europe*, vol. 1: *Des origines aux prémices de la revolution démographique* (Paris: Fayard, 1997), p. 309. See also S. L. Gilman, *Fat: A Cultural History of Obesity* (Cambrige: Polity, 2008), p. 166.

13. J. A. Brillat-Savarin, *Physiologie du goût* (Paris, 1848), méditation 21, p. 210.

14. This literature is best represented by titles from the 1830s that all feature the notion of "physiology": *Physiologie du bourgeois, Physiologie du bon vivant, Physiologie de la lorette*, etc. See A. Lhéritier, ed., *Les Physiologies, Catalogue des collections de la Bibliothèque nationale* (Paris: Bibliothèque nationale, 1958). See the lithographs of H. Daumier in *La Caricature* between 1830 and 1840.

15. F. A. Barde, *Traité encyclopédique de l'art du tailleur* (Paris, 1834), pl. 32.

16. A. Bertall, "Le dimanche à paris," in G. Sand, P. Gavarni, J.-J. Champin, Bertall (C.-A. d'Arnould, dit Bertall), T. Lavallée, *Le Diable à Paris, Paris et les Parisiens* (Paris, 1845), 1:300.

17. H. de Balzac, *Illusions perdues* (1843), in *Oeuvres complètes* (Paris: Alexandre Houssiaux, 1925), 7:474, with engravings by H. Monnier.

18. See J. Dargent, *Le Corps obèse: Obésité, science et culture* (Seyssel: Champ Vallon, 2005), p. 45.

19. H. de Balzac, *La Maison Nucingen* (1837), in *La Comédie humaine*, 5:595.

20. Ibid., p. 602.

21. H. de Balzac, *Le Père Goriot* (1834), ibid., 2:994.

22. H. de Balzac, *Splendeurs et Misères des courtisanes*, ibid., 5:776.

23. E. Sue, *Les Mystères de Paris* (Paris, 1842), 1:79.

24. H. de Balzac, *L'Illustre Gaudissart* (1832), in *La Comédie humaine*, 4:12.

25. Ibid., p. 21.

26. Ibid., pp. 14–15.

27. H. Daumier, "Le député ventrigoulard achevant sa fonction législative ou digestive," *La Caricature*, May 22, 1834.

28. See, for example, H. Daumier, "Qui en veut?" *Le Charivari*, January 4, 1835.

29. "Cette adorable boule est celle de Boulay," *Revue comique* (1848): 188.

30. J. Mainzer, "La marchande de poissons," in *Les Français peints par eux-mêmes*, 5:305.

31. H. de Balzac, *La Vieille Fille* (1836), in *La Comédie humaine*, 4:255.

32. A.-J.-B. Parent-Duchâtelet, *De la prostitution dans la de Paris* (Paris, 1837 [1836]), 1:195.

33. Ibid.

34. Ibid.

35. *Les Français peints par eux-mêmes*, 2:122.

36. L. Huart, "La grisette," in *Bibliothèque pour rire*, p. 16.

37. *Les Français peints par eux-mêmes*, 2:102.

38. F. Pyat, "Le Solognot," ibid., 7:233.

39. Ibid.

40. Ibid., p. 234.

41. A. Hugo, *France pittoresque ou Description pittoresque, topographique et statistique des départements et colonies de la France* (Paris, 1835), 1:226.

42. See L. R. Villermé, "Examen des causes qui déterminent une différence de la mortalité dans les divers quartiers de Paris et dans les grandes villes," *Annales d'hygiène publique et de médecine légale* 3 (1830): 294, and "Taille de l'homme en France," *Annales d'hygiène publique et de médecine légale* 1 (1929): 351.

43. H. de Balzac, "Le Notaire," in *Les Français peints par eux-mêmes*, 2:105–7.

44. H. de Balzac, *La Femme de trente ans* (1828–1844), in *La Comédie humaine*, 2:781.

45. J. Csergo, "Quand l'obésité des gourmands devient une maladie de civilisation: Le discours médical, 1850–1930," in J. Csergo, ed., *Trop gros? L'obésité et ses représentations* (Paris: Autrement, 2009), p. 16.

46. H. Monnier, "Le bourgeois," in *Bibliothèque pour rire*, p. 43.

47. H. de Balzac, *Le Contrat de marriage* (1835), in *La Comédie humaine*, 3:114.

48. H. de Balzac, *Le Cabinet des antiques* (1837), ibid., 4:366.

49. C. Charle, *Histoire sociale de la France au XIXe siècle* (Paris: Seuil, 1991), p. 57.

50. "Le système ancien," *La Caricature*, no. 1 (1833).

51. See, for example, F. Demier, *La France du XIXe siècle, 1814–1914* (Paris: Seuil, 2000), p. 212: "The mid-size and small bourgeoisie find themselves excluded from the political system by the poll tax regime."

52. P.-J. Stahl, ed., *Scènes de la vie publique et privée des animaux: Études de moeurs contemporains* (Paris, 1842), 1:98, 99, 102.

53. See, in particular, the metamorphosis of King Louis-Philippe into a pear, *Le Charivari*, January 17, 1834.

54. S. Peytel, *Physiologie de la poire* (Paris, 1832), p. 66.

55. Balzac, *L'Illustre Gaudissart*, 4:21.

56. Note the jackets whose chest areas are "convex, closed hemispheres" (La Silhouette, 1830), p. 25. See also J. Harvey, *Men in Black* (Chicago: University of Chicago Press, 1995), p. 195.

57. T. Gautier, "Gavarni," in *Oeuvres complètes* (Paris, 1846), 1:n.p.

58. See the entry for "Ceinture," in A. Dubourg, *Dictionnaire des ménages: Répertoire de toutes connaissances usuelles, Encyclopédie des villes et des campagnes* (Paris, 1836), vol. 1.

L. Maigron, *Le Romantisme et la Mode* (Paris: Champion, 1911), p. 69. A. Dumas, T. Gautier, and A. Houssaye, *Paris et les Parisiens au XIXe siècle* (Paris, 1856), p. 439.

59. Balzac, *Le Père Goriot*, 2:894, and *Eugénie Grandet* (1833), in *La Comédie humaine*, 3:509.

60. Sue, *Les Mystères de Paris*, 1:80.

61. H. de Balzac, *Le Bal de Sceaux* (1829), in *La Comédie humaine* (Paris: Gallimard, 1979), 1:124.

62. Cited in J. Léonard, *Archives du corps: La santé au XIXe siècle* (Rennes: Ouest France, 1986), p. 206.

63. A. de Vigny, *Le Journal d'un poète* (1831), in *Oeuvres complètes* (Paris: Gallimard, 1948), 2:937.

64. H. Monnier, "Scènes de la vie bureaucratique," in *Scènes populaires* (1835–1839) (Paris: E. Dentu, 1879), 1:383ff.

65. *Journal des jeunes personnes* (1835), 3:332.

66. Balzac, *Le Père Goriot*, 2:875.

67. H. de Balzac, *Béatrix* (1838–1844), in *La Comédie humaine*, 2:339.

68. Ibid., p. 415.

69. Balzac, *Le Père Goriot*, 2:874.

70. Balzac, *Béatrix*, 2:377.

71. Balzac, *La Vieille Fille*, p. 255.

72. H. de Balzac, "La femme comme il faut," in *Les Français peints par eux-mêmes*, 1:25.

14. From Chemistry to Energy

1. See, "Hydropsie," in *Gazette médicale de Paris* (1836): 452.

2. J.-B. Bouillaud, "Hydropsies partielles et obliterations des veines," *Archives générales de médecine* 2 (1823): 190.

3. Ibid., p. 200.

4. Ibid., p. 37. See also A. Drouard, "Perspectives historiques sur la notion de nutrition," in F. Audouin and F. Sabban, eds., *Un aliment sain dans un corps sain* (Paris: PUF, 2007); in particular, "Nutrition became a science at the same time as chemistry," p. 97.

5. See, for example, the chapter on fat in J.-A. Chaptal, *Éléments de Chymie* (Paris, 1796 [1790]), 3:346.

6. See the entry for "Engraissement," in L. Vivien, ed., *Cours complet d'argiculture, ou Nouveau Dictionnaire d'agriculture théorique et pratique* (Paris, 1834).

7. See "L'engraissement des bestiaux," in C.-F. Bailly, A. Bixio, and F. Malpeyre, eds., *La Nouvelle Maison rustique du XIXe siècle, Encyclopédie d'agriculture pratique* (Paris, 1835), 2:397.

8. See the entry for "Comburant" and the remark "Lavoisier called oxygen the most excellent *comburant*," in É. Littré, *Dictionnaire de la langue française* (Paris, 1866). 1:675. The entry in this dictionary can be consulted at the Internet archive, http://archive.

org/details/1883dictionnaireo1littuoft. For other searches, begin at the Web site of Lexilogos: http://www.lexilogos.com/francais_moderne.htm.

9. J. Liebig, *Chimie organique appliquée à la physiolgie animale et à la pathologie* (Paris, 1842 [1827]), p. 24.

10. M. Lévy, *Traité d'hygiène publique et privée* (Paris, 1857 [1835]), 1:700.

11. Liebig, *Chimie organique*, p. 90.

12. Ibid., p. 101.

13. See, J.-B. Dumas and J.-B. Boussingault, *Essai de statique chimique des êtres organisés* (Paris, 1844), p. 11.

14. S. Carnot, *Réflexions sur la puissance motrice du feu et sur les machines propres à développer cette puissance* (Paris, 1824).

15. J. Cruveilhier, *Traité d'anatomie pathologique générale* (Paris, 1849), 1:1.

16. See, J.-F. Braunstein, *Broussais et le Matérialisme, Médecine et philosophie au XXe siècle* (Paris: Klincksieck, 1986).

17. See X. Bichat, *Traité des membranes* (Paris, 1799), an VIII. Note that the word *structure* is used starting in article 1, p. 1.

18. See "Remarques sur les affections des membranes muqueuses," ibid., p. 76.

19. Cruveilhier, *Traité d'anatomie*, pp. 1–2.

20. Lévy, *Traité d'hygiène*, 1:299.

21. Ibid., 1:254.

22. August-François Chomel speaks of "prédisposition" (*Éléments de pathologie générale* [Paris, 1817]), while Michel Lévy speaks of "imminence morbide" (*Traité d'hygiène*, p. 258ff.).

15. From Energy to Diets

1. J. A. Brillat-Savarin, *Physiologie du goût* (Paris, 1848), méditation 22, p. 225. Limet, who had a bakery in the rue Richelieu in the 1820s, produced deluxe breads famous for being light and white. Achard was a pastry chef based in Lyon famous for his cookies and especially his vanilla-flavored waffles.

2. Ibid., méditation 5, p. 64. On the career of Jean Anthelme Brillat-Savarin, see P. Ory, *Le disours gastronomique français, Des origines à nos jours* (Paris: Gallimard/Julliard, 1998), especially "L'âge des physiologies," p. 98.

3. Brillat-Savarin, *Physiologie du goût*, méditation 6, p. 70.

4. Ibid., méditation 22, p. 226.

5. B. Constant, cited by A. J. Tudesq, "La France romantique et bourgeoise, 1815–1848," in G. Duby, ed., *Histoire de la France* (Paris: Larousse, 1971), 2:360.

6. A. de Tocqueville, *De la démocratie en Amérique* (Paris: GF-Flammarion, 1981 [1835, 1840]), volume 2, part 3, chapter 13.

7. Brillat-Savarin, *Physiologie du goût*, méditation 3, pp. 27–28.

8. Ibid.

9. Ibid., p. 30.

10. Ibid., méditation 4, p. 33.

11. See Ory, *Le Discours gastronomique*, p. 55, especially the evocation of the "Caté-chisme de l'art de bien vivre," by A.-B.-L. Grimod de la Reynière.

12. J.-P. Aron, *Le Mangeur du XIXe siècle* (Paris: Robert Laffont, 1973), especially pp. 162 and 170 on the theme of "bodily happiness" subtly claimed by a "society decidedly full of itself."

13. Ibid., p. 161.

14. A. Dinaux, *Les Sociétés badines, bachiques, chantantes et littéraires, Leur histoire et leurs travaux* (Paris, 1867), 1:387.

15. L. Gozlan, *Balzac intime* (Paris, 1866), p. 15.

16. E. and J. de Goncourt, *Journal: Mémoires de la vie littéraire*, vol. 1, *1851–1865* (Paris: Robert Laffont, 1989 [1887–1896]), p. 46.

17. Ibid.

18. L. Reybaud, *Jérôme Paturot à la recherché d'une position sociale* (Paris, 1845), p. 27.

19. E. Briffault, *Paris à table* (Paris, 1846), p. 4.

20. See Ory, *Le Discours gastronomique*, p. 69.

21. A.-B.-L. Grimod de Reynière, "Les méditations d'un gourmand," in *Almanach des gourmands* (Paris, 1803).

22. See, P. Parkhurst Ferguson, *Accounting for Taste: The Triumph of French Cuisine,* (Chicago: University of Chicago Press, 1992), especially "Between the Old Regime and the New," p. 50ff.

23. M.-A. Carême, *L'Art de la cuisine française au XIX siècle: Traité élémentaire et pratique*, 2 vols. (Paris, 1833).

24. *Physiologie du bon vivant* (Paris, 1845), p. 16.

25. W. Wadd, *L'Embonpoint considéré comme maladie, avec un examen critique des opinions anciennes et modernes relatives à ce sujet, ses causes, sa guérison* (Paris, 1838 [1829]), p. 25. W. Wadd, *Comments on Corpulency: Lineaments of Leanness, Mems on Diet and Dietetics* (London: J. Ebbers, 1829).

26. A. Bossu, *Anthropologie ou Étude des organes, fonctions, et maladies de l'homme et de la femme* (Paris, 1857 [1846]), 2:139.

27. M. Lévy, *Traité d'hygiène publique et privée*, 3d ed. (Paris, 1857 [1835]), 1:302.

28. See the entry for "Régime," in M. Courtin, ed, *Encyclopédie moderne ou Dictionnaire abrégé des sciences, des lettres et des arts* (Paris, 1830).

29. Brillat-Savarin, *Physiologie du goût*, méditation 21, p. 209.

30. "Une femme à la mode," *Journal des coiffeurs*, October 15, 1838, pp. 283–84.

31. G. Sand, *Oeuvres autobiographiques* (Paris: Gallimard, 1970), 2:75.

32. On the history of the corset, see F. Libron and H. Clouzot, *Le Corset dans l'art et les moeurs du XIIIe au XXe siècle* (Paris, 1933).

33. *Moniteurs de la mode*, August 10, 1845.

34. E. Briffault, "L'école de natation," in *Paris à table*, p. 138.

35. J. A. Brillat-Savarin, *Physiologie du goût*, méditation 22, p. 230.

36. É. Daurant-Forgues and J.-J. Granville, *Les Petites Misères de la vie humaine* (Paris, 1843), p. 298.

37. Ibid., see especially the title of the chapter on the obese, "Gros, gras et triste," p. 289.

38. See P. Pachet, *Les Baromètres de l'âme: La naissance du journal intime* (Paris: Hatier, 1990), especially the evocation of the "Aptitude au dédoublement et à l'auto-observation," p. 80.

16. The Dominance of Aesthetics

1. Crafty, *Paris à cheval* (Paris, 1884), p. 237.

2. See "On the weight and price of bikes," *Manufacture d'armes et de cycles de Saint-Étienne: Catalogue, Chasse, pêche, velocipede* (1893, n.p.).

3. A. Millaud, *Physiologies parisiennes* (Paris, 1887 [1886]), p. 237.

4. G. de Maupassant, "Mes vingt cinq ans" (1885), in *Contes et nouvelles* (Paris: Robert Laffont, 1988), 2:543–46.

5. *La Vie parisienne* (1896): 266.

6. *Le Printemps: Moniteur des modes illustrés*, April 1, 1890.

7. See "Le poids," in É. Duponchel, *Traité de médecine légale militaire: Conseils de revision* (Paris, 1890), p. 293.

8. "Je me pèse," *L'Illustré national*, December 23, 1901.

9. "Un truc de ces sacrés Parisiens," *L'Illustré national*, January 19, 1902.

10. See the ad for "L'Exupère" in *Archives générales de médecine* (1903).

11. See the entry for "Obésité" by J.-A. Sicard, in É Brissaud, A. Pinard, and P. Reclus, eds., *Pratique medico-chirurgicale* (Paris, 1907).

12. J. Verne, *Karaban le têtu* (Paris, 1883). I thank Sylvie Roques for telling me about this text.

13. Body mass index (*Indice de masse corporelle*), defined as weight in kilograms divided by the square of the height in meters, is put forward today as the unit of measure of all gradations in size.

14. See the earlier discussion of Quetelet in chapter 12.

15. L. A. de Saint-Germain, *L'Obésité et son traitement: Extrait des leçons cliniques d'orthopédie, par le Dr. de Saint-Germain, recueillies et publiées par le Dr. Pierre-J. Mercier* (Paris, 1891).

16. A. Proust and A. Mathieu, *L'Hygiène de l'obèse* (Paris, 1897), p. 4.

17. E. Zola, *Le Ventre de Paris* (1873), in *Les Rougon-Marquart: Histoire naturelle et sociale d'une famille sous le Second Empire* (Paris: Gallimard, 1966), 1:637.

18. Ibid., 1:667.

19. Ibid., 1:653.

20. Ibid., 1:861.

21. *Le Messager des modes*, April 1, 1880.

22. Zola, *Le Ventre de Paris*, 1:739.

23. G. Flaubert, *L'Éducation sentimentale* (1869), *Oeuvres*, Paris: Gallimard, 1952), 2:454.

24. Zola, *Le Ventre de Paris*, 1:739.

25. L'obésité," *Journal de beauté*, November 28, 1897.

26. *Le Caprice*, January 1, 1900.

27. Zola, *Le Ventre de Paris*, 1:674–75.

28. Ibid., 1:736.

29. See H. Boutet, *Autour d'elles, le lever, le coucher* (Paris, 1899), p. 100.

30. See the ad for *pilules persanes* in *Le Printemps: Moniteur des modes illustrées*, November 1, 1890, where corpulence is described as a *léger défaut* (a small defect).

31. *Le Charivari*, July 20, 1876.

32. *La Vie parisienne* (1880): 466.

33. J. Michelet, *La Mer* (Paris, 1875), p. 392. For more on this new "scandal," see J. D. Urban, *Sur la plage: Moeurs et coutumes balnéaires* (Paris: Payot, 1994), p. 128. Michelet, ibid.

34. H. Rebel, *Les Nuits chaudes du cap français* (Paris: UGE, 1985 [1903]), p. 420.

35. *Le Charivari*, July 13, 1885, July 14, 1866, July 29, 1880, July 1, 1889, July 17, 1884. Cham, "Je vous avais prise pour une baleine!" ("I mistook you for a whale!"), in *Douze Années comiques, 1868–1879* (Paris, 1880), p. 97. *Le Charivari*, July 28, 1889.

36. *Journal de beauté*, September 23, 1899. *La Vie parisienne* (1898): 560.

37. See S. Melchior-Bonnet, *Histoire du miroir* (Paris: Imago, 1994), p. 103.

38. See the entry for "Verrerie," in *Dictionnaire universel théorique et pratique du commerce et de la navigation* (Paris, 1861), vol. 2.

39. É. Zola, *Carnets d'enquêtes: Une ethnographie inédite de la France*, ed. H. Mitterand (Paris: Plon, 1986), p. 321.

40. E. and J. de Goncourt, *Manette Salomon* (Paris: Gallimard, 1996 [1867]), p. 304.

41. See the drawing with the caption "Mes parents m'ont réussi," in *La Vie parisienne*, May 23, 1896.

42. *La Vie parisienne*, April 25, 1896.

43. *La Vie parisienne*, January 14, 1899.

44. *La Vie parisienne* (1878): 62.

45. É. Zola, *Nana* (Paris: Gallimard, 1977 [1880]), p. 388.

46. See Y. Lequin, "Les chemins croisés de la mobilité sociale," in Y. Lequin, ed., *Histoire des Français, XIXe-XXe siècle*, vol. 2: *La Société* (Paris: Armand Colin, 1983), p. 311ff.

47. Proust and Mathieu, *L'Hygiène de l'obèse*, p. 18.

48. *Le Caprice* (1900): 52.

49. G. de Maupassant, *Boule-de-Suif* (1880), in *Contes et Nouvelles*, 1:19.

50. E. and J. de Goncourt, *Journal: Mémoires de la vie littéraire*, vol. 1, 1851–1865 (Paris: Robert Laffont, 1989 [1887–1896]), 1:161.

51. O. Mirbeau, *Le Journal d'une femme de chambre* (Paris: Gallimard, 1984 [1900]), p. 72.

52. Ibid., p. 56.

53. É Zola, *L'Assommoir* (1877), in *Les Rougon-Marquart*, 2:771–72.

54. A. Bertall, *La Comédie de notre temps: La civilité, les habitudes, les moeurs* (Paris, 1874), 1:105.

55. Ibid., p. 105–6.

56. See chapter 13.

57. Bertall, *La Comédie*, 1:109.

58. Ibid.

59. See K. Becker, "L'embonpont du bourgeois gourmand dans la littérature française du XIXe siècle," in J. Csergo, ed., *Trop gros? L'obésité et ses représentations* (Paris: Autrement, 2009), p. 63. "It is only toward the end of the century that doctors succeed in communicating the physiological dangers for obese people."

60. *Le Charivari*, August 24, 1888.

61. See Becker, "L'embonpoint"; also the testimony about Léon Gambetta by Eugène Paz in a letter edited by *Le Jockey*, January 24, 1888. I thank Maxime Paz for sharing this document with me.

62. Flaubert, *L'Éducation sentimentale*, 2:125.

63. Cham, "Vous êtes gras," in *Douze Années comiques*, p. 49.

64. Cham, "Je te demande un peu," ibid., p. 173.

65. Cham, "Y penses-tu?" *Le Charivari*, April 27, 1884.

66. See the testimony of Eugène Paz, *Le Jockey*, January 24, 1888.

67. See P. Antomattei, *Gambetta, héraut de la République* (Paris: Machalon, 1999), p. 398.

68. G. de Maupassant, *Toine* (1885), *Contes et Nouvelles*, 2:540.

69. Ibid.

70. Ibid., p. 543.

71. See at the same entry for "bedonnement," in A. Rey, ed., *Dictionnaire historique de la langue française* (Paris: Le Robert, 1992).

72. Bertall, *La Comédie*, 2:109.

73. F. Lagrange, *Physiologie des exercices du corps* (Paris, 1888), p. 252.

74. G. Demenÿ, *Les Bases scientifiques de l'éducation physique* (Paris, 1902), p. 244.

75. Ibid., p. 165.

76. On the history of anatomy and the associated representations of the body, see R. Mandressi, *Le Regard de l'anatomiste* (Paris: Seuil, 2004).

77. See B.-A. Richerand, *Nouveaux éléments de physiologie* (Paris, 1802). Richerand is the first physiologist to speak of "partial movements."

78. See G. Vigarello, *Le Corps redressé: Histoire d'un pouvoir pédagogique* (Paris: Delarge, 1978), p. 142ff.

79. "Ne me trouvez-vous pas passable?" *Le Charivari*, August 19, 1888.

80. J.-L. Forain, *La Comédie parisienne, Deux cents cinquante dessins* (Paris, 1892), p. 12.

81. Ibid., p. 24.

82. See F. Demier, *La France du XIXe siècle, 1814–1914* (Paris: Seuil, 2000), p. 364: "the radicaux, guardians of the republican identity."

83. Ibid.

84. See P. Birnbaum, *Le Peuple et les Gros, Histoire d'un mythe* (Paris: Grasset, 1979), p. 13.

85. "A. Rotschild, le roi des grinches," *Almanach du père Peinard* (1897): 60.

86. "Capital et travail," *Almanach du père Peinard* (1894): 32.

87. See F. Le Play, *Les Ouvriers des deux mondes: Études publiées par la Société d'économie sociale à partir de 1856 par Frédéric Le Play* (Paris: À l'enseigne de l'arbre verdoyant, 1883), pp. 149, 256, 292.

88. See A. Gautier, *Cours de chimie* (Paris, 1892), 3:795.

89. See É Duponchel, *Traité de médecine légale militaire*, p. 224.

90. E. Weber, *Fin de siècle: La France à la fin du XIXe siècle* (Paris: Fayard, 1986), p. 172.

91. Zola, *Le Ventre de Paris*, 1:894.

92. Ibid.

93. Ibid., 1:812

94. Ibid., 1:733.

95. Demier, *La France du XIXe siècle*, p. 374.

96. "Nos rois d'aujourd'hui," *Le Triboulet*, no. 2 (1882).

97. See J. El Gammal, "1815–1900: L'apprentissage de la pluralité," in J.-F. Sirinelli, ed., *Histoire des droites en France* (Paris: Gallimard, 1992), 1:509.

98. "À l'engrais, Étude naturaliste," *La Jeune Garde*, May 10, 1879.

99. É. Drumont, *La France juive, Essai d'histoire contemporaine* (Paris, 1888 [1886]), p. 800.

100. Ibid., p. 526.

101. See B. Tillier, *Cochon de Zola, ou les Infotunes caricaturales d'un écrivain engagé* (Paris: Séguier, 1998), pp. 135–37.

17. Clinical Obesity and Everyday Obesity

1. See P. Le Gendre, "Obésité," in C. Bouchard, É Brissot, and J.-M. Charcot, eds. *Traité de médecine*, 6 vols. (Paris, 1891–1894), 1:349: "The medical point of view is completely different."

2. A. Gautier, *L'Alimentation et les Régimes chez l'homme sain et chez les malades* (Paris, 1904), p. 501.

3. C. Bouchard, *Maladies par ralentissement de la nutrition* (Paris, 1885 [1882]), p. 128.

4. Le Gendre, "Obésité," p. 375

5. J.-A. Sicard, "Obésité," in É. Brissaud, A. Pinard, and P. Reclus, eds., *Pratique medico-chirurgicale* (Paris, 1907).

6. Bouchard, *Maladies*, p. 121.

7. See É. Demange, "Obésité" (1880), in A. Dechambre, ed., *Dictionnaire encyclopédique des sciences médicales* (Paris, 1864–1880), p. 16: "Étiologie et pathogénie."

8. Bouchard, *Maladies*, p. 118.

9. A. Proust and A. Mathieu, *L'Hygiène de l'obèse* (Paris, 1897), p. 19.

10. Le Gendre, "Obésité," p. 368. Demange, "Obésité," p. 13.

11. Bouchard, *Maladies*, p. 110.

12. Proust and Mathieu, *Hygiène de l'obèse*, p. 20.

13. Bouchard, *Maladies*, pp. 114, 64.

14. See M. V. Pettenkofer and C. Voit, "Über die Zersetzungsvorgänge im Thierkörper bei um Fütterung mit Fleisch und Kohlhydraten und Kohlhydraten allein," in L. Buhl, M. V. Pettenkofer, L. Radlkofer, and C. Voit, *Zeitschrift für Biologie* 9 (1873), reprint available from Nabu Press (2010).

15. G. Le Bon, *La Vie: Physiologie humaine appliquée à l'hygiène et à la médecine* (Paris, 1874), p. 77.

16. Proust and Mathieu, *Hygiène de l'obèse*, p. 80.

17. M. Berthelot, *Traité élémentaire de chimie organique* (Paris, 1872), p. 2: "Synthesis alone gives chemistry its character of completeness."

18. See the thesis by J.-L. de Montéty, "De la ration alimentaire en general, application au soldat" (Paris, 1887), p. 39.

19. H. Milne Edwards, *Leçons sur la physiologie et l'anatomie comparée de l'homme et des animaux* (Paris, 1877–1881 [1878]), 8:27.

20. Ibid.

21. J.-B. Fonssagrives, "Alimentation" (1865), in Dechambre, *Dictionnaire encyclopédique des sciences médicales*.

22. Bouchard, *Maladies*, p. 110.

23. Ibid., p. 57. The expression is borrowed from Friedrich Beneke, *Physiologische Vorträge, für Freunde der Naturwissenschaften niedergeschrieben* (Oldenburg, 1856).

24. Bouchard, *Maladies*, p. 58.

25. Sicard, "Obésité."

26. Proust and Mathieu, *Hygiène de l'obèse*, p. 82.

27. Demange, "Obésité," p. 21.

28. Ibid.

29. M. Labbé, *Régimes alimentaires* (Paris, 1910), p. 298.

30. M. Leven, *La Névrose: Étude clinique et thérapeutique, dyspepsia, anémie, rhumatisme et goutte, obésité, amaigrissement* (Paris, 1887), p. 236ff.

31. "Mort subite dans l'obésité et dans les familles névropathiques," *Revue de médecine et de chirurgie* (1892): 746.

32. Proust and Mathieu, *Hygiène de l'obèse*, p. 48.

33. See C. Bernheimer, *Decadent Subjects: The Idea of Decadence in Art, Literature, Philosophy, and Culture of the Fin de Siècle in Europe* (Baltimore: Johns Hopkins University Press, 2002).

34. J. Rengade, *Le Médecin de soi-même: Grands maux et grands remèdes*, 4 vols. (Paris, c. 1900), 1:100, 122.

35. V. Galippe, *L'Hérédité des stigmates de dégénérescence et les familles souveraines* (Paris, 1905), pp. 325–28.

36. C. Lombroso and G. Ferrero, *La Femme criminelle et la Prostituée* (Grenoble: Jérôme Millon, 1991 [1893]), p. 254.

37. See the article on "Obésité," in G. Cerfberr and M. V. Ramin, *Dictionnaire de la femme* (Paris, 1897).

38. L. S. Worthington, *De l'obésité* (Paris, 1877), p. 140ff.

39. Le Gendre, "Obésité," p. 375 *sq.*

40. Proust and Mathieu, *Hygiène de l'obèse*, p. 101 *sq.*

41. W. Banting, *De l'obésité* (Paris, 1864), p. 5. W. Banting, *Letter on Corpulence, Addressed to the Public* (New York: Cosimo, 2005 [1863]).

42. Proust and Mathieu, *Hygiène de l'obèse*, p. 243 sq.

43. Sicard, "Obésité," p. 619.

44. Cited by Proust and Mathieu, *Hygiène de l'obèse*, p. 146. Diet regimens extend in the same way to the associated maladies. See, for example, the regimen for *cardiaque obèse* in C. Fiessinger, *Le Régime du cardiaque* (Paris: Delagrave, 1907), p. 110. Sicard, "Obésité," p. 619. Gautier, *L'Alimentation*, p. 503.

45. Le Gendre, "Obésité," p. 31.

46. Ibid.

47. W. Banting, *De l'obésité*, p. 15.

48. K. Becker, "L'embonpont du bourgeois gourmand dans la littérature française du XIXe siècle," in J. Csergo, ed., *Trop gros? L'obésité et ses représentations* (Paris: Autrement, 2009), p. 66.

49. Sicard, "Obésité," p. 617.

50. Demange, "Obésité," p. 28.

51. Proust and Mathieu, *Hygiène de l'obèse*, p. 278.

52. Le Bon, *La Vie*, p. 426.

53. Demange, "Obésité," p. 28.

54. Proust and Mathieu, *Hygiène de l'obèse*, p. 278.

55. See G. M. Gould and W. L. Pyle, *Anomalies and Curiosities of Medicine: A Collection of Extraordinary Cases Derived from and Exhaustive Research of Medieval Literature, Abstracted, Annotated, and Indexed* (New York: Bell, 1896), p. 807.

56. See "L'obésité," *Journal de la beauté*, June 20, 1897.

57. See "L'obésité," *Journal de la beauté*, March 11, 1902.

58. Rengade, *Le Médecin de soi-même*, 1:258.

59. G.-H. Roger, *Digestion et Nutrition* (Paris: Masson, 1910), p. 375.

60. Ibid., p. 377.

61. J. Oertel, *Traitement de l'obésité et des troubles de la circulation (Affaiblissement du coeur, compensation insuffisante dans les lesions valvulaires, coeur gras, troubles de la circulation pulmonaire, etc.)* (Paris, 1886).

62. See F. Lagrange, *La Médication par l'exercice* (Paris, 1894), p. 261.

63. Gautier, *L'Alimentation*, p. 506.

64. See *Villes d'eaux, Histoire du thermalisme, Actes du 117e congrès national des sociétés savantes, sections Histoire moderne et contemporaine, Archéologie et histoire de l'art, Histoire des sciences* (Clermont-Ferrand, October 1992) (Paris: CTHS, 1994).

65. A. Joanne and A. Le Pileur, *Les Bains d'Europe* (Paris: Hachette, 1880), p. 34.

66. G. Bardet and J.-L. Macquerie, *Villes d'eaux de la France* (Paris: E. Dentu, 1885), p. 422.

67. Ibid.

68. See É. Philbert, *Observation d'un cas de polysarcie traité aux eaux de Brides (Savoie)* (Paris, 1877).

69. See C. S. Schindler-Barnay, *Traitement curatif et préservatif de l'obésité et de ses suites aux eaux de Marienbad* (Paris, 1869 [1865]).

70. "Les eaux de Stilba," *Le Charivari*, July 10, 1885.

71. Bardet and Macquarie, *Villes d'eaux de la France*, p. 361.

72. See T. Zeldin, *Histoire des passions françaises* (Paris: Encres, 1978 [1973]), 2:107, "Orgueil et Intelligence." T. Zeldin, *A History of French Passions, 1848–1945*, 5 vols. (Oxford: Oxford University Press, 1979–1981 [1973–1977]).

73. See J. Arnulf and R. Bercioux, *Évian les Bains et sa region: Guide illustré du Baigneur, du Touriste et du Cycliste* (Évian les Bains, n.d.), p. 51.

74. A. Millaud, *Physiologies parisiennes* (Paris, 1887 [1886]), p. 309.

75. Dr.Brière, *Les Bains d'Yverdon, Eau thermale, sulfurée, sodique* (Lausanne, 1869), p. 10.

76. See G. Appeldorfer, *Maigrir, c'est fou!* (Paris: Odile Jacob, 2000). Many advertisements from around 1900 are cited in this work.

77. "Pilules persanes," *Le Printemps, Moniteur des modes illustrées*, November 1, 1890.

78. "Pilules persanes," *Écho du Moniteur des modes*, 1887. "Thé indou," *Le Messager des modes*, November 1, 1905.

79. "Pilules Gigartina," *Le Messager des modes*, January 15, 1904. "Eau de Brahmes," *Le Triboulet*, January 1882. "Ceinture Ismaël," *Le Printemps, Moniteur des modes illustrées*, April 16, 1890.

80. "Thé Beautygène," *Le Printemps, Moniteur des modes illustrées*, January 1, 1900.

81. "Chardon," *L'Illustré national*, January 26, 1902.

82. "Chardon," *Écho du Moniteur des modes*, 1888. "Poudre du docteur Homeland," *Le Printemps, Moniteur des modes illustrées*, September 11, 1887.

83. "Eau de Brahmes," *Le Triboulet*, January 1, 1882. "Chardon," *L'Illustré national*, January 26, 1902. "Poudre du docteur Homeland," *Le Printemps, Moniteur des modes illustrées*, January 1, 1900.

84. See "Ouvrier cordonnier Malakoff," in F. Le Play, *Les Ouvriers des deux mondes: Études publiées par la Société d'économie sociale à partir de 1856 par Frédéric Le Play* (Paris: À l'enseigne de l'arbre verdoyant, 1883), p. 285.

18. The Thin Revolution

1. J. Prévost, *Plaisirs des sports: Essais sur le corps humain* (Paris: Gallimard, 1925), p. 57.

2. See G. Durville, "L'homme normal c'est l'athlète," *Naturisme: La grande revue de la culture humaine*, July 15, 1936.

3. C. Fischler, *L'homnivore* (Paris: Odile Jacob, 1993 [1990]), p. 316. This text is extraordinarily rich and stands as the pioneering study in the contemporary analysis of obesity.

4. É. Bayard, *L'Art de reconnaître la beauté du corps humain: L'homme, la femme, l'enfant* (Paris: Ernest Gründ, 1926), pp. 204, 254, 271.

5. A. Dubout, "Le port de Marseille," *Le Rire*, April 1, 1933.

6. See P. Sorcinelli, "L'aliment et la santé," in J.-L. Flandrin and M. Montanari, eds., *Histoire de l'alimentation* (Paris: Fayard, 1996), p. 820.

7. Ibid.

8. G. d'Avenel, *Le Nivellement des jouissances* (Paris, 1913).

9. F. Heckel, *Maigre, Pourquoi? Comment? Conception et méthode nouvelles* (Paris, 1930), p. 17.

10. Ibid., p. 55.

11. J. Ruffier, "L'embonpoint des automobilistes," *Physis, Revue médicale de kinésithérapie et d'éducation physique* (January 1928): 1725. Note the remarks about "the fatal fattening up of automobilists" and "they're fat, way too fat."

12. L. Pascault, "L'arthritisme, maladie de civilization," *Revue des idées*, January 15, 1906, p. 1.

13. See A. Baubérot, *Histoire du naturisme: Le mythe du retour à la nature* (Rennes: Presses universitaires de Rennes, 2004).

14. Ruffier, "L'embonpoint des automobilistes," p. 1725.

15. F. T. Marinetti, "Manifeste futuriste," *Le Figaro*, February 20, 1909.

16. See the ad for the the White Company (1917), in E. J. Heimann, *All-American Ads, 1900–1919* (Cologne: Taschen, 2001), p. 179.

17. See M. Braunschvig, *La Vie américaine et ses Leçons* (Paris: Armand Colin, 1931), p. 147.

18. H. Béraud, *Le Martyre de l'obèse* (Monaco: Imprimerie nationale de Monaco, 1950 [1922]), p. 28.

19. Braunschvig, *La Vie américaine*, p. 49.

20. See "Le nouveau culte de l'homme actif," in C. McDowell, *Histoire de la mode masculine* (Paris: La Martinière, 1997), p. 113.

21. See, for example, Kuppenheimer good clothes (1924), in Heimann, *All-American Ads*, p. 466.

22. *Catalogue de la Manufacture de Saint-Étienne, Tarif-album* (Saint-Étienne, 1924), p. 370.

23. See the ad Michou, *Revue naturiste*, April 15, 1935.

24. Ibid.

25. Béraud, *Le Martyre de l'obèse*, p. 36.

26. Colette, *Le Blé en herbe* (1923), in *Romans, récits, souvenirs* (Paris: Robert Laffont, 2004), 2:305, 313, 314, 331.

27. *Vogue*, December 1, 1922.

28. See M. Perret, "Sortir," in G. Duby and M. Perrot, eds, *Histoire des femmes en Occident* (Paris: Plon, 1990–1991), 4:1991, "Le XIXe siècle."

29. C. Bart, *Les Garçonnes, Modes et fantasmes des années folles* (Paris: Flammarion, 1998), p. 7.

30. See Colette, *Le Blé en herbe*, p. 331: "a dry ankle, a leg of a slender animal."

31. G. Hébert, *L'Éducation physique feminine, Muscle et beauté plastique* (Paris: Vuibert, 1919), p. 71.

32. Colette, *Le Blé en herbe*, pp. 338, 308, 331.

33. H. de Montherlant, *Les Olympiques* (1924), in *Romans et oeuvres de fiction non théâtrale* (Paris: Gallimard, 1959), pp. 281–82.

34. M. Marelli, *Les Soins scientifiques de beauté* (Paris: Oliven, 1936), p. 9.

35. See the observations about the American periodical *Ladies' Home Journal*, in P. N. Stearns, *Fat History: Bodies and Beauty in the Modern West* (New York: New York University Press, 1997), p. 105.

36. See "La sur-marchandise," in E. Morin, *Les Stars* (Paris: Seuil, 1972), p. 98.

37. See Stearns, *Fat History*, p. 45. The author evokes a similar situation in the United States, underlining how patients insisted on getting medical treatment long before doctors. "Indeed, much of the causation of the growing medical concern about weight came from patient pressure, rather than the other way around."

38. L. Chauvois, *Les Dessanglés du ventre, Maladies par relâchement des parois et organes abdominaux* (Paris, 1923).

39. Ibid., p. 23.

40. P. Richer, *Nouvelle Anatomie artistique, Morphologie de la femme* (Paris: Plon, 1920), p. 71ff.

41. Hébert, *L'Éducation physique feminine*, pp. 23, 24, 135.

42. Ibid., p. 140.

43. A. Thooris, *La Vie par le stade* (Paris, 1924), p. 146ff.

44. See, for example, "Symptômes, complications et formes," in G. Mouriquand, *Précis de diététique et des maladies de la nutrition* (Paris, 1926), p. 528ff.

45. See, for example, F. Heckel, *Grandes et petites obésités: Cure radicale* (Paris, 1920 [1911]), p. 226, pl. 5, "Obésité monstrueuse."

46. See the introduction to part 4.

47. J. Vallès, *La Rue* (Paris, 1866), p. 121. See also J. Courtine, "Le corps anormal: histoire et athropologie culturelle de la difformité," in A. Corbin, J.-J. Courtine, and G. Vigarello, eds., *Histoire du Corps* (Paris: Seuil, 2005), 3:202.

48. Vallès, *La Rue*, p. 122.

49. See G. M. Gould and W. L. Pyle, *Anomalies and Curiosities, op. cit.*, p. 359.

50. See "Cannon, the heaviest man in the world, age 30," postcard (late 19th century); "Souvenir de Mlle Térésina," postcard (late 19th century). I thank Jean-Jacques Courtine for sharing these documents with me.

51. J.-J. Courtine, "Le corps animal," in Corbin, Courtine, and Vigarello, *Histoire du Corps*, 1:220.

52. See the collection at the Getty Web site of images from the early twentieth century.

53. See "Cas d'obésité monstrueuse, femme de 247 kg vue de dos," in Heckel, *Maigrir*, p. 314.

54. Ibid., p. 234.

19. Declaring "the Martyr"

1. R. Dubois, *Comment maigrir? Moyens efficaces, conseil pratiques* (Paris, 1912). F. Heckel, *Maigrir, Pourquoi? Comment? Conception et méthode nouvelles* (Paris, 1930). P. Mathieu, *Pourquoi on engraisse: Comment on maigrit* (Paris, 1931). A. Antoine, *L'Art de maigrir* (Paris, 1931).

2. Heckel, *Maigrir,* p. 142.

3. Ibid.

4. Ibid., p. 143. "It is not necessary that it show."

5. See R. Ghigi, "La beauté en question: Autour d'une histoire de la cellulite," DEA thesis, École des Hautes Études en Sciences Sociales, 2002, p. 31.

6. F. Wetterwald, *Qu'est-ce que la cellulite?* (Paris, 1932), p. 15.

7. See chapter 5.

8. Heckel, *Maigrir,* p. 139.

9. See "Complications," in H. and M. Feuillade, *Le Livre de l'obèse,* (Paris: Vigot Maloine, 1935), p. 20.

10. Ibid., "the parasitic origin of malignant tumors," p. 127.

11. See P. Darmon, *Les Cellules folles, L'homme face au cancer de l'Antiquité à nos jours* (Paris: Plon, 1993).

12. Heckel, *Maigrir,* pp. 114, 130.

13. E. Berillon, "La psychologie de la race allemande d'après ses caractères objectifs et spécifiques," *Association française pour l'avancement des sciences: Conférences,* February 2, 1917, p. 105.

14. Ibid., p. 122.

15. Feuillade and Feuillade, *Le Livre de l'obèse,* p. 19.

16. Heckel, *Maigrir,* p. 178–79.

17. Ibid., p. 180.

18. See "Fat as a Turn-of-the-Century Target, Why?" in P. N. Stearns, *Fat History: Bodies and Beauty in the Modern West* (New York: New York University Press, 1997), p. 48.

19. See *Annual Statistical Report: Metropolitan Life Insurance,* November 1922.

20. Heckel, *Maigrir,* p. 187.

21. See the ad for Continental Scale Works, "the new Health-O-Meter de Luxe," 1929, in S. Heller, *All American Ads of the 20s (Midi Series)* ed. J. Heimann (Cologne: Taschen, 2004), p. 276. This ad can be viewed at http://oldadvertising.blogspot. fr/2009/09/health-o-meter-scales-1929.html (accessed June 13, 2012).

22. Ibid.

23. *Fémina,* July 1935.

24. See the ad for Continental Scale Works.

25. See H. Schwartz, *Never Satisfied: A Cultural History of Diets, Fantasies, and Fats* (New York: Free Press, 1986).

26. Heckel, *Maigrir,* p. 187.

27. Feuillade and Feuillade, *Le Livre de l'obèse,* p. 113.

28. L. Caillon, *Guide du malade à Vichy* (Paris: Maloine, 1932).

29. G. and A. Durville, "L'automassage et le massage du ventre," *Naturisme, La grande revue de la culture humaine*, July 15, 1936.

30. E. Desbonnet, *Comment on devient athlète* (Paris, 1910 [1909]), p. 134.

31. See Mathieu, *Pourquoi on engraisse*, p. 39. For a complete panorama of techniques used in the field, see J. Monet, *La Naissance de la kinésithérapie* (Paris: Glyphe, 2009).

32. S. Voronoff, *Quarante-Trois Greffes de singe à l'homme* (Paris: Doin, 1924), p. 94.

33. P. Tissié, *La Fatique et l'Entraînement physique* (Paris, 1897), p. 3.

34. R. W. Emerson, "Self-Reliance" (1841), in *Essays and Lectures* (New York: Library of America, 1983), pp. 257–82.

35. J. de Lerne, *Comment devenir plus fort* (Paris, 1902). S. Roudès, *Pour faire son chemin dans la vie* (Paris, 1902).

36. See J. Defrance, *L'Excellence corporelle: La formation des activités physiques et sportives modernes, 1770–1914* (Rennes: Presses universitaires de Rennes, 1987), p. 135. See J. P. Muller, *My System: 15 Minutes Exercise a Day for Health's Sake* (London: Link House, 1904). Total sales are estimated at two million. An online version available at http://www.archive.org/details/MySystemByJ.P.Muller had been downloaded 23,360 times as of February 2012.

37. See chapter 11. For a synthetic study of all of these new experiments, see R. H. Chittenden, *Physiological Economy in Nutrition* (New York: Frederick A. Stokes 1904).

38. See W. O. Atwater and E. B. Rosa, "A new respiration calorimeter and experiments on the conservation of energy in the human body," *Physical Review*, September 1899.

39. See W. O. Atwater and F. G. Benedict, *Experiments on the Metabolism of Matter and Energy in the Human Body (1900–1902)* (Washington: Government Printing Office, 1903).

40. C. E. Ruppli, *Le Métabolisme basal: Essai d'étude générale, techniques et résultats* (Bordeaux, 1929), p. 68.

41. See chapter 17.

42. M. Labbé and H. Stévenin, *Le Métabolisme basal* (Paris, 1929), p. 219. "Bouchard's theory is ruined." Subsequent precise studies will be less affirmative about the basal metabolism of obese subjects. See G. Besse, *Morphologie et Physiologie animales* (Paris: Larousse, 1953), p. 452.

43. Ibid., p. 218. See also G. Laroche, *Le Métabolisme basal en clinique* (Paris, 1931), p. 7. "In cases of obesity, basal metabolism is generally normal, but it may be lowered by low thyroid function and by the genital glands."

44. Feuillade and Feuillade, *Le Livre de l'obèse*, p. 37.

45. Heckel, *Maigrir*, p. 51.

46. Labbé and Stévenin, *Le Métabolisme basal*, p. 220.

47. Ibid., p. 219.

48. "Pour maigrir," *Le Printemps, Moniteur des modes illustrées*, no. 3, 1921.

49. M. Riva, *Marlene Dietrich par sa fille* (Paris: Flammarion, 1993), p. 133.

50. Heckel, *Maigrir,* pp. 194, 221.

51. *Votre beauté,* April 1937.

52. H. Béraud, *Le Martyre de l'obèse* (Monaco: Imprimerie nationale de Monaco, 1950 [1922]), pp. 19, 88, 114, 124, 149. Béraud's text is to be read with a certain distance. This 1922 narrative remains pathbreaking. The author's later works slip into political extremism and indignities—especially those written during the German occupation, which led to his condemnation.

53. Ibid., p. 43.

54. Ibid., see chapter 18.

55. Béraud, *Le Martyre de l'obèse,* p. 29.

56. Ibid., see chapter 10.

57. Ibid., p. 299.

Part 6. Changes in the Contemporary Debate

1. See B. M. Popkin and C. M. Doak, "The Obesity Epidemic Is a Worldwide Phenomenon," *Nutritional Reviews,* no. 56 (1998). For a more anthropological approach to the problem, see "Epidemic Obesity," in S. L. Gilman, *Fat: A Cultural History of Obesity* (Cambrige: Polity, 2008), p. 12.

2. See A. M. Prentice and S. A. Jeb, "Beyond Body Mass Index," *Obesity Reviews,* no. 2 (2001).

3. C. Collange and C. Gallois, *La Grosse et la Maigre* (Paris: Albin Michel, 1994).

4. R. Peto and G. Whitlock, "Body-Mass Index and Cause-Specific Mortality in 900,000 Adults: Collaborative Analysis of 57 Prospective Studies," *Lancet,* March 18, 2009.

5. See *Le Monde,* November 19, 2009.

6. See the ObEpi studies, undertaken in France every three years since 1997, online at www.lanutrition.fr/ObEpi.

7. See the speech by Bill Clinton on "The Weight of the Nation," July 27, 2009, at a conference sponsored by the Centers for Disease Control and Prevention.

8. See the ObEpi study for 2006.

9. M.-F. Rolland-Cachera and F. Bellisle, "No Correlation Between Adiposity and Food Intake: Why Are Working Class Children Fatter?" *American Journal of Clinical Nutrition,* no. 44 (December 1986): 779–87.

10. See J. Sobal and J. Stunkard, "Socioeconomic Status and Obesity: A Review of the Literature," *Psychological Bulletin,* no. 105 (1989).

11. See J.-L. Lambert, *L'Évolution des modèles alimentaires en France* (Paris: Lavoisier, 1987).

12. P. Delaveau and C. Jaffiol, *Expliquez-moi l'obésité, Comprendre, prévenir, traiter* (Paris: Pharmathèmes, 2005), p. 24.

13. Ibid., p. 27. See also "Obésité et mortalité," *La Lettre de la NSFA,* no. 21 (September 2006).

14. C. Emery, "Évaluation du coût associé à l'obésité en France," *La Presse médicale* 36 (June 2007).

15. S. Czernichow and A. Basdevant, "Conséquences medico-économiques de l'obésité," in A. Basdevant and B. Guy-Grand, eds., *Médecine de l'obésité* (Paris: Flammarion, 2004), p. 28.

16. See "Proposition de loi relative à la prevention et à la lutte conte l'obésité présentée par MM. R. Courtand, C. Saunier, M. Rainaud," Sénat, May 6, 2008, "Exposé des motifs."

17. J.-M. Le Guen, *Obésité, nouveau mal français, Pour une réponse politique à un fléau social* (Paris: Armand Colin, 2005).

18. Ibid., see also "Proposition de loi." *Enjeu de société:* R. Mazzoli, "La Lutte contre l'obésité," *Marketing Magazine*, December 1, 2004.

19. See the "health emergency" announcement, published by the association Obésité, online at www.obesipub.org.

20. Le Guen, *Obésité.*

21. See the first French study, C. Fischler, *L'homnivore* (Paris: Odile Jacob, 1993 [1990]). For a recent synthesis, see A. Basdevant, "Origines des obésités," in Basdevant and Guy-Grand, *Médecine.*

22. See C. Simon, "Alimentation, gain de poids et obésité," in Badevant and Guy-Grand, *Médecine*, p. 54. "The palatability of a food and the subjective judgment of the pleasant character of that food."

23. A. S. Cérisola and J. Mistral, "L'obésité aux États-Unis: Enjeux économiques et défis politiques," Washington, DC, French Embassy, working document of the agence-financière, March 2004.

24. Study INCA (Étude Individuelle Nationale des Consommations Alimentaires), AFFSSA (Agence Française de Sécurité Sanitaire des Aliments)/CREDOC (Centre de Recherche pour l'Étude et l'Observation des Conditions de Vie)/DGGAL (Direction de l'Alimentation), 1990.

25. Simon, "Alimentation."

26. Ibid., p. 55.

27. See Le Guen, *Obésité*, p. 41.

28. Nouvelobs.com, February 27, 2007.

29. *Le Monde*, September 18, 2007.

30. See "Proposition de loi."

31. See the interview with A. Badevant, *Le Monde*, November 19, 2009.

32. See the interview with A. de Danne, ibid.

33. See C. Durif-Bruckert, *La Nourriture et nous, Corps imaginaire et normes sociales* (Paris: Armand Colin, 2007), p. 166.

34. Ibid.

35. Ibid.

36. Ibid.

37. J.-P. Poulain, *Sociologie de l'obésité* (Paris: PUF, 2009), p. 115.

38. M. Le Barzic, "Déterminants psychologiques de l'obésité," in Basdevant and Guy-Grand, *Médécine*, p. 62.

39. See C. Durif-Bruckert, *La Nourriture, op. cit.*, p. 170.

40. See B. Waysfield, *Le Poids et le Moi* (Paris: Armand Colin, 2003), p. 72.

41. Ibid., p. 59.

42. Poulain, *Sociologie de l'obésité.*

43. Le Barzic, "Déterminants," p. 62.

44. For a pioneering study of this "syndrome," see A. Keys, J. Brozek, and A. Henschel, *The Biology of Human Starvation*, 2 vols. (Saint Paul: University of Minnesota Press, 1950).

45. Le Barzic, "Déterminants," p. 65.

46. Ibid. See also M. Corcos, *Le Corps insoumis, Psychopathologie des troubles et conduits alimentaires* (Paris: Dunod, 2005).

47. See J. Winand, *Aspects qualitatifs et quantitatifs du métabolisme lipidique de la souris normale et de la souris congénitalement obèse* (Paris: Maloine, 1970).

48. J. Nassier, "Taste, Food Intake, and Obesity," *Obesity Reviews*, no. 2 (2001).

49. K. Clément, "Déterminants géniques de l'obésité humaine," in Basdevant and Guy-Grand, *Médecine*.

50. Basdevant, "Origine des obésités," p. 42.

51. See chapter 17.

52. Ibid.

53. Basdevant, "Origines des obésités," p. 38. Simon, "Alimentation," p. 53. Basdevant, ibid. Clément, "Déterminants," p. 85. The leptin gene is described as an "orchestra conductor."

54. See S. C. Woods and R. J. Seeley, "Adiposity Signals and the Control of Energy Homeostasis," *Nutrition*, no. 16 (2000).

55. Basdevant, "Origine des obésités," p. 41.

56. Ibid., p. 35.

57. Le Barzic, "Déterminants," p. 60.

58. G. S. Barsh, I. S. Farroqi, and S. O'Rahilly, "Genetics of Body Weight Regulation," *Nature Genetics*, no. 404 (2000).

59. Clément, "Déterminants," p. 89. A. Basdevant, "Examen clinique," in Basdevant and Guy-Grand, *Médécine*, p. 95.

60. Y. Schutz, "Dépense énergétique et obésité," in Basdevant and Guy-Grand, *Médecine*, p. 73.

61. Clément, "Déterminants," p. 89.

62. Basdevant, "Origine des obésités," p. 45.

63. For one of the first prophetic texts on this subject, see D. Rorvik, *Quand l'homme devient machine: Une nouvelle étape de l'évolution* (Paris: Albin Michel, 1973). A translation of Rorvik and L. B. Shettles's best seller, *Your Baby's Sex: Now You Can Choose* (1971).

64. Poulain, *Sociologie de l'obésité*, p. 112.

65. P. Dupuy and C. Berberian, "Global Boboland," *Libération*, September 1, 2009. See P. Dupuy and C. Berberian, *Global Boboland* (Paris: Fluide Glacial-Audie, 2009).

66. Fischler, *L'Homnivore*, p. 354. "With the triumphant arrival of individualism, what the body is testimony to now is not so much (social) power, as (individual) mastery."

67. F. Dubet and D. Martucelli, *Dans quelle société vivons-nous?* (Paris: Seuil, 1998), p. 75. "L'individu se détache de la grande société."

68. A. Ehrenberg, *Le Culte de la performance* (Paris: Calmann-Lévy, 1991), p. 281. "L'individu est son apparence."

69. A. Janov, *Le corps se souvient: Guérir en revivant sa souffrance* (Monaco: Rocher, 1997). A translation of A. Janov, *Why You Get Sick, How You Get Well: How Feelings Affect Your Health* (West Hollywood, CA: Dove, 1996).

70. S. Marinopoulos, *Le Corps bavard* (Paris: Fayard, 2007).

71. T. Bertherat, *Le corps a ses raisons, Auto-guérison et anti-gymnastique* (Paris: Seuil, 1976).

72. J. Doazan, J.-C. Grosse, J. Mathis, C. Pellet, J.-L. Rebora, F. Senent, J. Serena, and J. Siccardi, *Le corps qui parle, Huit pieces courtes* (Paris: Les Cahiers de l'Égaré, 2001).

73. M. Gauchet, "Je suis mon corps," in *Qu'avons-nous fait de la liberté? Télérama*, special issue (2007): 44.

74. P. Pallardy, *Et si ça venait du ventre? Fatigue, prise de poids, cellulite, troubles sexuels, problèmes esthétiques, depression, insomnie, mal de dos* (Paris: Pocket, 2002).

75. Le Barzic, "Les Déterminants," p. 64.

76. *Mincir Zen*, no. 2 (2009).

77. See Waysfield, *Le Poids et le Moi*, p. 73.

78. Fischler, *L'Homnivore*, p. 343.

79. Poulain, *Sociologie de l'obésité*, p. 112.

80. F. Coupry, *Éloge du gros dans un monde sans consistence* (Paris: Robert Laffont, 1989).

81. Ibid., p. 191.

82. See, for example, the High Authority Against Discrimination and for Equality (HALDE), an independent administrative authority created by the law of December 30, 2004.

83. See the group's Web site at www.allegrofortissimo.com.

84. See the interview with Viviane Cacquière, president of Allegro Fortissimo, October 7, 2008, online at www.ma-grand-taille.com.

85. Waysfield, *Le Poids et le Moi*, p. 146.

86. Cécile, blogpost at www.allegrofortissimo.com, May 11, 2009.

87. J. Boucher, *La Grosse* (Paris: Hachette pratique, 2009), p. 91.

88. Ibid., p. 149.

89. Ibid.

INDEX

Photos are indicated by *p1, p2, etc.*

Abdomen, as source of inventiveness, 39

Abdominal muscles, 150–51

Abdominal type, 150

Adipose, ambiguity of, 10

Advertising, 164–65, 188

All That Glitters Is Not Gold, *p7*

Alpino, Prosper, 72

Ambiguity: contemporary identity and, 196–97; Enlightenment-era size, 89; in middle ages, 4, 9, 10–12, 14, 20, 28, 89; between phlegm and fat, 46; Renaissance-era, 42, 46, 62, 67, 74; in Restoration and July Monarchy periods, 119, 121, 124; skinniness, 42; of thresholds, 43–44; *see also* Gradations, of fat and fatness

Ambivalence, Renaissance period, 39–40

Anatomy: early nineteenth-century, 129; Enlightenment-era, 83–84, 220*n*19; 1920s graduated, 170–71

Anatomy Society, 129

Anemic obesity, 155–56, 158

Anglicus, Bartholomaeus, 11, 14

Animals, 106, 122, 161; fear of humidity in certain, 71, 104; Middle Ages and, 5; physiques of carnivorous, 105; Renaissance-era weighing of, 67

Anne of France, 29

Apoplexy, 47–49, 150

Appetite, civilized, 105

Aron, Jean-Paul, 133

Ascendancy and power, 5, 27, 43

Ascites, 12, 51

Atavistic obesity, 160–61

Atwater, Wilber Olin, 179–80

Aurelianus, Caelius, 10

Bacher, Georges-Fréderic, 100

Balance scale, 82–83, *p9*

Balneology, digestive malfunction and, 163–64

Balzac, Honoré, 114, 116, 119, 227*n*3; eating habits of, 133; ironic reversals of, 121–22; thin characters of, 123, 124

Banting, William, 159

Barygraphic curves, 178

Basal metabolic rate (BMR), 179, 180

Baths, 102, *p3, p10, p11*

Bayeux tapestries, 23

Bears, 6, 21, 25

Beaumont, Jean-Baptiste Élie de, 81–82, 94, 100, 136, 183–84

Beauty: Enlightenment-era, 220n29; in Middle Ages, 3–4, 28–29; in Renaissance era, 40, 67–68, 74; today's ideal of feminine, 170; turn-of-the-century, 144

Beggars, 33–34

Belly: abdominal muscles for masculine, 150–51; differing standards for men and women, 87–89, p5; Enlightenment-era nuance and, 86–87; as masculine image, 148–49; see also Bourgeois belly

Belts, 29, 75–76, p10

Benedict, Francis Gano, 179–80

Béraud, Henri, 168–69, 182–83, 184

Berbérian, Dupuy, 194

Bertall, A., 118, 148, 149, 150, 228n14

Berthelot, Marcelin, 157

Bertholon, Pierre, 102–3

Betrayal, 195

Bigness: ambivalence about, 39–40; ascendancy and power in, 5, 27, 43; degrees of, 87; evaluation of, 43, 64–67; health associated with, 26–27; Middle Ages ambiguity of fat and, 4, 9, 10–12, 14, 20, 28; stupidity linked with, 26; thresholds of acceptable, 43–44, 87; very big, 7–9; see also Degrees; Fat and Fatness; Gradations, of fat and fatness; Typologies; specific time periods

Black bile, 42

blood: circulation, 48; excess, 155–56

BMR; see Basal metabolic rate

Body: care, 178–79; exposure, 145–46; types, 150; see also Female body

Body mass index, 143

Bosse, Abraham, 59, 88

Boswell, James, 104

Bouchard, Charles, 155, 156, 157

Boucher, Joëlle, 196

Bouillaud, Jean-Baptiste, 126

Bourgeois belly, p7; ironic reversals about, 121–23; obesity type and, 118; prestige, 109; respectability for, 120–21, 123–24; social mores and, 118

Boutet, Henri, 144–45

Brantôme, 40

Breads, 131–32, 231n1

Breasts, 60, 75

Bright, Richard, 126

Bright, Timothy, 43

Brillat-Savarin, 114, 118, 120; chemistry of foods detailed by, 132–33, 134

Brueghel, Pieter, 40

La Bruyère, Jean de, 43

Buchan, William, 103

Buffon, G. L., 83, 84, 86, 87, 112; diet recommended by, 106

Burner, 154, 156, 180

Bustle, 147

Byron, George Gordon (Lord), 114–15

Calories, 156–57; combustion theory and specificities of, 139; treatment as reducing, 160

Cambrie, Giraud de, 4

Campanella, Tommaso, 52

Cappadoce, Arétée de, 12

Carbon accumulation, 128

Cardan, Girolamo, 65

La Caricature, 122

Caricature du roi Édouard VII d'Angleterre, Le Foudre de guerre, p8

Caricatures, 10, p7, p8, p11; contemporary, 194–95; Enlightenment-era, 86, 96; Renaissance-era, 40; Restoration and July Monarchy period, 117, 122, 123

Carnot, Sadi, 128

Carrache, Annibal, x

Castiglione, Baldassar, 65, 74

Causes, see Origins and causes, of fat

Cellulite, 175

Cerclage (special belt), 75
Cervantes, M. de, 39–40
Chair scale, 70, 79–80
Charas, Moyse, 61
Charivari, 115
Charles VI, 14
Charlotte, Elizabeth, ix, 66
Chauliac, Guy de, 15, 20
Chemistry: diet and, 131–33, 134; Enlightenment-era, 106–7; ethno-, 176; fat origin experiments, 127–28; hydropic urine, 126; of spa life, 162–64; of synthesis, 157; *see also* Combustion theory of food
Cheyne, George, 82, 104, 105
Childbirth, Renaissance period: prescriptions for after, 67–68; prevention of breast enlargement during, 75
Child of wealth, gout sufferer as, 54
Children, 92
Chodowiecki, Daniel, 86, 88
Circus shows, 172
Clerics, 4, 18–19, 33
Clothes: 1870s women's, 147; evocation of "hidden" and, 144–45; personality conveyed in, 194; pressure exerted by, 65; tightness of, 64; *see also* Fashions
De la Clôture, Louis Le Pecq, 91, 93
Colette, Sidonie-Gabrielle, 169
Combustion theory of food, 109, 125, 127–28, 131, 134, 181; burner deficiency and, 154, 156; caloric specificities arising from, 139; diet and, 107, 110, 157; ruining of, 180
Commynes, P. de, 25
Contemporary debate, 185–97; collective mobilization against obesity, 187–88; criticism of fat in, 189, 193–95; genetic studies and, 191–92; obesity epidemic, 185, 186–87; rhetoric of hope in, 192–93; self-identity and, 193–96; thinness and obesity dynamics in, 188–89; thinness effects

perceived in, 189–90; vicious circle theme, 191
Contours: lack of distinctions between, *p2*; molding of, *p8*, *p12*
Corpimeter, 114
Corpulence, obesity replacing, 92
Corsets, 88, 164, 169, *p8*; archaic and modern, 135; open and closed, 144–45; Renaissance period invention of, 74–76
Coupry, François, 195
Court culture, 21–22, 35–36
Crafty, 141
Cranach, Lucas, 56–57
Criticism, of fat: affluence focus of, 95–97; contemporary, 189, 193–95; early 1900s, 168–69; Enlightenment-era centrality of, 96; in fifteenth-century iconography, 24–25; insensitivity and, 94–95; ironic reversals as, 121–23; medieval, 17, 23, 24–25; in modern times, x–xi; moral nature of medieval, 6–7, 25, 31; psychological nature of, xi–xii; *see also* Stigmatization
Cruveilhier, Jean, 129
CSIR, *see* International Scientific Commission on Nourishment
Cullen, William, 92, 101

Dairy consumption, 167
Dangers of excess, 1
Decadence, 153
Deformations, morbid imminence and, 130
Degeneration concept, 158–59
Degrees, 87, 155, 175–76; scale and, xi–xii, 201n14; *see also* Gradations, of fat and fatness
D'Ennery, Adolphe, 115
De Nogent, Barry, 89
Deregulated nervous systems, 158
Desbordes, Sieur, 81
Deveaux, Jean, 49

Dickens, Charles, 148–49
Dictionary definitions, diet, 134–35
Dictionnaire, 60, 92, 222*n*13
Dictionnaire de médicine, xii
Diderot, D., 95
Diet and dieting: chemistry and, 131–33, 134; combustion and, 107, 110, 157; contemporary, 189; dictionary entry for diet, 134–35; early nineteenth century, 131–34; Enlightenment-era ideas on, 103–7; exercise and, 71–73; meat-plant debates, 105–7; Renaissance restraints and, 69–71; slow nutrition concept, 157; social class and, 152; turn-of-the-century, 152, 159–62; *see also* Foods
Dietrich, Marlene, 182
Digestion, balneology and, 163–64
Dissection, hydropsy death and, 93
Doctors: Enlightenment-era, 82, 83, 92–93, 99–100, 102–5; Middle Ages, 27–28; modern, 182–84; Renaissance period, 45–54, 60, 70; Restoration and July Monarchy, 120, 126, 130; turn of the century, 149, 155–58, 162–63, 182–83; *see also* Medical texts, medieval; *specific doctors*
Double-breasted suit, 169
Dryness, Renaissance period and, 70–73
Du Chesne, Joseph, 46
Dürer, Albrecht, 40, 57, *p3*

Early nineteenth century, *see* Restoration and July Monarchy periods
Edema, *see* Hydropsy
Edward VII, *p8*
Electricity, 102–3
Elixirs, 165
Embonpoint, 61, 145
Energy model, 109–10, 156–58; *see also* Chemistry; Combustion theory of food
The English Depicted By Themselves, 116

Enlightenment era, 77–107; affluence criticism in, 95–97; attention to forms of obesity in, *p5*; beauty criteria, 220*n*29; chemistry revolution, 106–7; criticism centrality during, 96; exceptional cases publicized in, 81, 92, *p5*; first forms specifications, 84–87, *p5*; gradations and, 81–87, 220*n*17, 220*n*19; health focus in, 79–81; insensitivity feared in, 94–95; means of measuring invented in, 82–84; modernity concerns of, 106; nervous tension concerns, 90, 91–92, 222*n*12; obesity term introduced in, 91–93, 222*nn*13, 14; overview, 77–78; reproductive faculties concern in, 94–95, 97; size precision, 77, 81–82, *p5*; social and political dimension of fatness, *p5*; soft fibers concern in, 90, 91–92; statistical calculations, 83–84, 220*n*17, 220*n*18; stigmatizing powerlessness in, 90–98; treatments, 99–107; waist measurement in, 81–82, 219*n*12; waists of men and women, 87–89; weight measurement in, 79–81; *see also* Women, Enlightenment-era
Equilibrium, 79–80, 145
Ethno-chemistry, 176
Ettmüller, Michael, 67
Evacuation, 15–16, 72, 99
Evaluation, beginning of, 43, 64–67; numbers and, 109
Évian spas, 163
Exceptional cases: Enlightenment-era publicizing of, 81, 92, *p5*; 1920s study of monstrous, 171–73; potential discoveries from, 111–12
Excess: blood, 155–56; criticism of, 7–9; dangers of, 1; gout from wine, 53; skinniness, 69
Excitants, 101–2, 160–61
Excretion, balance between ingestion and, 79–80

Exercise, 71–73, 161–62

Fairs and carnivals, 115, 172
The Fall of the Damned, 57, *p4*
Faret, Nicolas, 35
Fashions: 1920s male, 169; 1920s
    women's, 169–70
Fat and fatness: discounting localiza-
    tion of, 50; double judgment of, 119;
    early ambiguity of adipose, 10; fight
    against, xii–xiii; fire and, 127–28, 157;
    heaviness and lack of intelligence,
    36; historical overview, ix–xiii; as
    malady, 92; in medieval texts, 10–12;
    opulence and disability distinction,
    8–9; pathology of, 92–93, 176–77;
    popular songs denigrating, 38; as
    public health threat, 187; Renais-
    sance rejection of, 38; Restoration
    period definitions of, 127–28; scale
    and degrees of, xi–xii, 155, 175–76,
    201n14; vulgarity and, 41, 96; *see also*
    Ambiguity; Ambivalence, Renais-
    sance period; Bigness; Criticism, of
    fat; Gradations, of fat and fatness;
    Origins and causes, of fat; Size;
    Thresholds; Weight; *specific time
    periods*
Feasts: in Middle Ages, 5, 8–9, 19, 27; in
    Renaissance, 35, 38–39; in Restora-
    tion and July Monarchy period,
    133–34
Female body: dominant humor of, 11;
    medieval view of ideal, 22; public con-
    demnation of, xi; turn of the century
    thinness of, 169–70
Feminine obesity: 1920s and, 175; turn-
    of-the-century types, 147–48
Fibers, soft, 90, 91–92
Fire: fat-burning, 127–28, 157; insuffi-
    cient, 158; Lavoisier's oxygen discov-
    ery and, 127, 230n8
Floyer, John, 80

Foix, Count of, 6
Foods: Brillat-Savarin's chemistry and,
    132–33, 134; CSIR on meat and dairy,
    167; drying, 71, 198; plastic, 127, 156;
    respiratory, 127–28, 156; stigmatiz-
    ing of, 132; weighing, 70; *see also*
    Combustion theory of food; Diet and
    dieting
Fougères, Etienne de, 28–29
Le Fournier, André, 68
Free time, 154
The French Depicted by Themselves, 116,
    119, 120
Friction, perspiration and, 101
Froissart, J., 6, 47–48
Futurist Manifesto, 168

Galippe, Victor, 158
Gambetta, Léon, 149
Gargantua, Renaissance giants and, 38
Gastronomy, 132–33
Gastrophoric men, 117–21
Gautier, Armand, 152
Genetic studies, 191–92
Giants, medieval mythical, 4
Glissenti, Fabio, 73
Globe imagery, 62–63
Glutton: bear as symbol of, 25; as gour-
    met, 134; in Middle Ages, 6, 19, 25, *p1*
Goncourt brothers, 133, 148
Gonthier, Nicole, 7
Gout: as malady of rich, 54; medieval
    view of, 14–15; Renaissance doctors
    on, 53–54
Gradations, of fat and fatness, xi–xii;
    Enlightenment sensitivity to, 81–87,
    220n17, 220n19; in Middle Ages,
    20–21, 27–28; modern period, 170–71,
    174; new terms toward increasing,
    55, 56; Renaissance period difficulty
    with, 43–44, 46–47; roundness and,
    60; of weight gain, 170–71; *see also*
    Degrees

Grandville, J. J., 122, 135–36
Le gras, x, 201*n*8
Grasse, 62
Le gros, x, 201*n*8
Grosse, Francis, 86
Guérard, Nicolas, 34
Guyon, Louis, 46, 55

Head and Face of a Hydropic Man, *p*2
Health: Enlightenment focus on, 79–81;
    fat as public health threat, 187; medi-
    eval bigness and, 26–27; medieval
    principles and practices, 28; medieval
    regimes for, 20
Health Diary of Louis XIV, 54
Health practitioners, 181
Hébert, George, 171
Height: measuring weight and, 83–84,
    112–13, 143; waist measurements
    ignoring, 81–82, 219*n*12
Heingarter, Conrad, 27–28
Henry IV, 46, 72
Hereditary factors, 155
Herriot, Édouard, 176
Hildegarde of Bingen, 11
Hippocrates, 10
Hips, turn-of the century attention on,
    146–48
History, of fat people, overview, ix–xiii
Hogarth, William, 86, 96
Horseback riding, 101
Household income, 186–87
The Household of the English Merchant, *p*5
The Human Comedy (Balzac), 116, 119
Humors, bodily: evacuating, 72; gout
    and, 14, 54; hydropsy and, 52; medi-
    eval views of, 11–12, 14; Renaissance
    focus on, 70–71
Hutchinson, John, 130
Hydropsy, 12–13, *p*2; cure for, 15; diagno-
    sis changes, 126; Enlightenment-era,
    93; Renaissance period and, 51–52;
    tonics for, 100

Hygiène de l'obèse (Mathieu/Proust),
    143
Hyperbolic exaggeration, 123
Hypothyroidism, 161

Identity: body and, 196; contemporary
    self-, 193–97; paradox, 196–97
*Imaginative Exercises of Different Human
    Characteristics and Forms* (von Goez),
    86
Impotence, skinniness and, 42
Impromptu of Versaille (Molière), 63
Inactivity, 34, 120
The Indiscreet Jewels (Diderot), 95
Inertias, xiii
Ingestion-excretion equilibrium, 79–80
Insensitivity, 94–95
Insults, Renaissance expressions and,
    36–38
Interior milieu, 161
International Scientific Commission on
    Nourishment (CSIR), 167
Intuitive contours, seventeenth century,
    66
Intumescences, 93, 103
Invasion theme, 187

Joubert, Laurent, 47
Journal de médicine, 81, 92, 219*n*12
July Monarchy period, *see* Restoration
    and July Monarchy periods

Knights, 5, 21

Laughing fat person, 40
Lavatar, Gaspar, 85
Lavoisier, A. L., 106–7, 123, 127, 135, 179,
    230*n*8
Legislation, 188
Lemons, 73–74
Leptin signals, 192
De L'Étoile, Pierre, 49, 75
Leucophlegmasia, 12

Leven, Manuel, xi

Lévy, Michel, 129

Liébault, Jean, 41, 68, 73, 74, 75, 222*n*14

Liebig, J., 127, 128, 156

Life insurance, 177

Linguistic changes, during Renaissance period, 59–63

Lining, John, 80

Lion, 21

Livre, 220*n*17

Louis VI (Louis the Fat), 8, 15

Louis XIII, 70

Louis XIV, 54

Louis XV, 89, 97–98

Louis XVIII, 114

Louis-Philippe, *p7*

Lourd (heavy), 36

Lymphatic obesity, 162

Lymphatic system discovery, 50

Maccary, Ange, 111

Margaret of Navarre (queen), 76

Margueritte, Victor, 170

Marivaux, P. de, 84–86

Marriage of the Virgin, p2

The Marvelous Effect of Lacing . . . a View of the Pretty Miller's Wife, p9

Massage, 178

Mathieu, Albert, 143, 158, 160

Maupassant, G. de, 142, 147–48, 150

Measurement: Enlightenment-era invention of, 82–84; oxygen, 179–80; waist, 81–82, 219*n*12; waist measurements ignoring weight, 81–82, 219*n*12; weight, 79–81; weight and height, 83–84, 112–13, 143

Meat consumption, 105–7, 152, 167; Middle Ages, 5–6

Mechanical explanations, 51–52

De Médici, Catherine, 47, 72

Medical texts, medieval, 10–12, 19–21; *see also* Doctors

Melancholy, 42–43, 94

Membranes, distinctions between mucous and fibrous, 129

Men: belly as masculine image, 148–49; gastrophoric, 117–20; Middle Ages descriptions of clerics, 4; 1920s fashions for, 169; obesity in early nineteenth-century, 135; waists of women and, 87–89

Mennell, Stephen, 105

Middle Ages, ix–x, 1–29; ambiguity in, 4, 9, 10–12, 14, 20, 28; ascendancy and power of bigness, 5, 27, 43; beautiful women described in, 3–4; beauty in, 28–29; behaviors and immorality criticisms in, 6–7, 25, 31; bigness and prestige in, 3–9; bigness types coexisting in, 17; from big to very big, 7–9; clerical model, 18–19; conflicting images of, 1; courtly model of, 21–22; criticism of fat in, 17, 23, 24–25; doctor recommendations for very big, 27–28; evacuation as cure in, 15–16; excess criticized in, 7–9; feasts of, 5, 8–9, 19, 27; gluttony in, 6, 19, 25, *p1*; gout viewed in, 14–15; healthy regime idea, 20; hunger context, 3; medical texts, 19–21; medical texts of, 10–12; mythical giants of, 4; slimming efforts in, 28–29; social class distinctions, 25–26; swellings viewed in, 12–14; *see also* Women, in Middle Ages

Milaud, Albert, 142

Military recruitment, 1800s, 114

Mirrors, 145–46

Modern period (twentieth century), x, 167–84; criticism of fat person in, x–xi; fashion, 169–70; feminine obesity and, 175; Gradations and, 170–71, 174; graduated anatomy of, 170–71; monstrosity theme, 171–73; 1920s narratives of suffering, 174–75; pathological diversity of 1920s, 176–77; stigmatization in, 174–75,

Modern period (*continued*)
    183; treatment narratives of, 181–84;
    see also Contemporary debate
Molière (Jean-Baptiste Poquelin), 63
Mondeville, Henri de, 11, 19
Monks, 18–19
Monnier, Henri, 118, 124
Monstrosities, 56, 171–73; swimwear
    allowing view of, 145
Morality, medieval criticism based on,
    6–7, 25, 31
Morbid imminence, 129–30
Moreau the Younger, 88
Mundy, Françis, 106
Muscles: abdominal, 150–51; tone, 166
Mythical giants, 4
Myxedema, 161

Nana (Zola), 146
National Healthy Nutrition Program
    (PNNS), 188
Natural History (Buffon), 83
Neck, 48–49; squashed, 57
Nephritis, 126
Nervous tension: deregulated nervous
    systems, 158; Enlightenment-era
    focus on, 90, 91–92, 222n12; regimen,
    103–5
The New Game, p11
1920s, *see* Modern period
Nineteenth century, *see* Restoration and
    July Monarchy periods
Nollet, Abbé, 102
Numbers: Buffon's, 84; early nineteenth-
    century presence of, 111–12; 1800s
    evaluations using, 109; Enlightenment
    concern with, 79–81; history and, 198;
    Restoration period and, 131; Turn of
    the century precision and, 161–62
Numerical curiosity, 79–81
Nutrition, Bouchard's retarding, 157

"Ob" (mouse) research, 191–92

Obesity: anemic, 155–56, 158; anti-obesity
    advertising in 1900s, p10; atavistic,
    160–61; attention to forms of, 84–87,
    p5; changes in use of word, 175;
    degrees of, 155, 175–76; dynamics of
    contemporary thinness and, 188–89;
    Enlightenment-era introduction of
    term, 14, 91–93, 222nn13; epidemic of,
    185, 186–87; feminine, 175; as health
    threat, 187; household income and,
    186–87; masculine, 135; nutrition-
    retarding factor in, 157; phenomenal
    cases of, p5; scientific period of, 154;
    suffering dimension of, 135–37; turn-
    of-the-century female types, 147–48;
    see also Gradations, of fat and fatness;
    Treatment; Typologies
Oily aspect of skin, 62
One's Own Doctor (Deveaux), 49
Opulence: disability distinguished from,
    8–9; stigma of, 14
Orange, princes of, 48
Origins and causes, of fat: chemistry
    experiments, 127–28; Renaissance
    period views, 70–71; Restoration-
    period views of, 127–28; turn-of-the-
    century views of, 157–58
Overall roundness, 56
Oxygen, 157; discovery of, 107, 123, 127,
    230n8; measuring, 179–80

Pallardy, Pierre, 194–95
Paré, Ambroise, 34
Pathology, of fatness: classification, 93;
    Enlightenment-era, 92–93; turn-of-
    the-century diversifying of, 176–77
The Patriotic Weight-Loss Machine, p6
Pear image, 123
Pepys, Samuel, x, 66, 216n11
Personal testimonies: contemporary,
    185–86; treatments and, 139
Perspiration: Floyer's comparison, 80;
    friction and, 101; imperceptible, 70, 80

Petit, Antoine, 100, 101

De Peysonnel, Charles, 91

Philipon, Charles, 122

Philippe IV (Le Bel), 19

Philosophical Dictionary (1764), 106

Phlegm, 11, 14, 46; leucophlegmasia, 12

Phlegmatic person, 156

Physical thickness, 79

Physiology of Taste (Brillat-Savarin), 114, 132

Pickwick Papers (Dickens), 148–49

Pig, 98

pinched waist, 123

Pinguis (big), 7, 27–28

Pisan, Christine de, 13–14, 19

Plastic foods, 127, 156

PNNS, *see* National Healthy Nutrition Program

polysarcia, 160

Poquelin, Jean-Baptiste; *see* Molière

Portrait of a Young Woman, p4

Portraits, p4; realism in, 58–59

"Portraits" (Carrache), x

Powerlessness, xiii, 77–78, 90–98

Praepinguis (very big), 7, 27–28

Preparatory Studies (Rubens), 57–58

Prestige, 3–9, 35, 89, 109

Prévost, Jean, 166

Proust, Adrien, 143, 158, 160

Public health threat, narrative of, 187

Quest of the Holy Grail, 21

Quetelet, Adolphe, 112–13, 143, 186

Rabelais, F., 39, 59–60, 72; giants of, 38

Reactivity, fiber and, 91

Realism, 23, 24, 55–59

Regulatory system, 192

Relational suffering, 184

Renaissance period, 31–76; activity and passivity, 33–36; ambivalence, 39–40; apoplexy in, 47–49; beauty manuals in, 67–68; corsets invented in, 74–76;

court model of, 35–36; diets and restraints of, 69–71; dramatic representations of fatness in, 45–47; evaluation beginning in, 64–67; fat rejected in, 35–38; feasts in, 35, 38–39; flesh overflow explored in, 57–59; giants and, 38–39; gout viewed in, 53–54; hydropsy viewed in, 51–52; images and realism of features in, 55–59; insults and new expressions during, 36–38; linguistic changes in, 59–63; obscurity of fatness during, 49–50; origin of fat viewed in, 70–71; overview, 31–32; popular songs denigrating fatness, 38; resistances and fascinations, 38–41; roundness and, 56, 58, 59, 60, 62–63; skinniness refused in, 41–44; weighing rarity in, 66, 216*n*11; women's dress in, 74–76; women's slimming emphasized in, 73–74; *see also* Women, in Renaissance period

Rengade, Jules, 158

Reproductive faculties, Enlightenment-era concern with, 94–95, 97

Respiratory foods, 127–28, 156

Respiratory type, 150

Resting metabolic rate (RMR), 180

Restoration and July Monarchy periods, 109–37; bourgeois men, 120–21, 123–24; criticism and ironic reversals of, 121–23; diets in, 131–34; fat definitions in, 127–28; feasting in, 133–34; fire and fat in, 127–28, 230*n*8; morbid imminence in, 129–30; numbers and, 111–12; self-weighing in, 113–15; slimming techniques, 114–15, 134; suffering dimension of obesity, 135–37; thinness in, 123–24; thin waists and, 123–24; typology of sizes for men and women, 117–20, 228*n*14; waist-weight relation during, 112–13; water and fat viewed in, 125–26; *see also* Women, Restoration and July Monarchy period

Retarding nutrition, Bouchard's concept of slow or, 157

Retz, Noël, 103

Reverendissimo Vivo—V. H. Huntington, p6

Riolan, Jean, 48–49, 49

RMR, *see* Resting metabolic rate

Robinson, Bryan, 80

Roman de Renart, 1

Ronsard, P., 59

Rosa, Edward Bennett, 179–80

Roundness: degrees of, 86; globe imagery for, 62–63; natural, 59; Renaissance descriptions, 56, 58, 59, 60, 62–63

Rousseau, 105–6

Rowlandson, Thomas, *p6*

Royal Pharmacopia (Charas), 61

Royalty, bear as emblem of, 6

Rubens, Pierre Paul, 57–59, *p4*

Saint-Simon, Louis de Rouvroy duc de, x, 43

Sanctorius, 70, 79–80, *p9*

Sand, George, 135

Satire, 96, 151–53

Sauvages, Boissier de, 83, 93

Scale (physical), xii, *p10*; apartment, 142; chair, 70, 79–80; daily use of, 177–78; Desbordes request to install public, 81; at fairs, 115; public personal, 178; rarity of, 115; Sanctorius's, *p9*; Wyatt's invention of balance, 82–83

Schwilgué, C. J. A., 102

sciatica, medieval term for, 14

Science of monsters, 56

Scientific period, 154

Scot, Michael, 12

Sealed chamber experiments, 107

Sedentariness, 168, 175

Self-esteem, 196

Self-identity, 193–97

Self-weighing, Restoration period and, 113–15

Seyssel, Claude, 34

Shakespeare, William, 36–37

Short neck, 48–49

Sicard, Jean, 155

Sienna, Aldebrandin, 11

Silhouettes, 85, 87, 197–98, *p11*; coinage of term, 88; Enlightenment-age importance of, 85, 87, 88; passive sculpting of, *p12*; in Restoration and July Monarchy period, 116; turn-of-the-century's thinner, 166

Singular types, Enlightenment age identification of, 86, 220*n*29

Size: ambiguity, 89, 119, 121, 124; categories, 155–56; charts, 143–45; first attention to degrees of, *p5*; precision about, 77, 81–82; typologies of, 117–20, 228*n*14

Skinniness: ambiguity of, 42; excesses of, 69; nuancing, 62; refusal of, 41–44; Renaissance worries over, 61–62

Slack tissue, 92, 93, 99, 100, 126

Slimming: baths for, 102; belts and corsets for, 75–76; drying out for, 71–73; Enlightenment-era regimens for, 99–107; Middle Ages efforts toward, 28–29; Renaissance slow cultural, 32; Renaissance techniques for, 69–71; Renaissance women and, 73–74; Restoration period, 114–15, 134; turn-of-the-century, 149; vinegar and lemon for, 73–74

Slimming Bath Salts, Clark's, *p11*

Slow nutrition, 157

Small obesity, 155

Soap pills, 100

Social class, 25–26, 153, 167–68, *p5*; contemporary obesity and, 186–87; meat consumption and, 152

Social suffering, 199

Spas, 142, 162–64, *p10*

Spectator, 79–80

Spiromètre, 130

De Statica medicina, p9

Statistics: averages, 112–13; contemporary, 186–87; Enlightenment-age emergence of, 83–84, 220n17, 220n19; obesity epidemic, 186; turn-of-the-century focus on, 177; waist-weight relation and, 112–13; weight gain study and, 171

Stigmatization: changes over time, 197–99; of degeneration, 158–59; Enlightenment-era, 90–98; of foods, 132; lack of will as contemporary, 195; of laziness and weakness, 34; modern period, 174–75, 183; 1920s, 174–75; opulence, 14; powerlessness and, xiii, 77–78; Restoration period, 119–20; of ugliness, 151–53; victimization replacing, 185; *see also* Criticism, of fat

Strangled waist, 87–89, 123, p5

Straparola, Gianfranco, 40–41

Stupidity, bigness linked with, 26

Sue, Eugène, 118

Suffering: changes over time periods in, 183–84; 1920s narratives of, 174–75; privation and, 135–37; social, 199; treatment failures and, 179–81; treatment narratives of, 183

Sugar, 60–61, 131, 132, 189

Suger, L'Abbé, 8, 15

Swellings: drying out to cure, 72–73; Enlightenment-era writings on, 92–93; hydropsy, 51–52; in medieval texts, 12–14; seventeenth-century perceptions of, 66; *see also* Hydropsy

Swift, Jonathan, 81

Swimwear, 145

Sydenham, Thomas, 52

Tables of gentlemen, 27

Teas, 164

Tenon, Jacques (Parisian doctor), 83, 84, 220n19

Thermal spas, 162–63

Thermal weighing machine, p10

Thinness: contemporary, 188–90; in court culture of Middle Ages, 21–22; dynamics of contemporary obesity and, 188–89; early 1900s male, 168–69; 1920s concern with, 174; Renaissance model of, 35; Restoration and July Monarchy, 123–24, 135; thin revolution of 1920s, 166–73; turn-of-the-century female, 169–70; turn-of-the-century will to, 144; weight gain from obsession with, 190; women's obligatory, 22, 124, 197, p5; *see also* Skinniness

The Thirty Year Old Woman (Balzac), 121

Thresholds, 87; ambiguity of, 43–44

Tissot, Samiel, 90, 100, 101

Tonics, 99–100

Treatment: calorie reduction as, 160; electricity as, 102–3; Enlightenment-era, 99–107; excitants, 101–2; failures, 179–81; graded obesity and, 160; modern narratives of, 181–84; nerve regimen, 103–5; personal testimonies, 139; preoccupation with, 181; severe forms of, 160; therapeutic multiplicity, 177–79; tonics, 99–100; turn-of-the-century causes and, 159–62

Treatment of Secret Remedies for Female Maladies (Liébault), 75

Turn of the century, 139–67; advertising campaigns of, 164–65; aesthetics, 143–44, 151–53; body exposure and, 145–46; causes and treatments discussed in, 159–62; defect of civilization view of early 1900s, 167–68; degeneration and, 158–59; diets of, 152, 159–62; male thinness and fat denunciation in, 168–69; masculine waist, 148–51; monstrosity theme, 171–73; overview, 141–42; size chart

Turn of the century (*continued*)
conflicts, 143–45; thin revolution,
166–73; ugliness and ridicule in,
151–53; widespread weighing in,
142–43; women's clothes in 1870s,
147; women's hips and, 146–48; *see
also* Women, turn-of-the-century era
Twentieth century, *see* Modern period
Two-Penny Whist, p5
Tympanites, winds and, 13
Typologies: Abdominal type, 150; body,
150; bourgeois obesity, 118; Enlightenment era's singular, 86, 220n29;
Middle Ages bigness, 17; Restoration and July Monarchy period size,
117–20, 228n14; turn-of-the-century
female obesity, 147–48

Ugliness, turn of the century ridicule
and, 151–53
Urine, hydropic, 126

Valetudinarians, 79–80
Valois, Élisabeth de, 65
Van Eyck, J., 28
Vegetable Pantagruelism, 133
Vegetarianism, 105–6
Vercellio, Cesare, 76
Verville, Béroalde de, 39
Vichy waters, 97, 163, 178, p10
Victimization, 185
Villeneuve, Arnaud de, 13
Vincent-Cassey, Mireille, 18
Vinegar, 73–74, 134
Viollet, p12
Visions (Pisan), 13–14
Vogue, 170
Voltaire, 81, 82
Von Goez, Franz, 86
Vulgarity, 41, 96

Waist: Enlightenment-age measurement of, 81–82, 219n12; freedom of

men's, 87–89; measuring only, 81–82,
219n12; relation of weight and, 112–
13; Restoration and July Monarchy
thinness of, 123–24; strangulation of
women's, 87–89, 123, p5; turn-of-the-
century masculine, 148–51; women's
obligatory tight, p5
Walpole, Horace, 104
Water: medieval view of fat and, 12–13,
14; Restoration and July Monarchy
periods view of fat and, 125–26; Vichy
town spas, 97, 163, 178, p10
Weak constitution, 114
Weighing, p10; food, 70; foodstuffs and
waste, 80; public, 115; Renaissance
king's bet as rare case of, 66, 216n11;
self-, 113–15; treatment and, 178;
widespread, 142–43
Weight: calculation of animal, 67; curve,
142; Enlightenment concern with
average body, 84; measuring height
and, 83–84, 112–13, 143; numerical
measuring of, 79–81; progression of,
117, 130; relation of waist and, 112–13;
Renaissance-era weight watching, 74;
waist measurement replacing, 81–82,
219n12
Weight gain: study of gradations of, 170–
71; thinness obsession causing, 190
William the Conqueror, 8, 17, 205n2
Wind, 13–14
Wine: gout caused by excess, 53; misuse
of, 58
Women: beauty ideal for contemporary,
170; changed status of, 197–98; early
nineteenth-century, 117–20; obligatory thinness, 22, 124, 197, p5; *see also*
Female body
Women, Enlightenment-era: Marivaux's
nuanced language about fat, 85; waist
strangulation in, 87–89, p5
Women, in Middle Ages: beautiful, 3–4;
belts worn by noble, 29

Women, in Renaissance period: baths of, 73, *p3*; beggars, 34; belts and corsets for, 75–76; country, 68; decorative beauty of, 74; drawings of, 57; manuals on dress of, 74; seductiveness of big, 40; slimming emphasis in, 73–74; voluptuous, 34

Women, Restoration and July Monarchy period: cause of fat in, 127–28; thinness importance, 135; thinness types in, 124; typologies of, 117–20, 228*n*14

Women, turn-of-the-century era: beauty, 144; clothes style in, 147; focus on hips, 146–48; obesity types specified in, 147–48; thinness of early 1900s, 169–70

Women Bathing, p3

Wyatt, John, 82–83

Zanzibar, 5

Zola, 142, 148, 152; aesthetics and variations in characters of, 143–44; friends on recovery of, 160; mirror scene in *Nana*, 146; satire on, 153

EUROPEAN PERSPECTIVES
A Series in Social Thought and Cultural Criticism
Lawrence D. Kritzman, Editor

Gilles Deleuze, *The Logic of Sense*

Julia Kristeva, *Strangers to Ourselves*

Theodor W. Adorno, *Notes to Literature*, vols. 1 and 2

Richard Wolin, ed., *The Heidegger Controversy*

Antonio Gramsci, *Prison Notebooks*, vols. 1, 2, and 3

Jacques Le Goff, *History and Memory*

Alain Finkielkraut, *Remembering in Vain: The Klaus Barbie Trial and Crimes Against Humanity*

Julia Kristeva, *Nations Without Nationalism*

Pierre Bourdieu, *The Field of Cultural Production*

Pierre Vidal-Naquet, *Assassins of Memory: Essays on the Denial of the Holocaust*

Hugo Ball, *Critique of the German Intelligentsia*

Gilles Deleuze, *Logic and Sense*

Gilles Deleuze and Félix Guattari, *What Is Philosophy?*

Karl Heinz Bohrer, *Suddenness: On the Moment of Aesthetic Appearance*

Julia Kristeva, *Time and Sense: Proust and the Experience of Literature*

Alain Finkielkraut, *The Defeat of the Mind*

Julia Kristeva, *New Maladies of the Soul*

Elisabeth Badinter, *XY: On Masculine Identity*

Karl Löwith, *Martin Heidegger and European Nihilism*

Gilles Deleuze, *Negotiations, 1972–1990*

Pierre Vidal-Naquet, *The Jews: History, Memory, and the Present*

Norbert Elias, *The Germans*

Louis Althusser, *Writings on Psychoanalysis: Freud and Lacan*

Elisabeth Roudinesco, *Jacques Lacan: His Life and Work*

Ross Guberman, *Julia Kristeva Interviews*

Kelly Oliver, *The Portable Kristeva*

Pierre Nora, *Realms of Memory: The Construction of the French Past*
   Vol. 1: *Conflicts and Divisions*
   Vol. 2: *Traditions*
   Vol. 3: *Symbols*

Claudine Fabre-Vassas, *The Singular Beast: Jews, Christians, and the Pig*

Paul Ricoeur, *Critique and Conviction: Conversations with François Azouvi and Marc de Launay*

Theodor W. Adorno, *Critical Models: Interventions and Catchwords*

Alain Corbin, *Village Bells: Sound and Meaning in the Nineteenth-Century French Countryside*

Zygmunt Bauman, *Globalization: The Human Consequences*

Emmanuel Levinas, *Entre Nous: Essays on Thinking-of-the-Other*

Jean-Louis Flandrin and Massimo Montanari, *Food: A Culinary History*

Tahar Ben Jelloun, *French Hospitality: Racism and North African Immigrants*

Emmanuel Levinas, *Alterity and Transcendence*

Sylviane Agacinski, *Parity of the Sexes*

Alain Finkielkraut, *In the Name of Humanity: Reflections on the Twentieth Century*

Julia Kristeva, *The Sense and Non-Sense of Revolt: The Powers and Limits of Psychoanalysis*

Régis Debray, *Transmitting Culture*

Catherine Clément and Julia Kristeva, *The Feminine and the Sacred*

Alain Corbin, *The Life of an Unknown: The Rediscovered World of a Clog Maker in Nineteenth-Century France*

Michel Pastoureau, *The Devil's Cloth: A History of Stripes and Striped Fabric*

Julia Kristeva, *Hannah Arendt*

Carlo Ginzburg, *Wooden Eyes: Nine Reflections on Distance*

Elisabeth Roudinesco, *Why Psychoanalysis?*

Alain Cabantous, *Blasphemy: Impious Speech in the West from the Seventeenth to the Nineteenth Century*

Luce Irigaray, *Between East and West: From Singularity to Community*

Julia Kristeva, *Melanie Klein*

Gilles Deleuze, *Dialogues II*

Julia Kristeva, *Intimate Revolt: The Powers and Limits of Psychoanalysis, vol. 2*

Claudia Benthien, *Skin: On the Cultural Border Between Self and the World*

Sylviane Agacinski, *Time Passing: Modernity and Nostalgia*

Emmanuel Todd, *After the Empire: The Breakdown of the American Order*

Hélène Cixous, *Portrait of Jacques Derrida as a Young Jewish Saint*

Gilles Deleuze, *Difference and Repetition*

Gianni Vattimo, *Nihilism and Emancipation: Ethics, Politics, and Law*

Julia Kristeva, *Colette*

Steve Redhead, ed., *The Paul Virilio Reader*

Roland Barthes, *The Neutral: Lecture Course at the Collège de France (1977–1978)*

Gianni Vattimo, *Dialogue with Nietzsche*

Gilles Deleuze, *Nietzsche and Philosophy*

Hélène Cixous, *Dream I Tell You*

Jacques Derrida, *Geneses, Genealogies, Genres, and Genius: The Secrets of the Archive*

Jean Starobinski, *Enchantment: The Seductress in Opera*

Julia Kristeva, *This Incredible Need to Believe*

Marta Segarra, ed., *The Portable Cixous*

François Dosse, *Gilles Deleuze and Félix Guattari: Intersecting Lives*

Julia Kristeva, *Hatred and Forgiveness*

Antoine de Baecque, *History/Cinema*

François Noudelmann, *The Philosopher's Touch: Sartre, Nietzsche, and Barthes at the Piano*

Roland Barthes, *How to Live Together: Novelistic Simulations of Some Everyday Spaces*